ANTARCTICA

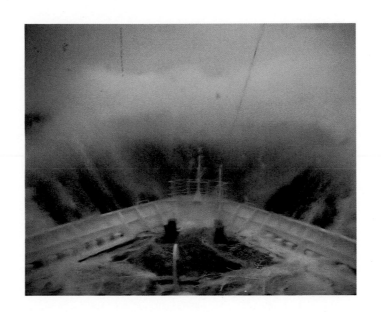

Dedication

For Betty, Denali and Carys
As a reminder of family journeys shared in Antarctica and for endless support in Hedgehog House.

For Garth Varcoe ("The Duck")
Who died under Mt Erebus after giving so much to the New Zealand Antarctic Research Programme.
Thanks for your friendship and sharing knowledge, both in Antarctica and while weathering winter
blizzards in the Antarctic Division's office.

For Gary Ball
New Zealand mountain guide and raconteur who lies at rest on Dhaulagiri, Nepal.
For bringing spirit, laughter, and professionalism to both the New Zealand and German Antarctic
programs and for your summit hug on Pik Kommunizma in the Soviet Pamirs.

For Rob Hall
"Kiwi Mountaineer" and gentle friend who is at rest on the south summit of Mt. Everest.
As the first New Zealander to climb K2, Makalu, and Lhotse, and in guiding over forty people to the
top of Everest, reaching the summit yourself five times, you brought the spirit of
mountaineering into our homes.
In assisting the New Zealand Antarctic Research Programme and in guiding remote peaks,
you brought a high standard of professionalism to Antarctica.

Acknowledgments

My journeys to Antarctica could not have been undertaken without considerable support
from many individuals and organizations, including the New Zealand Antarctic Research
Programme, Lindblad Travel, Society Expeditions, and in recent years Quark Expeditions, Polar
Journeys, and Adventure Network International. Particular thanks are due to Mike McDowell,
Greg Mortimer, Margaret Werner, and Anne Kershaw.
The text in this book has been markedly improved by comments from Dr. Howard Conway, Dr. Paul
Broady, Greg Mortimer, Peter Cleary, Lou Sanson, Jeni Bassett, Linley Earnshaw, Tui De Roy, Alan
Gurney, and in particular Betty Monteath. Their assistance is greatly appreciated.
The artwork of John Herbison considerably enhances the map of Antarctica and five-year-old
Andrew Woolley's poster art concludes the book with a powerful message.
Thank you both for your vision.
Editor Tracey Borgfeldt and designer Chris O'Brien and the team at David Bateman Ltd. have
skillfully nurtured this book from idea to finished product. Thank you kindly.

ANTARCTICA

BEYOND THE SOUTHERN OCEAN

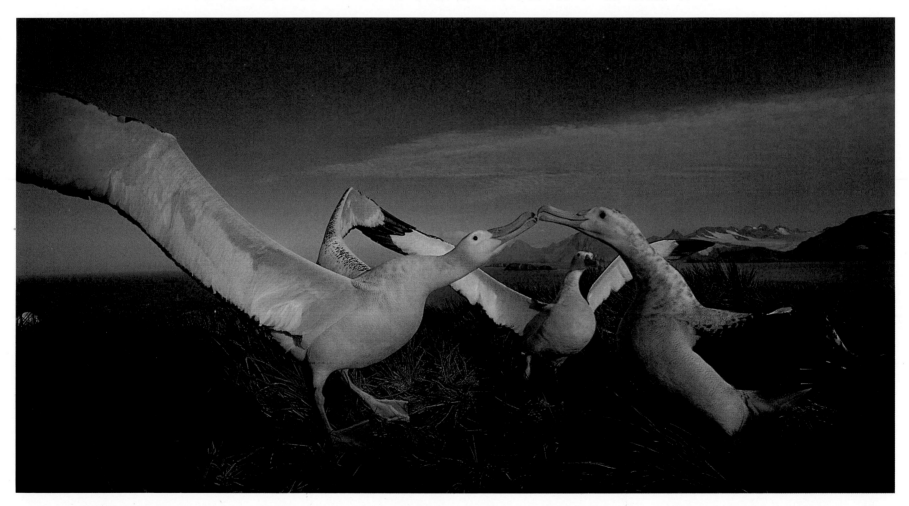

COLIN MONTEATH

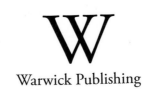

Warwick Publishing

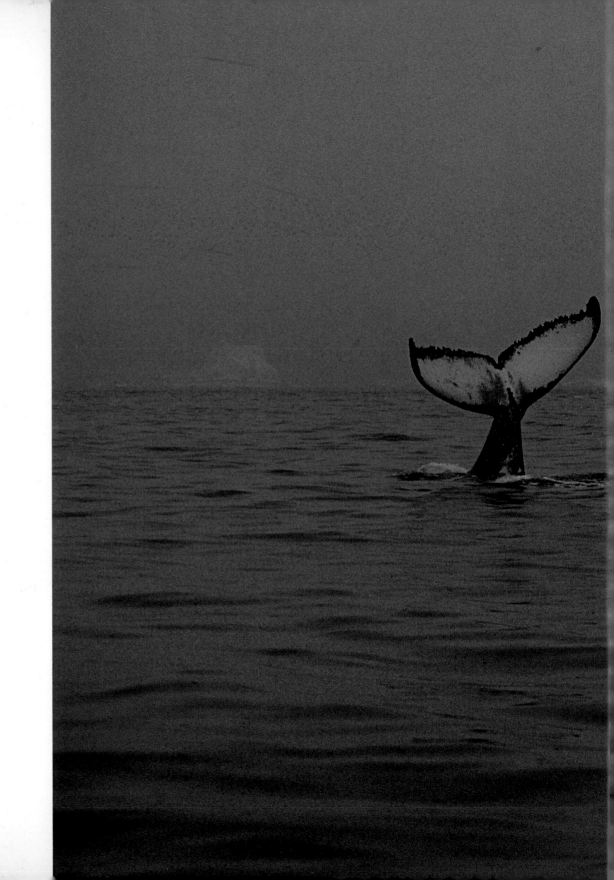

Front cover: *Old blue iceberg, South Sandwich Islands.*
Back cover: *Inquisitive Hooker's sea lion pups on Enderby Island, New Zealand subantarctic islands.*
Author portrait, back flap: *Colin Monteath on the summit of Vinson Massif, highest peak in Antarctica. [Photo: Greg Mortimer]*
Endpapers: *Marbled ice, Bransfield Strait, Antarctic Peninsula.*
Page 1 (half-title): *Southern Ocean wave breaking over bow of MV* Frontier Spirit, *Ross Sea.*
Page 3 (title page): *Wandering albatrosses in courtship dance, Albatross Island, South Georgia.*
Pages 4 and 5 (opposite): *Humpback whale sounding near iceberg, Petermann Island, Antarctic Peninsula.*

First published in 1996 by David Bateman Ltd, Tarndale Grove, Albany Business Park, Albany, Auckland, New Zealand

We acknowledge the financial support of the Government of Canada through the Book Publishing Industry Development Program for our publishing activities.

ISBN: 1-894622-60-X

Published in North America by Warwick Publishing Inc.
161 Frederick Street, Suite 200
Toronto, Ontario M5A 4P3 Canada
www.warwickgp.com

Distributed in Canada by
Canadian Book Network
c/o Georgetown Terminal Warehouses
34 Armstrong Avenue
Georgetown, Ontario L7G 4R9
www.canadianbooknetwork.com

Distributed in the United States by
CDS
193 Edwards Drive
Jackson TN 38301
www.cdsbooks.com

Design by Chris O'Brien/Pages Literary Pursuits
Printed in China through Colorcraft Ltd., Hong Kong

CONTENTS

6

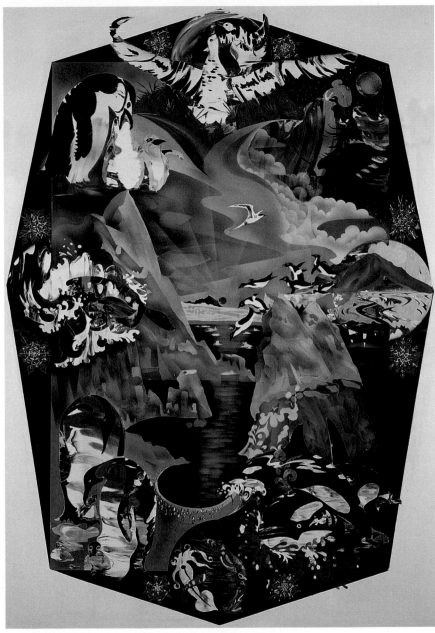

"Wild and Free" — painting by John Herbison/Hedgehog House.

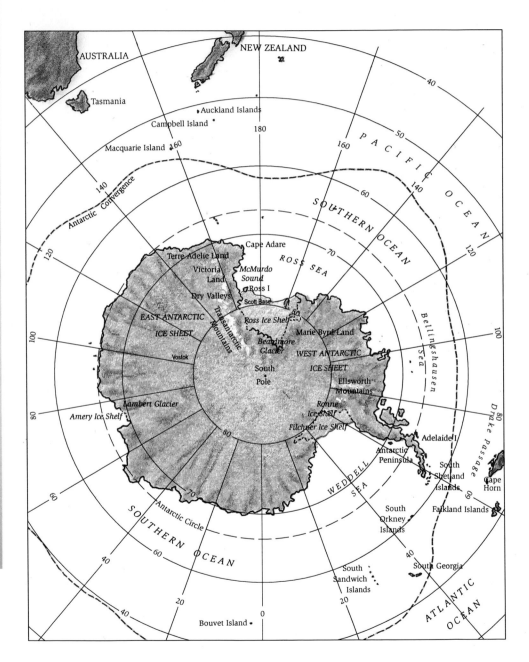

PREFACE

After twenty-one seasons in Antarctica I feel a need to reflect on what has drawn me to the polar regions. Why was my imagination captured by this icy realm? As a photographer, were my eyes simply enchanted by Antarctica's extremes, by vast mountain ranges, by unique animal life, by extensive seascapes juxtaposed with textures of delicate beauty and above all by the sheer magnetism of this land of silence? Perhaps it was the romantic derring-do of the early explorers? Maybe, in a world under pressure, I only wanted to grapple with the concepts of solitude and wilderness?

This passion for Antarctica stems from my teenage days growing up in Sydney. I was enthralled to read Boy Scout journals describing how the New Zealand Antarctic Research Programme had, each summer since the early 1960s, taken scouts to Scott Base to help with the running of an Antarctic station. The mere possibility of such fantastic polar adventures filled my youthful dreams.

For a youngster like myself, living near a Sydney beach, Antarctica was tantalizing, remote, seemingly unreachable; a shining beacon of ice hovering beyond the Southern Ocean. Above all, despite being a neighbor, Antarctica was in such sharp contrast to the red heart and blistering heat of my homeland. University breaks spent rockclimbing in the Blue Mountains soon developed into a lifelong fascination with big mountains. To improve my mountaineering skills I undertook an apprenticeship in New Zealand's Southern Alps. By 1972, with six seasons in the Alps behind me, I was able to start work in the Mt. Cook National Park as a guide and rescue team member. By then, a compelling desire to visit Antarctica had evolved.

My first season in Antarctica as a mountaineer with the New Zealanders became reality in 1973. This short-term position had matured into a full-time job by 1975; I worked out of Scott Base during the summer and planned future science expeditions in the winter months from the Antarctic Division's Christchurch office. As Field Operations Officer for the NZARP for the next nine seasons, I was in a privileged position to immerse myself in a wide range of projects and to work alongside gifted scientists, professional mountaineers, and Antarctic veterans from around the globe.

During those remarkable years with the NZARP, I gradually developed an overriding interest in polar photography. I tried hard to document my association with the Kiwi huskies, with expeditions to Mt. Erebus and the Transantarctic Mountains, with a visit by H.R.H. Prince Edward to the South Pole, and even with the aftermath of the Air New Zealand DC-10 crash in 1979. In both image and word, vignettes from these adventures appeared in 1985 in the Reader's Digest book *Antarctica*, and in *Wild Ice — Antarctic Journeys* published in 1990. Previously unpublished images from this period of government service have also been selected for this book. They help to illustrate how people live and work in the heart of the Antarctic and complement more recent images from my next decade of private Antarctic travel, largely in coastal regions.

In my ten years with the NZARP, based on Ross Island, I hardly ever saw the open sea. It was always frozen. So frozen, in fact, that the biggest aircraft and heaviest tractors could safely operate on it. I was used to working in the mountains, on crevassed glaciers and on windblown ridges. In setting out to earn a living as a freelance photographer and Antarctic guide in 1984, I was thrown into the deep end with Antarctic seaborne tourism. Initially I was not comfortable with the idea of handling small boats on a wild Southern Ocean. My subsequent adventures at sea have been as thrilling and challenging as any in the mountains.

Working on vessels such as the *Lindblad Explorer* and, in recent years, on Russian ships chartered by Quark Expeditions, has enabled me to visit a host of places largely unfamiliar to much of the Antarctic community. These journeys have helped to balance my knowledge of geography, history, science, and politics with that already gained from the Ross Sea sector. Since 1983, I have been fortunate to make repeated voyages to the Falklands, South Georgia, South Sandwich Islands, and the Antarctic Peninsula. These visits have allowed me to document elements of change and human interaction in modern-day Antarctica. In a kaleidoscope of photographic images, I have also tried to portray the many fleeting though beautiful moments to be experienced on the coastal fringe of the continent.

Arctic journeys in the 1990s have given me experiences in radically different environments in marked contrast to those of Antarctica. In 1991 I accompanied the first surface vessel traverse of the Arctic Ocean via the North Pole on a Soviet nuclear-powered icebreaker. This voyage enabled me to make my first observations of Arctic animals such as walruses, polar bears, and the clown-like puffins. Coming from Antarctica, which lacks land predators, I found it stunning to watch polar bears devour a seal on the pack ice. Apart from cruising in Zodiacs beside orcas, I had never been so close to powerful creatures like bears that were so self-assured and so obviously in perfect control in such an unforgiving environment.

The second voyage that year took me along the Siberian coast through the icy sea-lanes known as the Northeast Passage. It was highly exciting to discover hairy mammoth tusks preserved for 30,000 years in the permafrost of Siberian islands. I also visited nomadic Chukchi reindeer herders in their summer camps. Seeing indigenous people continuing to carve out an existence on the tundra, as they have done for thousands of years, again drove home how foreign this was from life in the Antarctic.

Before traversing the Greenland icecap with a team of huskies in 1993, I was able to witness something of the native Greenlanders' lives in the coastal villages of this massive island. It was striking to see the space-age technology of a missile radar base, DYEII, high on Greenland's icecap, which contrasted sharply with non-militarized Antarctica.

Antarctica: Beyond the Southern Ocean is a visual celebration of two decades of visits to the polar regions. It is primarily an Antarctic book, although a few Arctic images have been included to provide a comparison between the two poles. The book is also a plea to raise awareness of the need to respect Antarctica as a wilderness. Most people will never venture across the Southern Ocean. No matter. What is important is that we know enough about Antarctica to appreciate the significance of our stewardship of a whole continent that no one owns.

In March 1990, while waiting to reboard a ship at Cape Royds in the Ross Sea after a private climbing expedition, I was confronted with a few home truths. Normally, when climbing in far-flung mountains, I am getting further away from my family. This time my wife Betty and daughters Denali (13) and Carys (10) were getting closer by the minute as the ship rounded the Cape and entered McMurdo Sound. After years of being left behind while I roamed the continent, they were actually here experiencing the wonder of Antarctica for themselves. I'll never forget the sparkle in their eyes as the helicopter engine wound down and I crossed the heli-deck to hug them. Youngsters like Denali and Carys will inherit Antarctica soon enough. For them to continue to seek out wilderness is also to seek out that wild place in their hearts. The preservation of Antarctica as wilderness is vital to their spirit and essential to the well-being of the planet.

8

INTRODUCTION

Norwegian Roald Amundsen, leader of the first expedition to reach the South Pole in 1911, used words like "fairytale" in his journal, intimating that the majesty and peacefulness of Antarctica far outweighed its hostility. Many since have found the "otherworldliness" of this land of extremes so removed from their other experiences that traveling there seemed almost as alien as a journey into space. As for astronauts in a capsule, human survival in Antarctica is only possible with a comprehensive lifeline of fuel, food, shelter, and insulated clothing. Despite ski-equipped aircraft, icebreaking ships, tracked vehicles, reliable radios, and cozy bases, living and traveling in Antarctica remains fraught with problems. Truly beautiful it is, but no one can afford to treat Antarctica lightly.

Antarctica is much colder than the Arctic. Only on the coastal fringe of the Antarctic Peninsula during summer could temperatures be described as reasonable, occasionally reaching 50°F. In the interior, on the plateau-like ice sheets, the dry numbing cold ranges from 4°F to a crippling low of −128°F. Cold dominates every aspect of human endeavor and even with modern apparel the danger of frostbite is ever present. Wind too plays a crucial role. When one is caught in a blizzard, the simplest of tasks becomes nearly impossible.

Antarctica is an isolated mountainous continent perched on the crest of the globe. Its sheer immensity and far-reaching influence on global weather and ocean circulation are difficult to grasp. Antarctica is surrounded by the Southern Ocean, the wildest, coldest body of water imaginable. In winter, this freezes into a grinding iron-hard mosaic of sea ice, effectively doubling the size of the continent. In summer, the wind-lashed latitudes of the "furious fifties" and "screaming sixties" are studded with floating ice islands. The scale of these icebergs, released by massive glaciers and ice shelves, makes those of the Arctic seem tiny, almost friendly, by comparison.

And yet this brutal realm of seemingly barren ice and rock has a softer side. Antarctica is often laced with delicate colors that illuminate a rich array of patterns and textures. Importantly, Antarctica and the Southern Ocean support a profusion of wildlife, much of it found nowhere else. While there are few individual species, each exists in great numbers. As the foundation of the food web, myriads of microscopic zoo- and phyto-plankton sustain the crustacean krill that swarm in countless numbers while migrating through surface waters. Whales, seals, penguins and other seabirds, from the tiniest petrels to the great ocean wanderers, the albatrosses, depend on krill, squid, and fish for sustenance.

Although some snow petrels fly 124 miles inland to nest, most animal life is found breeding on coastal Antarctica or the subantarctic islands. Mosses and two flowering plants add a patina of plantlife restricted to specific niches. Primitive algae can thrive inside snowdrifts while thermophilic algae prefer volcanic hot spots. Hardy lichens cling to the southernmost rocks while others dodge life on the surface, craftily inhabiting the space between crystals inside rocks. Antarctica is perhaps best thought of as a simple rather than a fragile environment. If anything, the Antarctic environment is one of considerable resilience with ecosystems perfected by clever adaptations.

It is widely recognized that Antarctica is a precious scientific laboratory. Each spring researchers from over forty nations journey to bases scattered around "The Ice." During the short summer, they work long hours in continuous daylight, intent on extending the knowledge of their speciality. Sophisticated projects have now drilled into the ice sheets to recover cores that catalogue past climate. Others core sea-floor sediments to help elucidate the uplift of mountain ranges from the ancient supercontinent Gondwanaland. Both are huge tasks requiring dedication to precision work in difficult conditions.

Antarctic biologists are probing deeper into the mechanisms of polar ecosystems. Zoologists, aided by seaborne cruises, satellite tracking instruments, and diving programs, try to fathom biological puzzles such as the physiology of fish adapted to life in near-freezing water. The abundance and migration patterns of seals and penguins are also monitored in greater detail. Crucially, after many years' work, scientists are beginning to understand the complicated life cycle of krill. Freshwater biologists have made accurate chemical analyses of streams and lakes while botanists have built up a fascinating picture of the slow-growing, easily-damaged plants.

Science can be competitive; however, Antarctica's role in the International Geophysical Year (IGY) of 1957–58 sparked the neutrality of Antarctica, in essence creating the beginnings of a "World Park" concept. At that time, having established a network of bases around the continent, countries began sharing scientific data. This cooperation continues today.

The IGY was largely responsible for spawning the visionary policies of the Antarctic Treaty, which came into force in 1961. Still binding today, the treaty ensures the freedom of scientific investigation with member countries regularly exchanging information. This friendly working relationship, even among countries once bogged down by the Cold War, has created a mutual respect and camaraderie among expeditioners confronting the same obstacles in a punishing environment.

The Antarctic Treaty does not apply to the high seas and subantarctic islands north of 60° S. South of 60° S, it does ensure that military personnel, while legitimately employed to support science, cannot be armed. Nuclear explosions and the disposal of radioactive waste are prohibited. As long as the treaty remains in force, territorial claims are frozen, whereby the future activity of any country cannot affect the status quo of original claims to territorial sovereignty.

Today, both government and private expedition leaders are obliged to make an environmental impact statement before commencing an Antarctic project. This form of regulation is an important adjunct to the treaty. In addition to agreed measures to conserve Antarctic flora and fauna, there is a Code of Conduct that applies to any Antarctic visitor. Importantly, the Antarctic Treaty did not consider the possibility of the exploitation of minerals and hydrocarbons. Debated vigorously during the 1980s, the resultant Protocol on Environmental Protection includes a prohibition on mineral resource activity that can be reviewed after fifty years. This will become effective only after ratification by each individual government's internal legislation.

Antarctica: Beyond the Southern Ocean is in four parts. "Life on the Fringe" concentrates on the wildlife from the subantarctic islands. It also documents change stemming from recent political, military, and ecological upheaval. "Earth, the Ice Planet" examines the nature and effect of Antarctica's ice cover. Important concepts affecting global climate change are also discussed. "A Slippery Path" illuminates issues that deal with the human impact resulting from scientific, recreational, and commercial endeavors. "Wild and Free" delves into animal life on the continent itself, focusing in detail on two remarkable creatures — the emperor penguin and the Weddell seal. The photographic plates accompanying each chapter present a broad spectrum of images depicting both human activity and the natural world. Throughout the book, small Arctic images have been added underneath the main Antarctic plate in order to provide a comparison with the north polar region.

LIFE ON THE FRINGE

The idea of the roundness of the earth is the cause of inventing this fable of the antipodes....for these philosophers having once erred go on in their absurdities, defending one another. Is there anyone so foolish as to believe that there are antipodes with their feet opposite ours; people who walk with their heels upward and their heads hanging down? That there is a part of the world where the trees grow with their branches downwards and where it rains and snows upward?

Written before the fifteenth century by Christians in Rome referring to early Greek philosophers.

Terra Australis Incognita may not be quite the massive southern continent that the Greek philosophers believed it to be, but anyone who has fought through gnarled rata scrub in a blizzard on a subantarctic island knows that devilish branches definitely grow downward and it can rain and snow upward!

The subantarctic islands, like precious gems studding the northern fringe of the Southern Ocean, act as guardians and gateways to the Antarctic. Twelve main island groups cling to life in the windswept latitudes of the "roaring forties" and "furious fifties." Each has a distinct ecosystem, harboring a profusion of native flora and fauna. Although the islands still face the threat of introduced plants and animals, they remain isolated, relatively undisturbed sanctuaries. Claimed and administered by South Africa, France, the United Kingdom, Norway, Australia, and New Zealand, these unique wildlife refuges must be sheltered from excessive intrusion in the future.

Navigators began sighting the fogbound coastlines of these islands as early as 1522 (Ile Amsterdam), though many appeared on charts from the late 1600s and throughout the 1700s (South Sandwich Islands, South Georgia, Prince Edward Islands, Bouvetoya). The sealing industry, sparked by Captain

Cook's reports following his landings in South Georgia and his discovery of the South Sandwich Islands in 1775, led to the finding of Macquarie, Campbell, Heard, Auckland, the South Orkneys, and the Crozet Islands in the 1800s.

The subantarctic islands are clustered around the Antarctic Convergence Zone, an ever-changing oceanographic boundary. Macquarie, Campbell, Kerguelen, and the Falklands lie north of the Convergence, while others, for instance South Georgia, South Sandwich, the South Orkneys, and the Heard Islands, are to the south and hence biologically part of Antarctica. The zone occurs where cold Southern Ocean water sinks below warmer northern waters. The Antarctic Convergence is a region where huge quantities of microscopic plants and animals thrive on upwelling nutrients. The resultant massive plankton blooms support vast stocks of krill, squid, and fin fish, the major source of food for whales, seals, and penguins and other seabirds.

Fur and elephant seal populations took a terrible battering from the late 1700s through 1840. Prized for their pelt and oil, these creatures were nearly extinct by 1810. The fur seal trade was extremely lucrative so sealers were secretive about productive beaches, withholding geographical discoveries and navigational information from charts and reports. Violent confrontations between British and American sealers took place in the South Shetland Islands. The scarcity of animals pushed the sealers further and further afield. Some of the wildest and remotest of all islands, in the South Sandwich group, suffered a period of exploitation starting in 1818.

Benefiting from a scarcity of predators, abundant food, and the 1972 Convention for the Protection of Flora and Fauna, fur seal numbers have recovered to their level prior to decimation. Many beaches are so crowded that it is nearly impossible to gain a foothold for fear of being bitten by these nimble marine mammals. Scientists are concerned about the damage the seals cause to slow-growing plant life.

The other prolific subantarctic seal is the belching blubber-fat elephant seal. While the grotesque bulbous-nosed males return to sea after impregnating their harem and molting, the beaches are littered with muddy wallows of lumbering females that lie over each other like spilled jelly beans. Nearby, dozens of weaner pups play, cavorting on the sand or among swirling kelp in the shallows. Adorable as these round-eyed pups are, they soon turn into snotty-nosed multi-ton behemoths. Halitosis takes on a new meaning after a close encounter with elephant seals.

Kings, the showiest of penguins, strut disdainfully among the pods of smelly elephant seals, commuting to and from their own equally pungent colonies higher up in the tussock grass. Kings congregate to breed in huge colonies on South Georgia, Crozet, Kerguelen, and Macquarie Islands. With big chicks to rear, kings have developed the unusual breeding cycle of rearing only two chicks every three years.

The subantarctic islands are host to several other penguin species — the gentoo, chinstrap, and crested penguins such as the royal, the Snares-crested, and the macaroni. The orange-plumed macaroni is found in huge numbers, with one colony on South Georgia estimated at 80,000 breeding pairs. Magellanic and rockhopper penguins exist happily in close proximity to the sheep farms in the Falklands. In contrast, penguin life is far more treacherous in New Zealand. The rarest penguins in the world, the shy yellow-eyed and the furtive Fiordland-crested, battle for survival against stoats, cats, and scorching scrub fires. Fortunately the yellow-eyed also breeds on subantarctic islands south of New Zealand. Every effort is made to keep these islands predator-free.

The specter of a south Atlantic subsea hydrocarbon industry looms. Of more immediate concern to the environment and wildlife is the increase in the number of fishing fleets around Falkland and South Georgia waters since 1982. Overfishing could result in starvation for elephant seals and king penguins, which are highly dependent on fish and squid. Significantly, once-clean beaches in the Falklands have become littered with plastic pollutants dumped from fishing vessels. The most evil offenders are old nets and fishing lines that can hopelessly entrap wildlife. Every year, visitors to the Falklands and South Georgia make concerted attempts to catch fur seals and penguins with ropes and nets biting deep into their chests.

To protest against the depletion of fin-fish stocks in the Southern Ocean is one reason Greenpeace launched a decade-long Antarctic campaign in the 1980s. After building a base on Ross Island, they publicized a variety of abuses in the Antarctic. The environmentalists helped condemn the concept of mineral and hydrocarbon extraction from the Antarctic. Greenpeace continues to harass bogus "scientific" whaling in subantarctic waters. Ostensibly killing in the name of population ecology, the Japanese persist in harpooning, electrocuting, and carving up minke whales for Tokyo delicatessens. Increasingly in the 1990s, British warships patrol the South Georgia waters to protect British interests in still-disputed territory by monitoring fleets fishing close to the island.

The haphazard ensnarement of fur seals in southern Atlantic flotsam is bad enough, but a more tragic story has emerged concerning the rare Hooker's sea lion found only around New Zealand's Auckland Islands. The past eight years have witnessed the death of over 500 Hooker's drowned in squid trawler nets. Despite protest, the industry persists in using nets instead of improved "jigger" technology. The Hooker's population throughout the 1980s was further threatened by large numbers of pups drowning in quagmires of mud formed by collapsing rabbit burrows. New Zealand took successful steps in 1994 to eradicate the rabbits that had been released in the 1800s as food for castaways.

Albatrosses, the most graceful of all seabirds, have long encircled the globe, utilizing strong winds in the roaring forties to cover enormous daily distances in search of food. In recent years, however, disaster has struck. The fishing industry is taking a toll of albatross species such as the wandering, royal, and black-brow. Up to 44,000 drown each year after being hooked in long-line bluefin tuna fishing operations. The losses could be much higher; figures from some Japanese and Chinese vessels are unobtainable. Juvenile nonbreeding albatrosses, under ten years old, seem most prone to being hooked when they dive for the squid bait as the line spins out from the stern deck. Even if the industry markedly improved its technique to sink the bait rapidly beyond the reach of the birds, so many immature birds have already died that albatross populations will continue to crash for at least the next decade. For every breeding bird killed, a chick will also die. Sadly, the remaining adult is unable to feed a chick on its own. It is heart-rending to think that these noble birds, the greatest of fliers and navigators, are in dire jeopardy.

A more subtle though potentially more devastating, widespread, and long-lasting form of human impact is the effect of stratospheric ozone depletion on the productivity of the Southern Ocean. The worldwide use of chlorofluorocarbons (CFCs) as refrigerants and in aerosols has affected the protective band of ozone to such an extent that increased amounts of ultraviolet radiation are reaching the Earth's surface. First reported by British Antarctic Survey scientists in 1985, the ozone depletion reaches its max-imum in the southern hemisphere's cold spring month of October. As big as the Antarctic itself, the so-called ozone hole seems to repair itself by December. To a lesser extent, ozone depletion is also evident over the warmer Arctic.

High UV levels cause sunburn and cancer in humans and can affect other forms of life from bacteria to higher plants. The marine ecosystem of the entire Southern Ocean may be at risk. During the short Antarctic summer, microscopic plants called phytoplankton convert sunlight and chemicals into nourishment for themselves and other organisms in the food chain. Increased UV hitting the ocean surface means that some species of phytoplankton can lose up to 10 percent of their photosynthetic ability. By seriously affecting the base of the food web, UV-induced changes in the Antarctic could have serious ramifications for the ecosystem. Even if CFCs were totally banned today, it will take many years for the ozone layer to stablize and recover.

The problem of ozone depletion is compounded by the possible con-sequences of greenhouse warming (see next chapter). The "greenhouse effect" impinges on the subantarctic world faster than elsewhere. Australian scientists on Macquarie Island have observed a sudden crash in the elephant seal population by 50 percent to 100,000. Similarly, Heard Island's pop-ulation has halved to only 30,000. Rockhopper penguin numbers on Macquarie, Campbell, and in the Falklands are all plummeting. Part of the reason could be that seawater temperature, measured at Macquarie, has increased from 40.1°F to 41.7°F in recent years. A one-and-a-half degree shift may not sound like much, but squid and krill, the principal food for penguins and elephant seals, are intolerant of warmer water and so have moved further south. A significant number of subantarctic seals and penguins are starving. While this could be a natural cyclical event, the world could do well to heed the indicators of change in the subantarctic.

A different kind of change occurred in 1982 when warfare erupted in the subantarctic islands. Violent British-Argentine skirmishes centered on South Georgia. When I first went to Grytviken in 1983, the bay was filled with somber British warships. Heavily armed soldiers were dug into camouflaged pits surrounded by coils of barbed wire encircling Shackleton's memorial cross. Black-faced soldiers with machine guns patrolled the beaches and surrounding mountains. Others, wearing backpacks filled with detergent, sprayed a thick oily sludge that clogged the foreshore. This pollution was the result of bored off-duty soldiers taking pot-shots at the storage tanks dating from the whaling era. Although rumored to be soon phased out, British combat troops still occupy King Edward Point at Grytviken. Should armed surveillance on Antarctica's doorstep be acceptable?

North of latitude 60°S, beyond the influence of the Antarctic Treaty, human intrusion into the subantarctic realm is subject to regulations enforced by governments that lay claim to the various islands. On the whole, environmental rules are tight, with the management plans tailored to each ecosystem. Some perplexing activities do still occur. In 1979, the South African military was rumored to have tested nuclear-capable missiles near Marion Island. And in 1987, the French Navy sank the 193-foot Australian trawler *Southern Raider* after raking it with heavy-caliber machine gunfire while it sheltered from a storm near St. Paul Island. What military operation was the French government hiding in the Kerguelen/St. Paul Islands that was so sensitive it warranted the sinking of a foreign vessel? Newspaper reports at the time discussed the French shifting their nuclear test program from Muroroa to Kerguelen.

To the southeast of South Georgia, Thule Island is part of the South Sandwich group and is claimed as British territory. At 59°30'S, Thule is a mere half-degree of latitude outside Antarctic Treaty protection, which rigorously prohibits military action. British forces removed the Argentines at gunpoint from their meteorological base during the 1982 conflict. Twelve months later, Royal Navy vessels returned to the island. Despite the base being in the middle of a penguin colony, plastic explosive charges were laid and every building was blown to smithereens. To do this in the political heat of the aftermath of war is perhaps understandable. To ignore the desecration of the environment for over a decade is inexcusable.

Leaving the forlorn destruction on Thule behind in December 1993, I rejoined the icebreaker *Khlebnikov* to visit other nearby islands. That the South Sandwich Island group is subject to violent natural forces was reinforced by a helicopter flight I made around the ice-encrusted summit cone of Saunders Island. Steam belched constantly from the active crater of this volcano, which forms part of the fiery rim of islands known as the Scotia Arc. Antarctica contains ancient rocks dating back 3.1 billion years, whereas brand-new rocks are being continually formed under the Scotia Arc which extends from the South Sandwich Islands to Deception Island near the tip of the Antarctic Peninsula. Change in many forms is guaranteed for these restless dots in the Southern Ocean. Hopefully the future pace of change for landform and ecosystem will be influenced by the gamut of natural processes rather than by the rapidity and severity of change caused by human-induced pressure. Life on the fringe of Antarctica warrants our respect.

Opposite: King penguins cross river, St. Andrew's Bay, South Georgia.

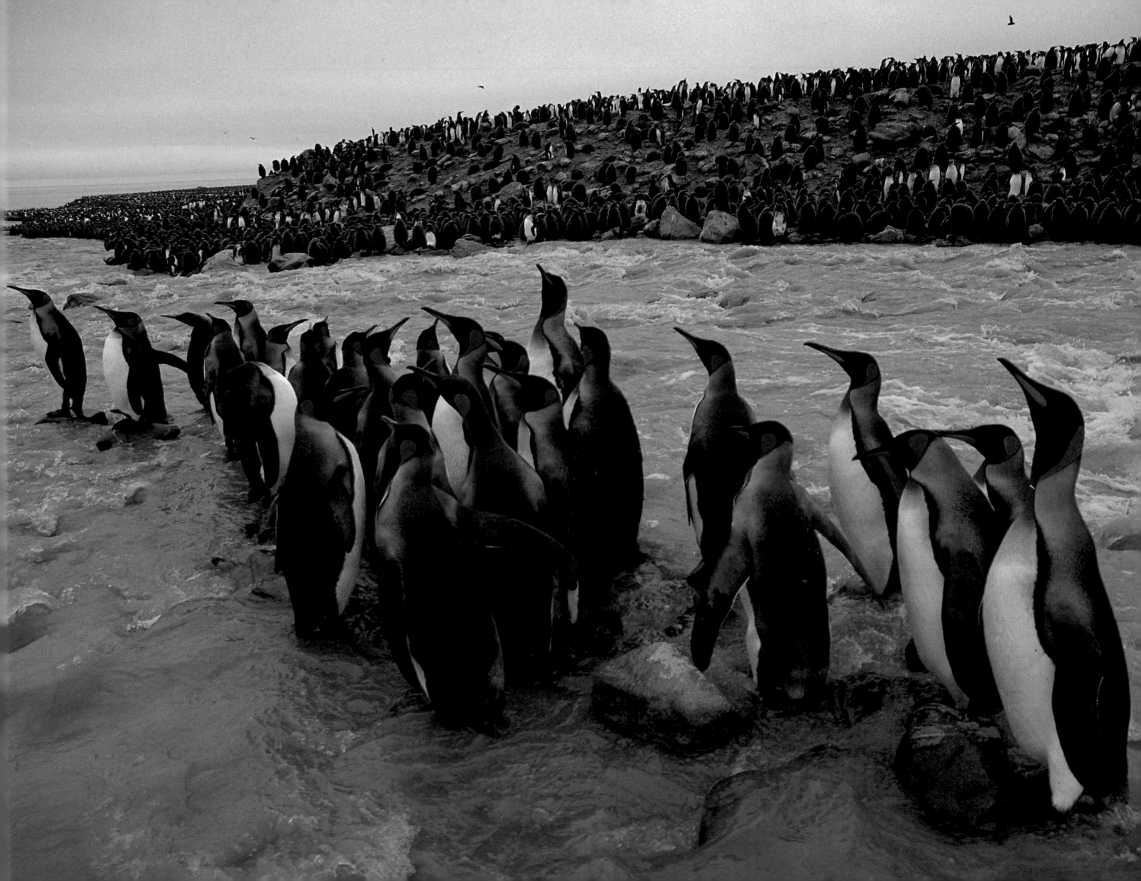

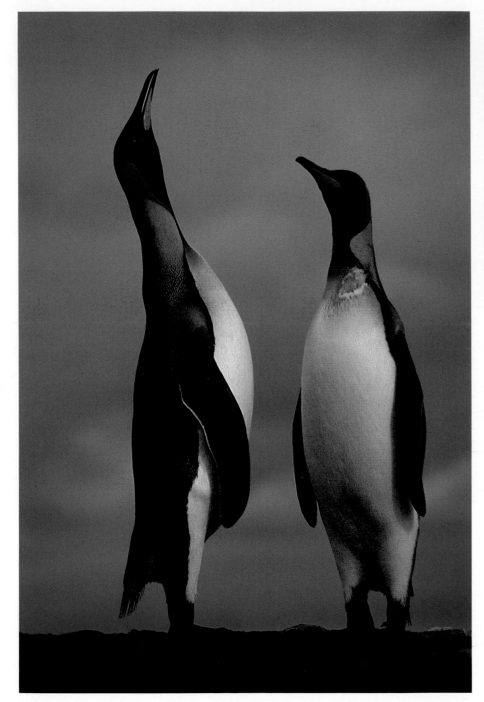

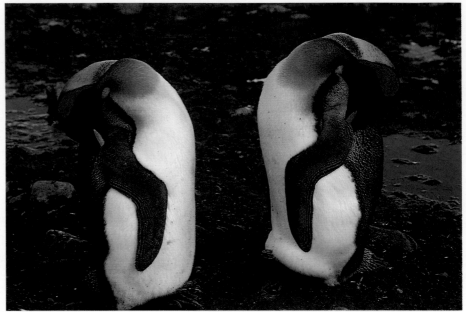

Above: Two of South Georgia's king penguins (*Aptenodytes patagonicus*) sleep on the beach at Royal Bay with beaks tucked under their flippers.

Left: King penguins greet each other on Salisbury Plain, South Georgia, by going through an elaborate ritual of "skypointing," calling and mutual preening. Standing just under three feet tall, the king penguin is only slightly shorter than its Antarctic cousin, the emperor penguin. The more slender king weighs about 40 pounds, whereas the emperor weighs twice as much. With a bright yellow-orange neck and throat feathers and a bright flash of orange on its bill, the king is perhaps the most elegant of all penguins. King penguins inhabit many subantarctic islands including South Georgia, Prince Edward, Crozet, Kerguelen, Heard, and Macquarie. There is even a small colony established further north on the Falkland Islands.

Feeding chicks throughout the winter on squid and small fish, kings need year-round access to subantarctic waters that don't freeze over. Kings are great divers, swimming extremely fast after prey. Depending on how far they must swim to find food, they return to the colony every two or three days to feed their hungry chick. Their main predator is the fearsome leopard seal although some are undoubtedly taken by orcas.

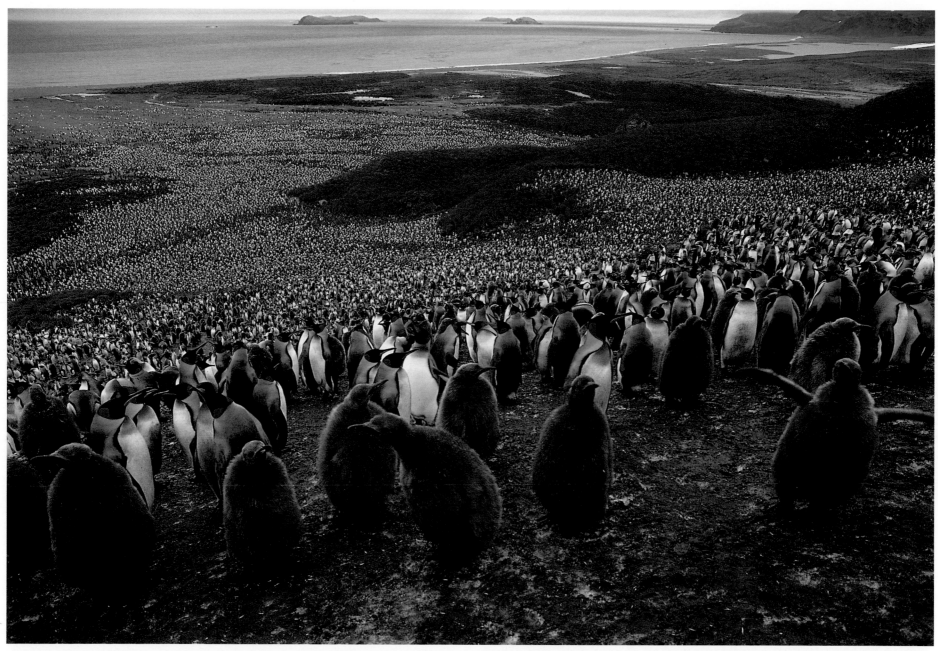

Covered in brown down feathers, roly-poly king penguin chicks start to explore their colony above South Georgia's Bay of Isles. Adult kings identify their chicks even in an extensive colony by listening for the chick's unique high-pitched whistle. Kings have an unusual breeding cycle, producing two chicks every three years. Kings require no nest and form colonies of up to several hundred thousand breeding pairs.

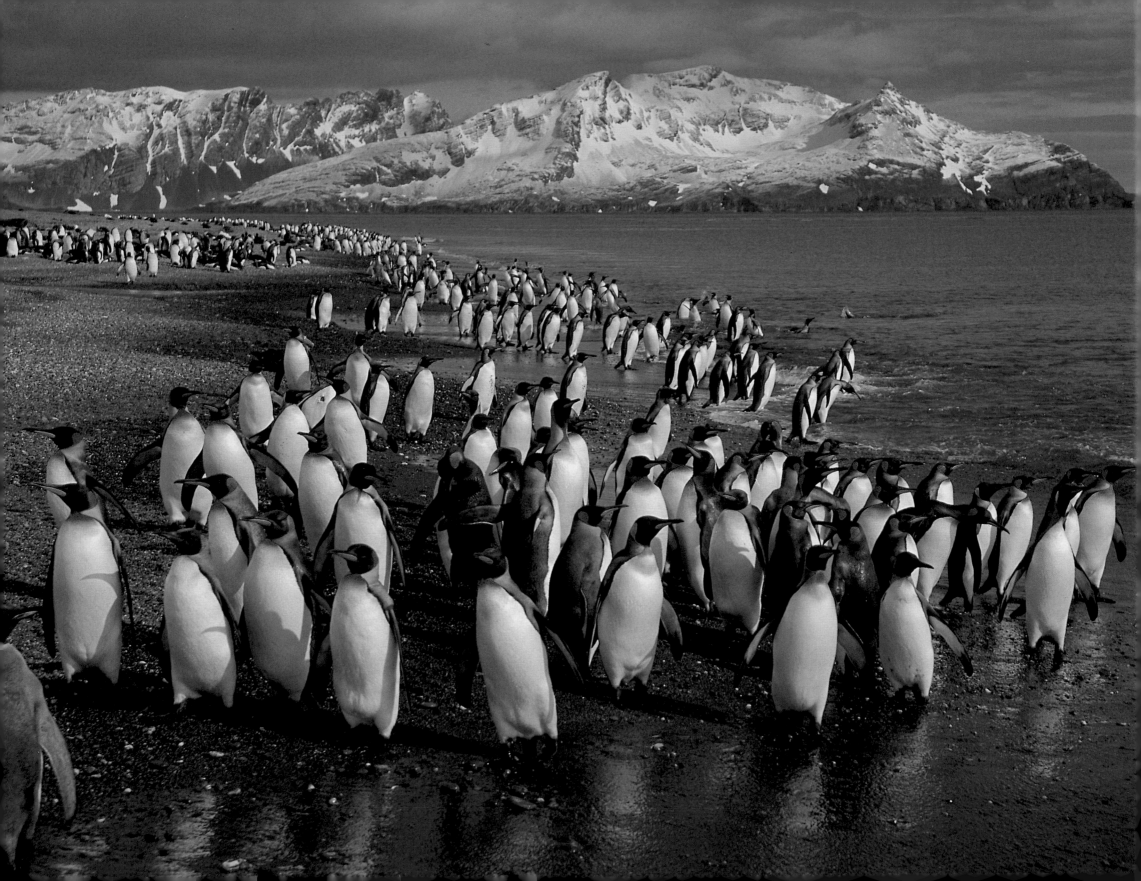

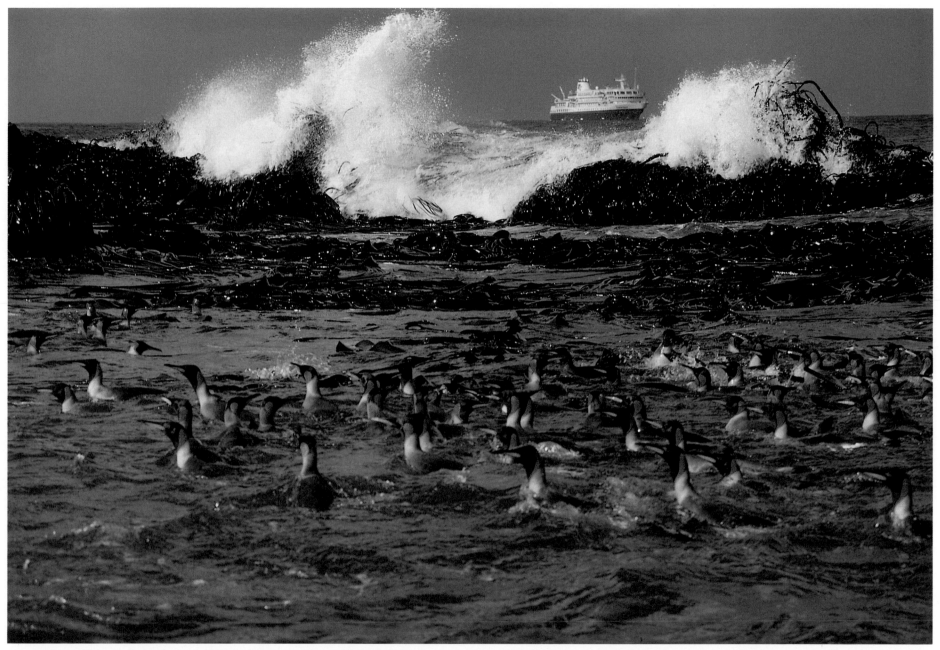

19

Above: Inquisitive king penguins swim through Macquarie Island's pounding surf to greet visitors from the MV *Frontier Spirit*. Macquarie Island's king penguin population is no longer threatened the way it was before Douglas Mawson stopped the killing of kings for oil in 1919.

Opposite: King penguins enjoy a swim in South Georgia's Bay of Isles.

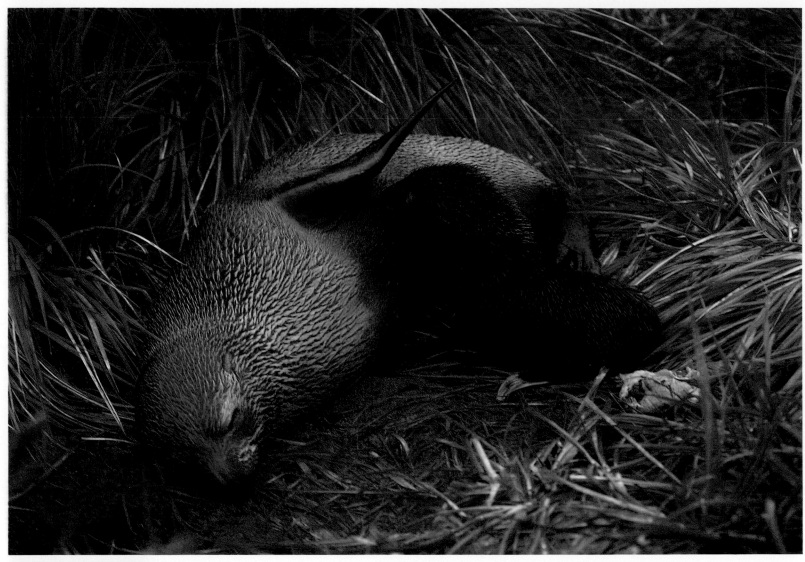

Above: A newborn Antarctic fur seal pup (*Arctocephalus gazella*) suckles while lying in thick tussock grass on Prion Island, South Georgia. Tussock grass and other flowering plants growing on subantarctic islands are being damaged by the resurgent fur seal populations.

Left: At 80° N, Franz Josef Land is only 600 nautical miles from the North Pole, yet it is covered in thick moss beds. The equivalent latitude in Antarctica supports only hardy lichens.

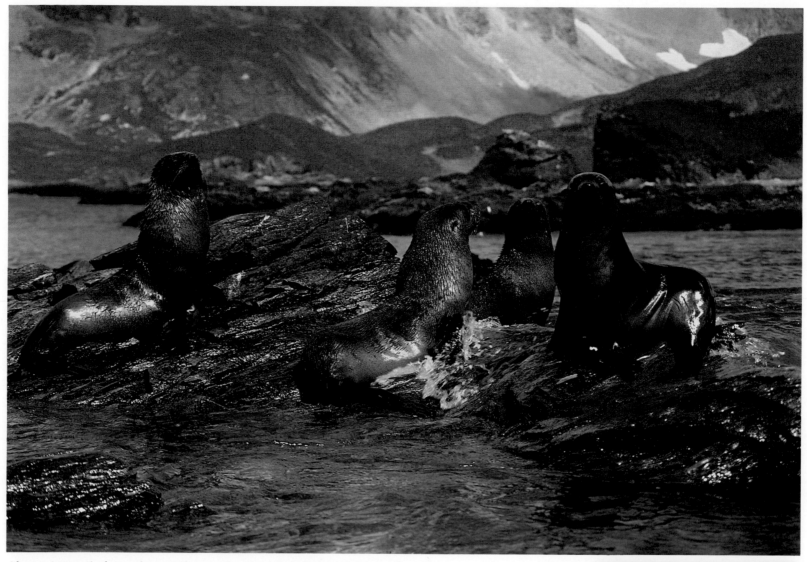

Above: Antarctic fur seal pups play on the rocky foreshores of Cooper Bay, South Georgia. Antarctic fur seals inhabit most subantarctic islands with some roaming south to the Antarctic Peninsula. As members of the Otariidae eared seal family, fur seals have external ears and are able to bring their hind flippers forward, enabling them to be agile on land.

Right: Found only in the Arctic, walruses (*Odobenus rosmarus*) have no external ears. Due to the remoteness of Siberia's Bennett Island, these walruses have eluded exploitation for their ivory tusks.

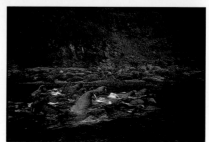

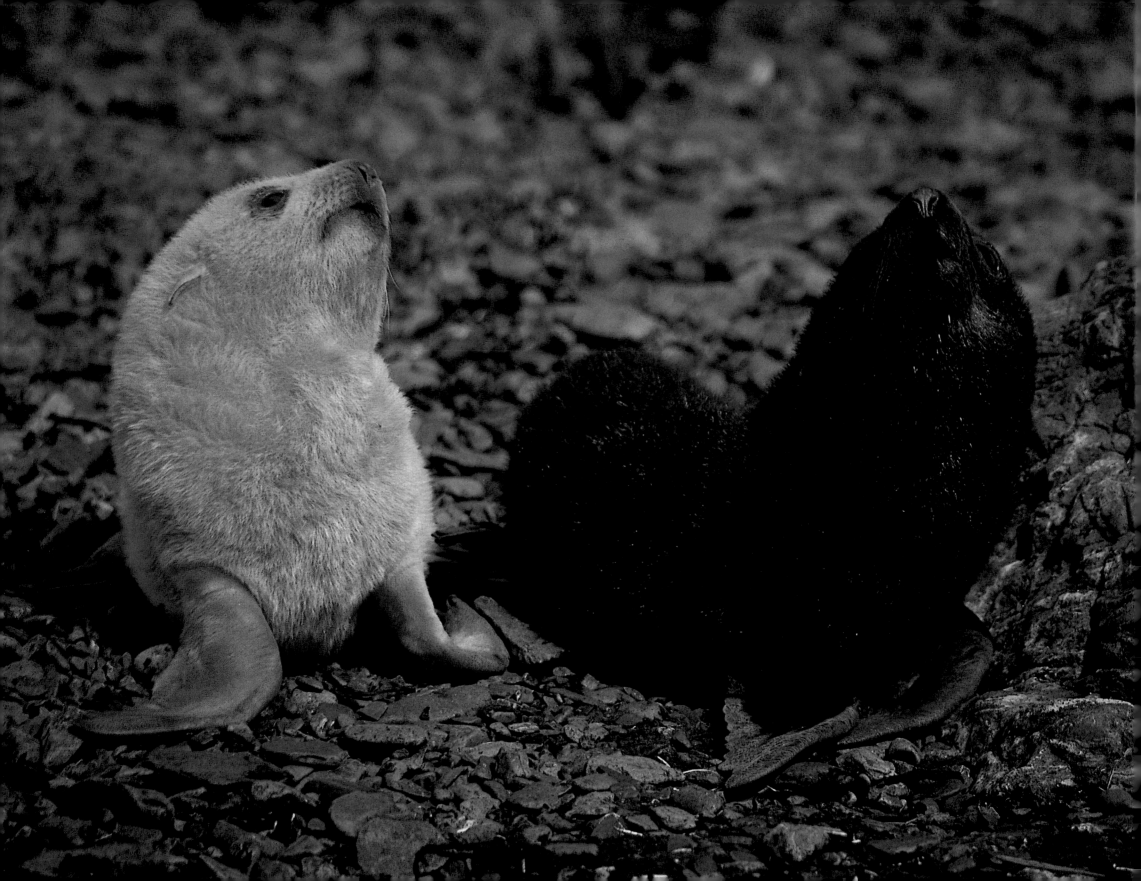

Opposite: Like Yin and Yang, a blond Antarctic fur seal pup plays with a black friend on South Georgia's Albatross Island. Not true albinos, blond fur seals are reasonably common on South Georgia.

Right: On the northern tip of South Georgia, Elsehul Bay and neighboring Undine Harbour play host to thousands of Antarctic fur seals. Throughout the sub-antarctic realm in the early 1800s fur seals were exploited to near extinction for their pelts. In recent years they have made a spectacular comeback. Fish and squid are eaten, although their main diet is krill (*Euphausia superba*). An increased availability of krill due to the decimation of whales is one reason for a rapidly expanding fur seal population.

Below: Male Pacific walruses crowd together on Arakamchechen Island on Siberia's Chukchi Peninsula. Appearing pink, these walruses have flushed blood to the surface of their thick hides so they can regulate body heat during the warm summer months of July and August. Although Inuit people throughout the Arctic have a traditional right to hunt walrus for meat and hide, the value of tusk ivory is marking the walrus as another creature at the whim of human greed.

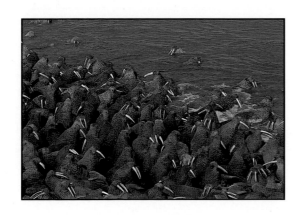

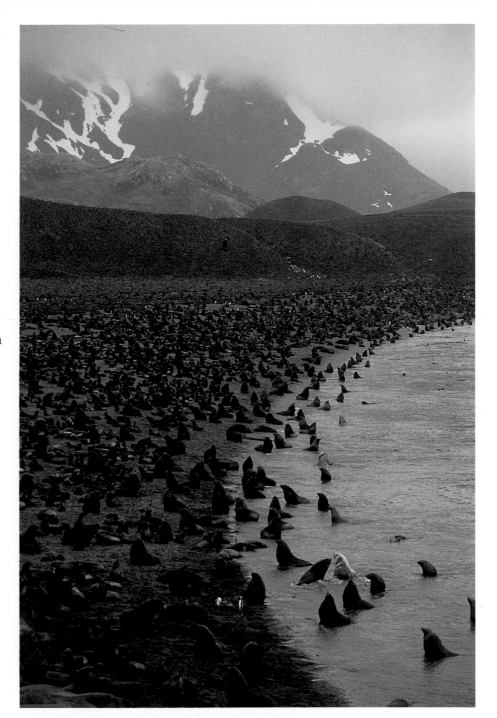

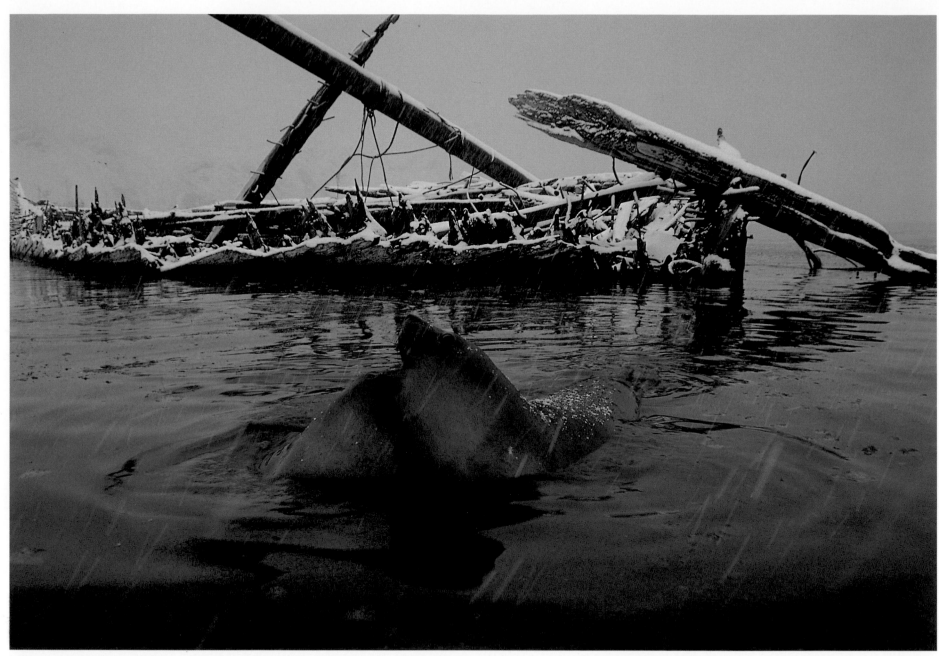

Young elephant seals (*Mirounga leonina*) swim together in a snowstorm beside the wrecked coal ship *Louise* at Grytviken whaling station on the northern coast of South Georgia. Once heavily exploited for the oil in their blubber, juvenile elephant seals can now enjoy play-fighting as they grow up for a life mostly spent at sea.

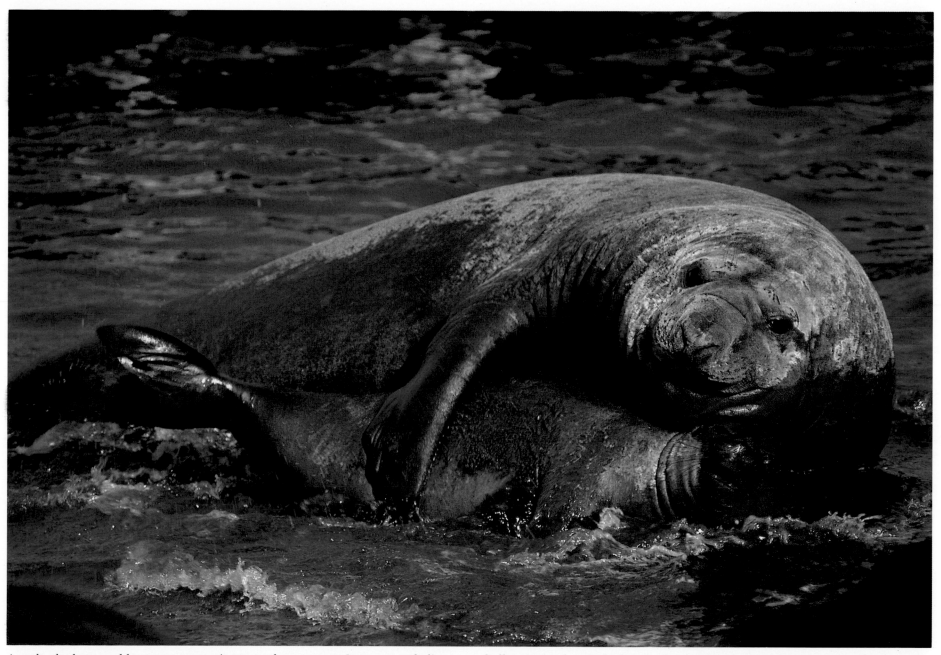

A male elephant seal becomes aggressive toward a pup near Stromness whaling station, South Georgia. The southern elephant seal breeds on all of the sub-antarctic islands. Males, with their large snout, weigh up to four tons. Fending off challenging males on the beach, the dominant male impregnates his harem in the spring, then departs to feed at sea, returning later to molt.

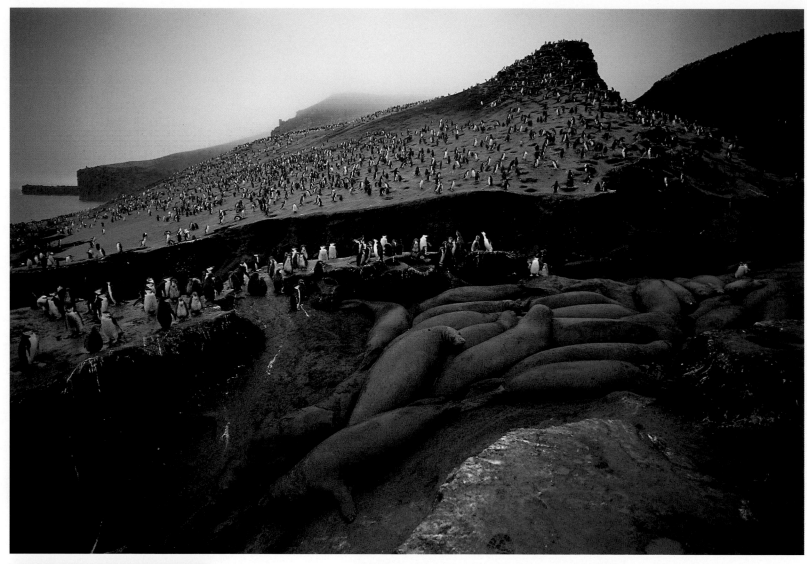

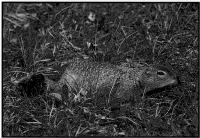

Above: Female elephant seals have crawled high up on Saunders Island, a volcano in the remote South Sandwich group. Oblivious of thousands of chinstrap penguins, the seals wallow in a muddy gully enjoying each others' company and warmth while they shed old skin, which looks like pieces of curled-up sandpaper.

Left: An Arctic ground squirrel on Siberia's Arakamchechen Island scurries to its burrow. With Arctic trees dwarfed to a few inches it is difficult for squirrels to evade capture by Arctic foxes. Neither animal is found in Antarctica.

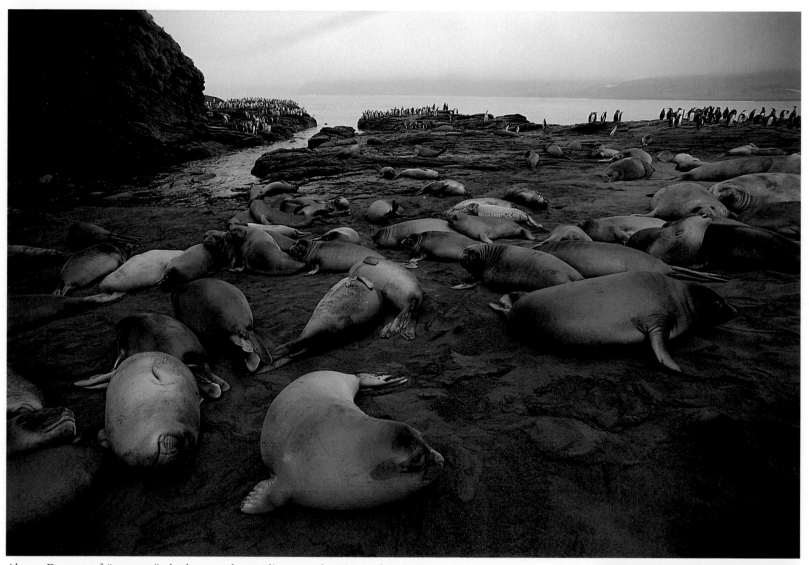

Above: Dozens of "weaner" elephant seal pups lie around at St. Andrew's Bay, South Georgia, while king penguins look on disdainfully. Young pups are often squashed by large males as they lumber toward the sea. Pups that have finished suckling begin to forage for crustaceans before graduating to a fish and squid diet at sea.

Right: Chukchi nomads from the Siberian tundra continue to live off reindeer, utilizing skin, meat, and antlers. South Georgia still has reindeer, which were introduced in 1909 by Norwegian whalers.

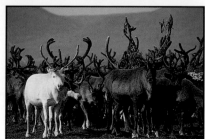

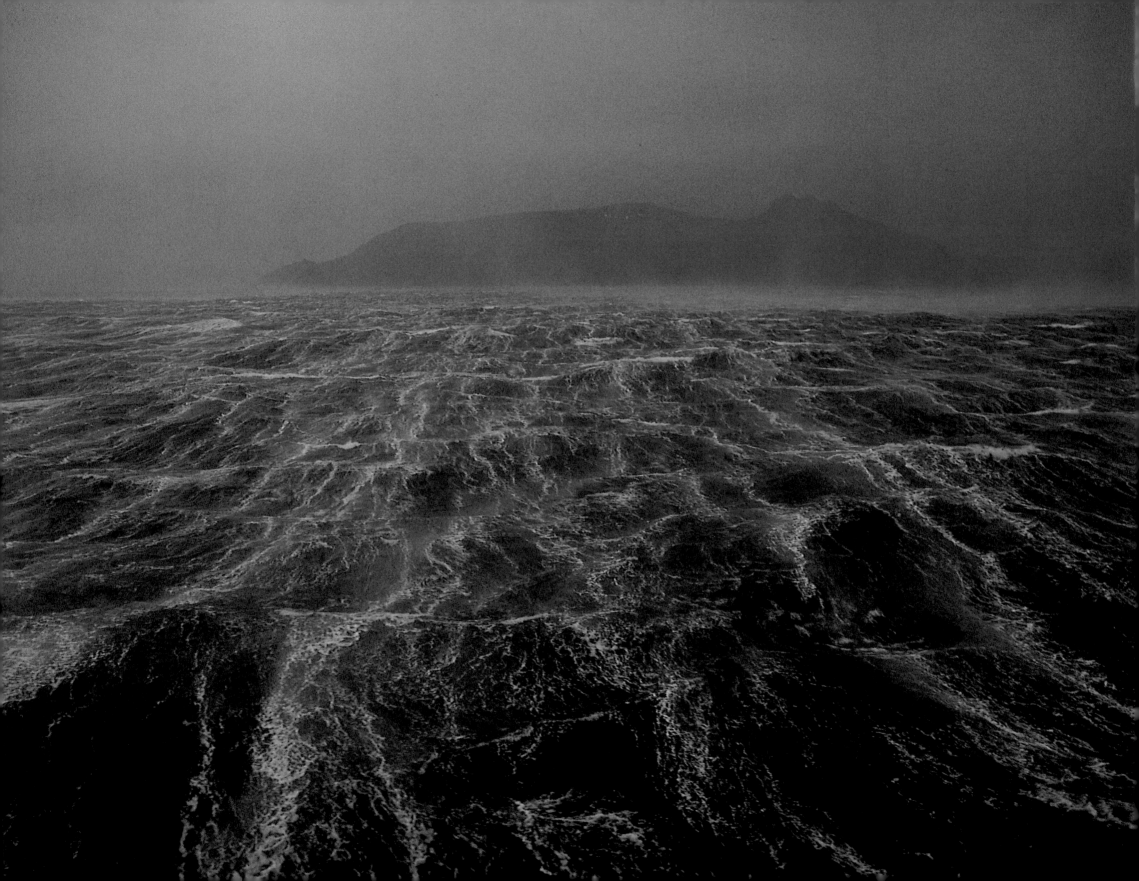

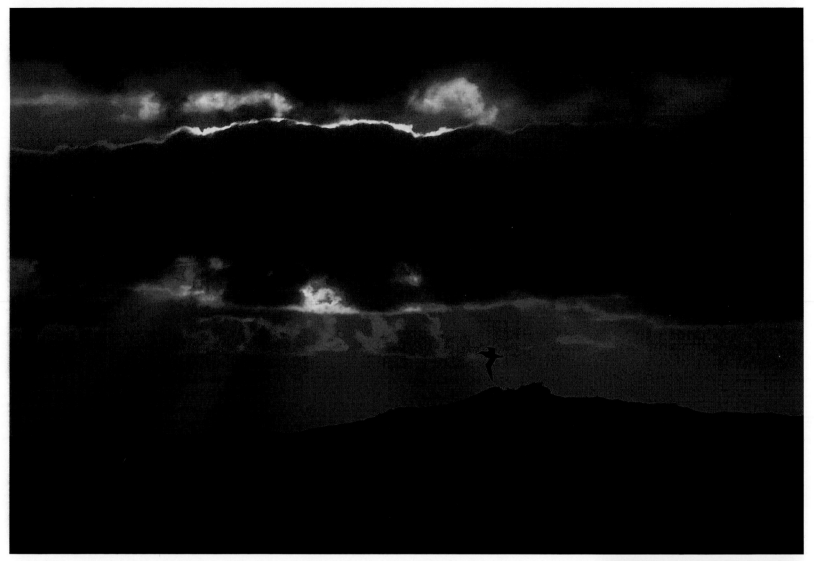

Above: A wandering albatross roams the Southern Ocean at sunset. The Drake Passage can have peaceful moods when the wind and swells moderate.

Opposite: With 80-knot winds and mountainous seas, the storm-tossed Drake Passage is often a fearsome place. Cape Horn is barely visible as sky and whipped-up waves merge.

Right: The tranquillity of an Arctic Ocean sunset on Wrangel Island. Unlike the Antarctic at the equivalent latitude, Wrangel, at 72° N, is home to a native population of Siberians, and is the breeding ground for many wild fowl.

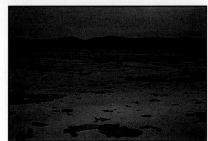

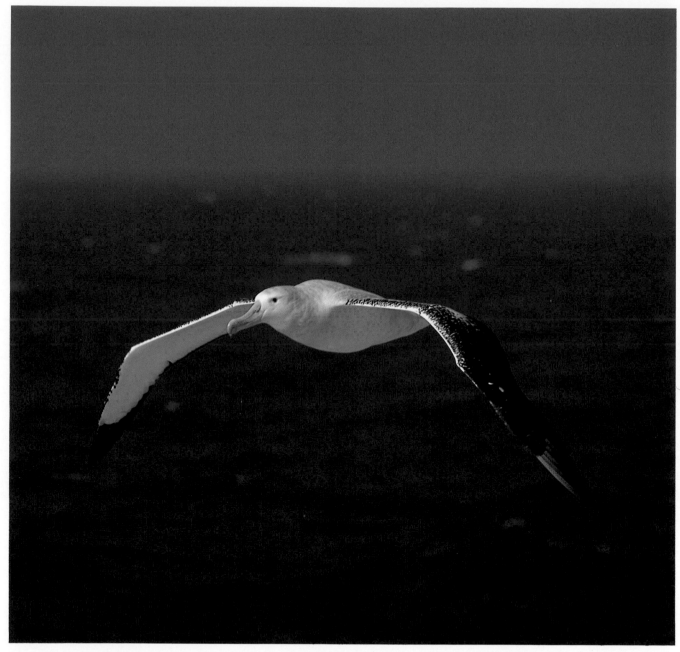

The wandering albatross (*Diomedea exulans*) is the largest seabird, with a wingspan of nearly ten feet. Juvenile wandering albatrosses circle Antarctica for years, finally returning to breed on an island such as South Georgia. The parent wanderer returns periodically during the course of the full year that it feeds its chick.

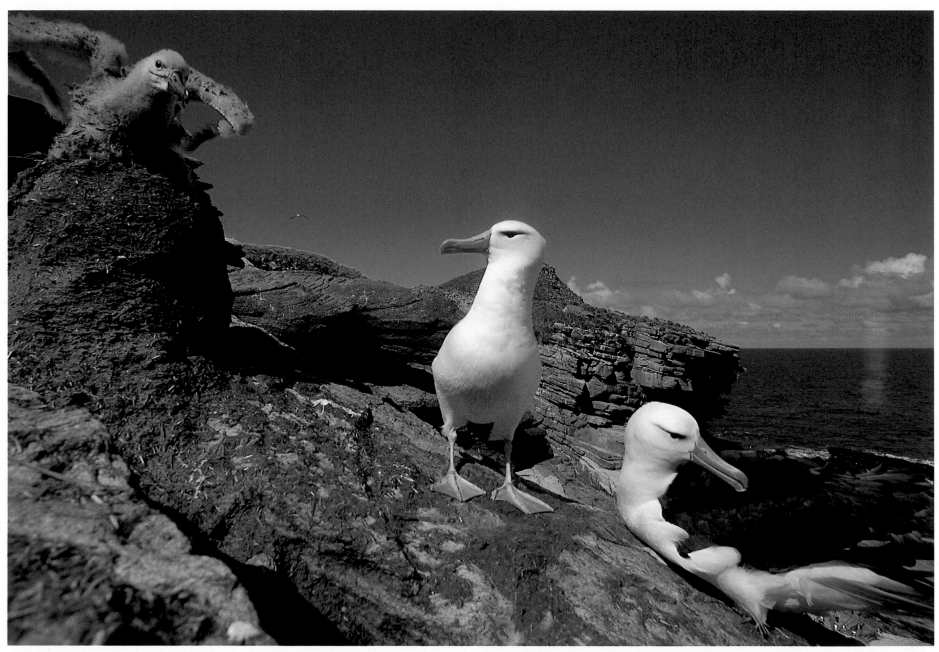

Proud parents look on as a black-browed albatross chick (*Diomedia melanophris*) unfolds its wings from the mud and grass pedestal of a nest on the cliff edge at New Island in the Falklands. Black-browed albatrosses, with the distinctive charcoal flash around their eyes, have a circumpolar range from Macquarie and Campbell Islands to South Georgia and South America.

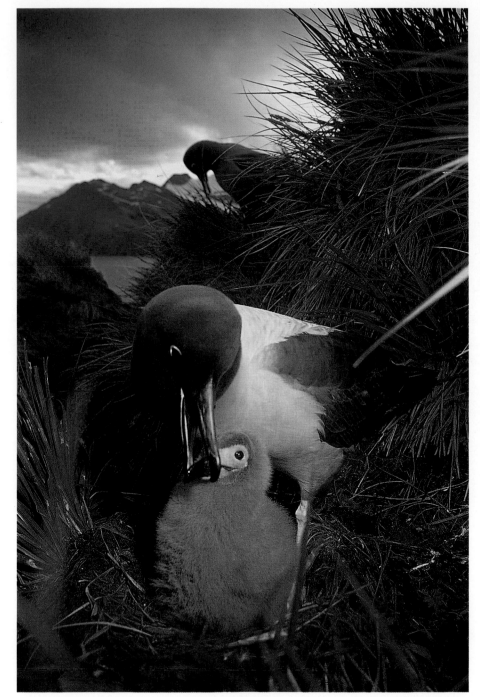

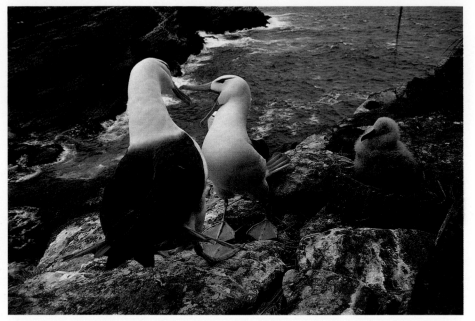

Above: Like all albatrosses returning to a mate already at the nest with a chick, black-browed albatrosses go through an elaborate and sensual sequence of mutual preening, strutting dances, and calls of recognition. This pair have built their nest on the sandstone cliff at West Point Island in the Falklands. Though smaller than the royal or wandering albatrosses, the black-brows are also great fliers and are commonly found many hundreds of miles from land using air currents across the tops of waves to glide effortlessly over the Southern Ocean.

Left: The light-mantled sooty albatross (*Phoebetria palpebrata*) is perhaps the most beautiful of all albatrosses, with the soft grey tones of its feathers and the white ring around its eyes. While one adult keeps watch on the tussocky headland above Gold Harbour on South Georgia, the other parent feeds an oily slurry of squid, krill, and fish to their down-covered chick. Many subantarctic islands have introduced pests; the worst on South Georgia is the brown rat, which takes a toll on fledgling petrels and albatrosses.

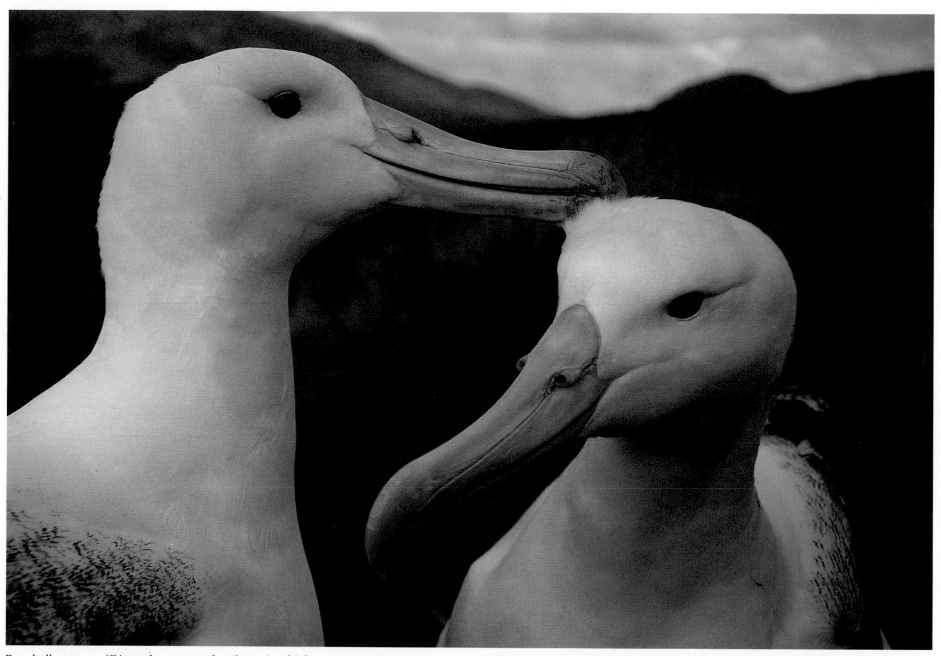

Royal albatrosses (*Diomedea epomophora*) nesting high on a tussock-covered ridge on New Zealand's subantarctic Campbell Island are tenderly preening and nibbling each other to reinforce the pair bonding. Albatrosses mate for life and can live up to sixty years. Although royals only breed on New Zealand's subantarctic islands, they are commonly found as far away as the Drake Passage.

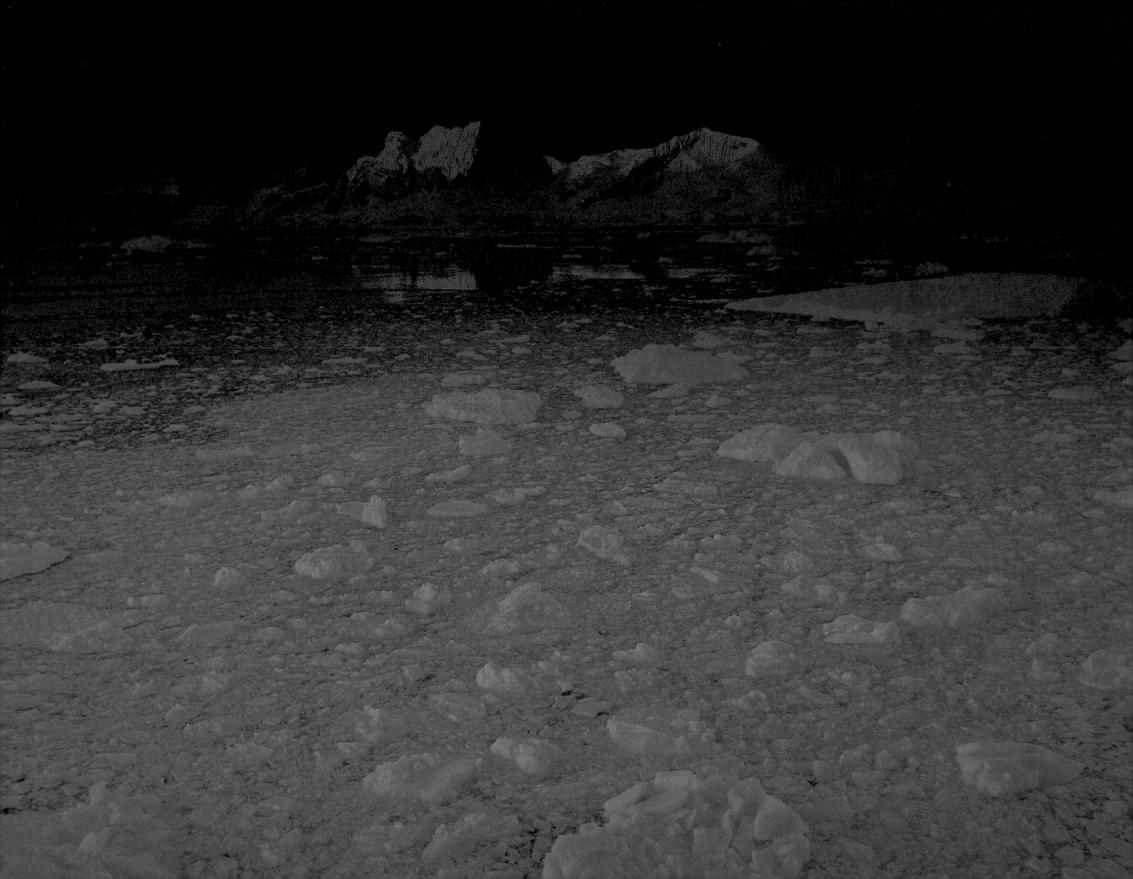

EARTH, THE ICE PLANET

To enter Greater Antarctica is to be drawn into a slow maelstrom of ice. Ice is the beginning of Antarctica and ice is its end. As one moves from perimeter to interior, the proportion of ice relentlessly increases. Ice creates more ice and ice defines ice. Everything else is suppressed...Earth — the fabled water planet is also an ice planet.
The Ice — A Journey to Antarctica, Stephen Pyne

While many people are attracted to Antarctica by images of its wildlife, it is ice that creates the most profound emotional impact. Outliers of the Antarctic domain, icebergs and pack ice entice us into a mysterious world that captures the imagination. Ice, in all its alluring hues and textures, radiates a peaceful beauty. The infinite shapes and sizes of icebergs adrift on a powerful ocean impart a profound feeling of antiquity and grandeur that enhances Antarctica's great blessing of silence. Confronting the sheer immensity of Antarctic ice further south leaves an indelible imprint on the senses unrivaled elsewhere. Arctic ice seems trivial by comparison.

Big ice-clad mountains the world over engender feelings of awe and humility. The unbridled majesty of icescape Antarctica goes far beyond this. Master of such a forbidding environment, ice forces us to ponder our frailty and vulnerability as humans on this incredible planet. And yet, the arrogance of human "rule" of the planet has created havoc through overpopulation and misuse of resources. In Antarctica, it is humbling to realize that ice makes all the rules. Ice dominates to such an extent that even during a brief encounter it can relegate the concept of a warm green world of plants beyond the northern horizon to hazy memory. Encountering

Opposite: Brash ice fills Paradise Bay as the sun lights up peaks on the Antarctic Peninsula.

vast expanses of ice can be as awesome as trying to grasp the magnitude and remoteness of stars. It is difficult to comprehend the idea that the effective area of Antarctica doubles during winter with the formation of sea ice. Ice challenges us to understand more of the nature of the Southern Ocean, of the consequences of climatic change, and of the influence of Antarctica's vast ice sheets on the rest of the Earth.

Antarctica has not always been so cold and so extensively glaciated. Coal beds and fossilized remains of the fern *Glossopteris* appear in sedimentary outcrops throughout the Transantarctic Mountains, indicating that the climate was once much warmer than today. Fossilized coniferous tree trunks lie scattered on sandstone ledges high up in Victoria Land's Dry Valleys while ancient turtles, whales, dolphins, and penguins have been found on coastal sites such as Prydz Bay near the Australian Davis base and Seymour Island in the Weddell Sea. Recently, a meat-eating dinosaur dating back 185 million years was discovered high on Mt. Kirkpatrick only 372 miles from the South Pole. Fossils of a berry-eating marsupial have also been found. This fossil record has helped piece together the geological history of Antarctica.

It is now recognized that Antarctica is the "keystone of Gondwanaland," the central landmass of the ancient southern supercontinent. Moving almost at the rate fingernails grow, tectonic plate action started to split Gondwanaland apart about 200 million years ago, gradually separating the landmasses of Africa, India, Australia, and South America from Antarctica. At the same time, Gondwanaland drifted from an equatorial position to one closer to the South Pole. The final break took place some 50 million years ago when the Antarctic Peninsula separated from the South American Andean chain. This gave birth to the 620-mile-wide Drake Passage and formed the

Southern Ocean. Distinct weather patterns then evolved and strong westerly winds started to blow continuously. In association with the winds, an ocean current known as the West Wind Drift began circulating. Unimpeded by continental landmasses, the cold circumpolar ocean and the persistent westerly winds combined to deflect warm surface waters northwards. It was the resultant cooling which initiated the large-scale glaciation of Antarctica.

The modern-day Antarctic ice sheets consist of about 39.2 billion cubic yards of ice spread over an area of 5.5 million square miles — nearly twice the size of Australia. Only a smattering of rocky summits and coastal icefree areas avoid complete inundation by this blanket of ice. Many of Antarctica's glaciers take on enormous proportions. The world's largest glacier, the Lambert, situated near the Australian science bases Davis and Mawson, is 250 miles long by at least 60 miles wide. The Lambert is further extended where it flows out to sea to form the Amery Ice Shelf. If the weight of Antarctic ice was removed from the continent, the land would rise from 985 to 3,300 feet. In fact, Antarctica's incredible mass causes the Earth to be slightly pear-shaped.

Antarctica is divided into the West and East Antarctic ice sheets by the 1,860-mile long Transantarctic Mountains, which are up to 14,700 feet high. Much of the West Antarctic Ice Sheet rests on bedrock that is well below sea level. The East Antarctic Ice Sheet by comparison is much larger and rests on a base that is predominantly above sea level. Massive ice domes in East Antarctica reach up to 13,120 feet. The North Pole and surrounding Arctic Ocean are often referred to by geographers and mapmakers as the "top of the world." In reality, with the geographic South Pole at over 9,840 feet and with a mean elevation of over 6,000 feet, Antarctica is by far the highest of all continents.

Severe cold temperatures in Antarctica vary with latitude, elevation and distance from the sea. The lowest on record is an almost inconceivable −128.2°F measured at Vostok, a Russian base in the interior of East Antarctica. Boiling water thrown into the air at Vostok immediately explodes into ice dust! Described as a "shining white lantern" from space, Antarctica is truly desert-like, receiving minuscule amounts of precipitation, often in the form of ice crystals known as angel dust. Antarctic travelers often observe angel dust create a variety of optical effects including "sundog" halos around the sun. Compared with the warmer Antarctic Peninsula, where annual snowfall can be as much as twelve feet, interior Antarctica receives little snow, only two inches. What snow does fall does not melt and is simply redistributed by wind, often forming concrete-like ridges called "sastrugi." The combination of low snow accumulation and cold temperatures makes the interior of Antarctica ideal for obtaining information about past climate.

It is now known that some climate variations over the last 50 million years have been caused by changes in the orbit of the Earth which directly affect the amount of incoming solar radiation. Less certain are the effects of meteorite impacts which may also influence Earth's orbit, volcanic activity which releases aerosols into the atmosphere to block sunlight, and of course, the greenhouse effect from the increased burning of fossil fuels. Deep ice cores recovered from places like Vostok are used to study past climates. By analyzing particles, the composition of isotopes and gases like CO_2 trapped in ice bubbles from core samples, scientists gain information about past atmospheric conditions. The Vostok core, the deepest drilled in Antarctica, is about 9,840 feet deep and at its extremity the ice is 300,000 years old.

West Antarctica has been the focus of considerable recent glaciological research motivated by the potential consequences of rising sea levels causing the ice sheet (its base already below sea level) to float and collapse. Studies show that 90 percent of the ice discharge from West Antarctica occurs through ice streams that are typically 30 miles wide. Evidence from ground surveys and satellite photographs show the ice streams surge at speeds of several feet per day compared with motion in the surrounding ice of a few feet per year. The boundaries between the fast-moving ice and the slower ice are marked by zones of huge crevasses. Seismic and radar profiling and drill cores extracted from the bed of these ice streams indicate the bed consists of ground-up rock lubricated by liquid water under pressure. As some ice streams have "shut down" in the last 300 years, it seems that the dynamics of West Antarctica's glaciology are extremely complex.

It has been suggested that, once started, complete collapse of the West Antarctic Ice Sheet could occur in as little as fifty years. The resulting 16-foot sea-level rise would flood many low-lying heavily populated areas of the world such as Bangladesh. While this would be serious enough, the breakup and melting of both the West and the massive East Antarctic ice sheets, although unlikely, could mean a disastrous 240-foot global rise. Such possibilities lend an urgency and priority to further glaciologcal studies in Antarctica.

The ice shelves surrounding Antarctica may hold the key to understanding ice sheet collapse. Ice shelves are floating masses of ice that form where ice streams or large glaciers discharge into the ocean. Under pressure, ice streams and glacial ice flow through mountain ranges, carving a powerful path down to sea level. The ice then coalesces again into the single massive entity of an ice shelf which spreads out over the ocean. As sea water flows under an ice shelf all the way to the hinge zone where it abuts the continent, the entire ice shelf flexes with the movement of the tidal cycle. Ice shelves make up

about 14 percent of the total area of Antarctica. The largest, the Ross Ice Shelf south of New Zealand, is commonly equated with the size of France.

There is very little melt in the interior of Antarctica and most ice mass is lost by melting from the seaward underside of the ice shelves as well as by the calving of icebergs. The iceberg calving process is probably triggered by tidal cycles and ocean swells which stress the outer edge of the ice shelf until a section breaks off. With more satellites in polar orbit scientists are now increasingly aware of major calving events. They can also track the movement of the resultant mega-bergs on their wandering paths through the Southern Ocean. In 1995, a single berg measuring 46 miles by 22 miles and 590 feet thick broke away from the Larsen Ice Shelf to drift northwards into the Weddell Sea. Another even larger one, 95 miles by 22 miles, cut loose from the Ross Ice Shelf in 1987. If melted, the volume of water from an iceberg this big would provide enough fresh water for each person on Earth to have two glasses per day for more than 2,000 years!

Relatively little is known about calving processes but it is likely that the iceberg calving rate increases as the sea level rises and as the sea surface temperature rises. Monitoring changes around the sensitive margins of Antarctica may give the first clues about climate changes. For example, atmospheric warming from the greenhouse effect could cause the oceans to warm and the associated thermal expansion to force sea levels to rise. It is possible that the recent dramatic collapses of some of Antarctica's major ice shelves are in response to such factors. Indeed, the massive collapses of the Prince Gustav, the northern Larsen, and the Wordie Ice Shelves in the past few years are unprecedented events in glaciological history. The disintegration of ice shelves in itself does not necessarily mean that sea levels will rise even more, for floating ice is already displacing a significant amount of sea water. In contrast, rising temperatures can also mean additional evaporation from the sea, hence more cloud cover and the balancing effect of increased snowfall in interior Antarctica.

The average temperature on the Antarctic Peninsula has risen about 1.4°F in the past fifty years, which is a greater increase than anywhere else on Earth. What has always been described as a "brief Antarctic summer" on the peninsula has now lengthened from sixty to ninety days. Plants such as mosses and the grass known as *Deschampsia* are flourishing in once-hostile niches. No one knows if this fluctuation is a regional phenomenon, limited to the western side of the Antarctic Peninsula. Could it be part of a natural orbital cycle or a warning of more ominous events ahead?

The Greek philosopher Aristotle postulated the existence of a southern continent that balanced known landmasses in the north. Centuries later, in the 1770s, James Cook's remarkable voyages circumnavigated Antarctica below the fringe of subantarctic islands thereby dispelling the idea of a single gigantic "Terra Australis Incognita." Sailing south of the Antarctic Circle to 71°S, Cook encountered ice on a scale never seen before. His exploration paved the way for other seafarers to gradually delineate the present-day boundaries of the Antarctic continent and the Southern Ocean. While Cook found southern latitudes inhospitable and "useless," the global importance of this frigid realm is now well established. Antarctica's ice cover plays a crucial modifying role in world weather patterns. Also, the cold dense oxygen-rich water of the Southern Ocean flowing at depth reaches oceans north of the equator, affecting their vitality. Antarctica's zone of influence in the south is the equivalent to northern regions contained within a line linking Vancouver, London, Berlin, Mongolia, and northern Japan.

Opposite: Quark Expeditions' vessel *Professor Khromov* glides carefully past icebergs near Petermann Island, Antarctic Peninsula. By chartering small ice-strengthened Russian hydrographic vessels, which only take 38 passengers, Quark Expeditions fosters the concept of highly flexible, low-impact adventure cruises in Antarctica.

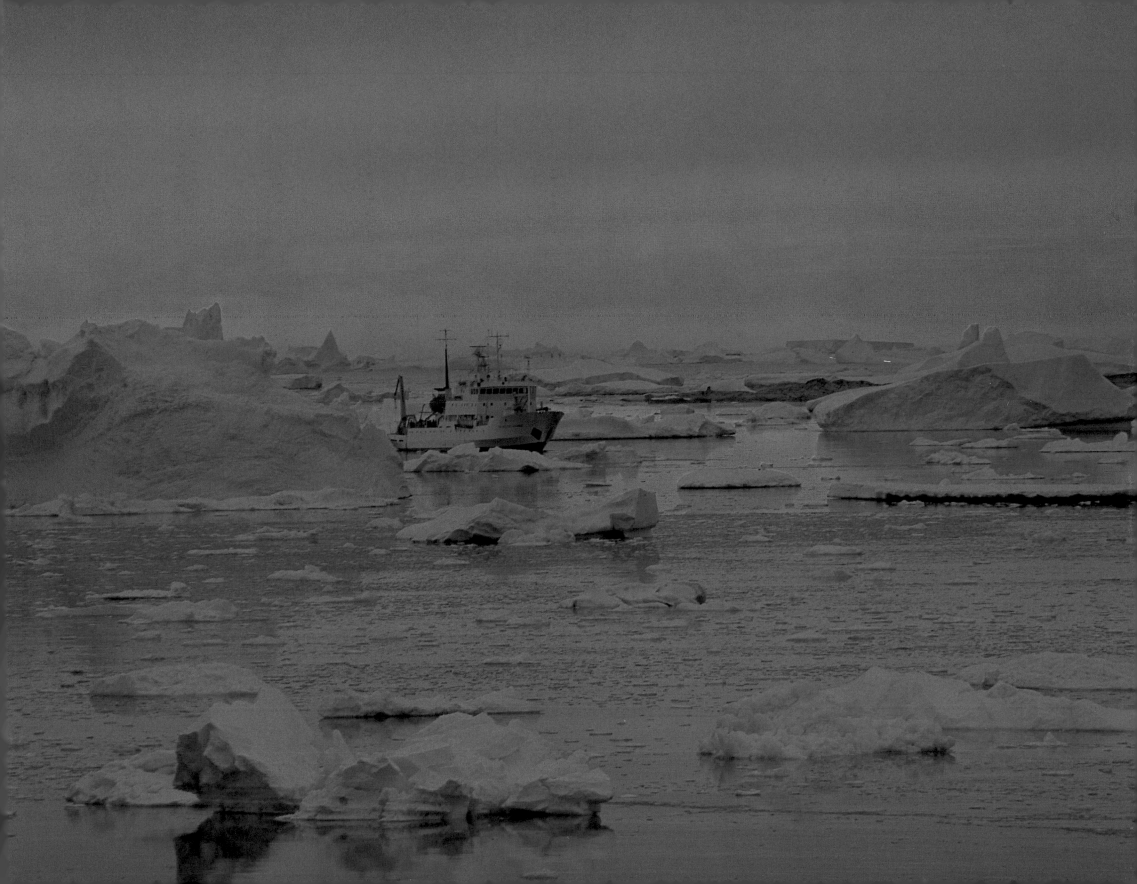

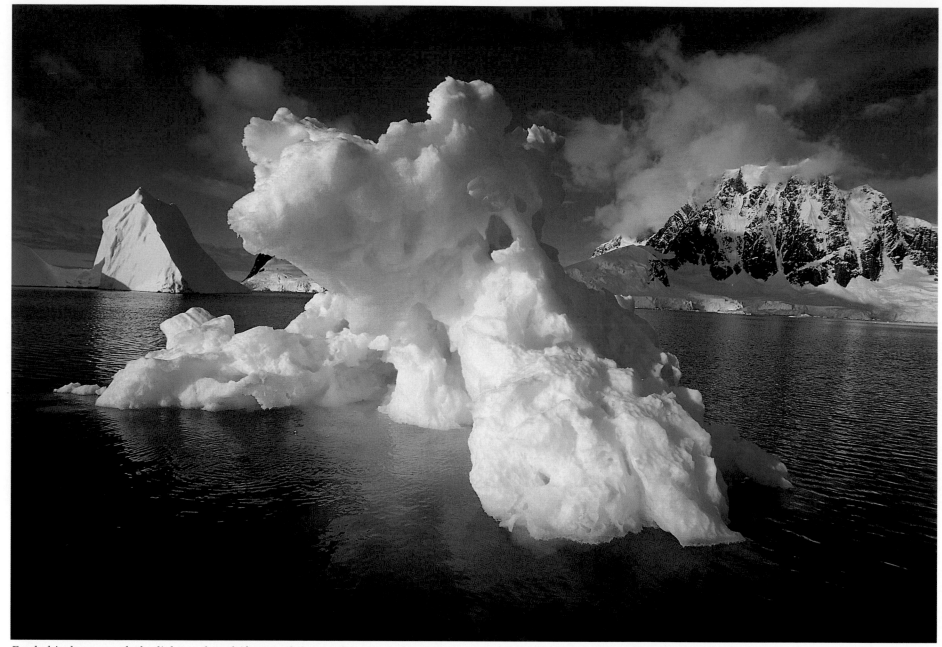

Eroded icebergs catch the light as they drift toward the southern end of Lemaire Channel on the Antarctic Peninsula. Two-thirds of an iceberg remain below the waterline. Icebergs often roll over and split apart as they are weathered by wave action and melting.

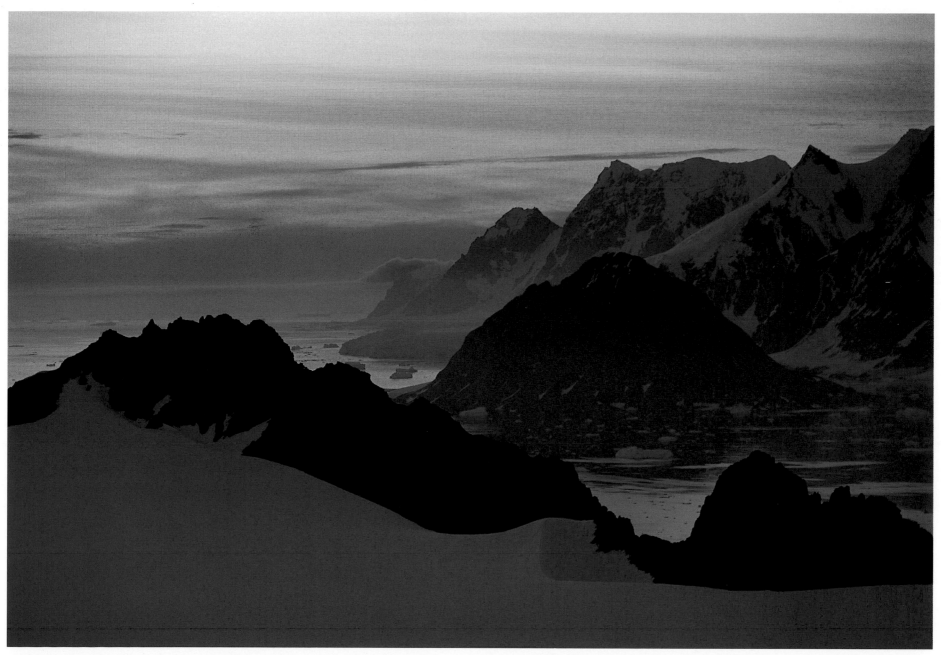

The view from the top of a peak on Adelaide Island encompasses other high summits above Marguerite Bay which are painted with Antarctica's midnight colors. At 67°S, Adelaide Island is just south of the Antarctic Circle. This image illustrates the extent of darkness during the height of summer. British Antarctic Survey's base Rothera with its newly completed hard-surface runway is located on the nearby coast.

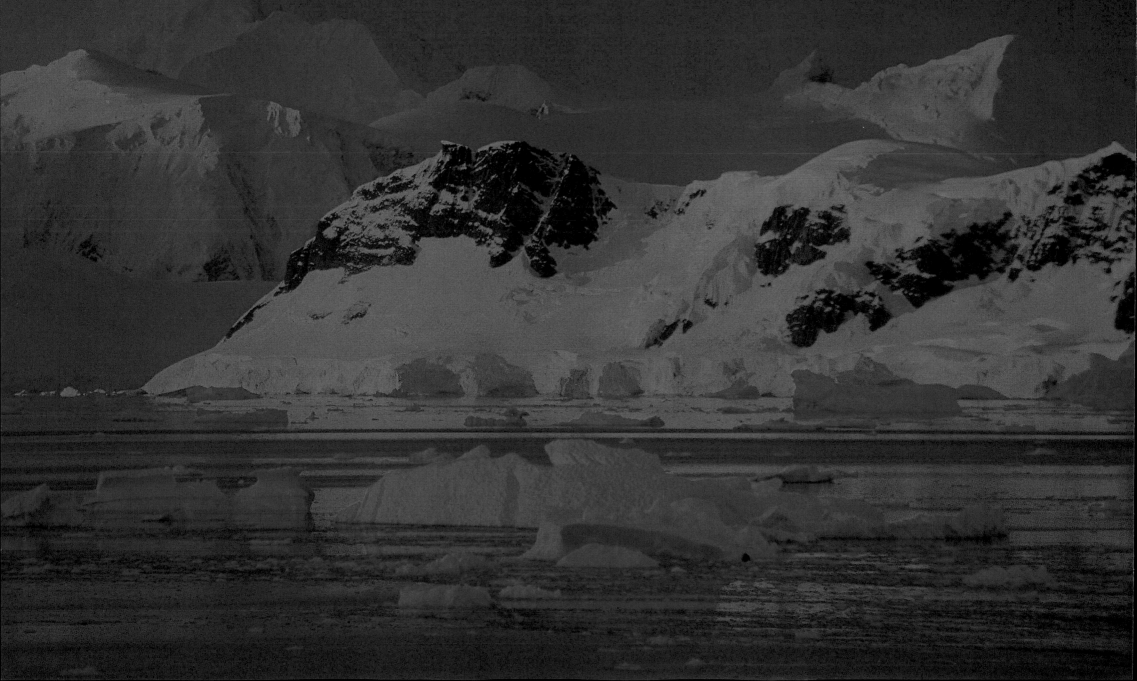

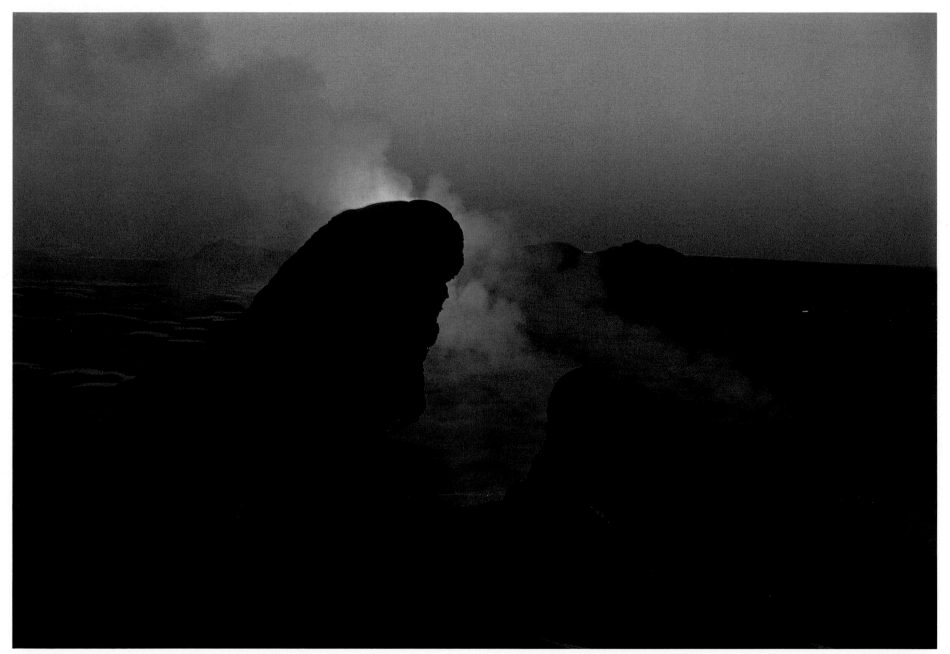

Above: The midnight sun over McMurdo Sound in Victoria Land silhouettes the sixty-five-foot high fumarole towers near the summit of the active volcano Mt. Erebus. The fumarole towers are hollow, formed when steam rising from hot soil freezes into a chimney-like structure. It is possible to have a sauna inside!

Opposite: Sunset on peaks in Paradise Bay, Antarctic Peninsula.

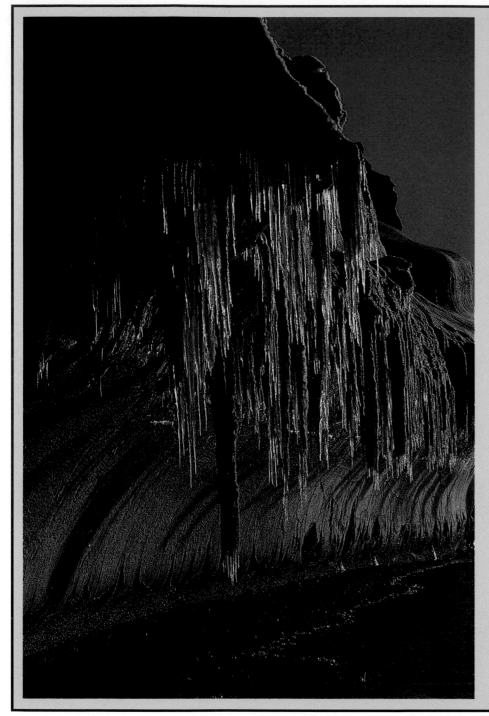

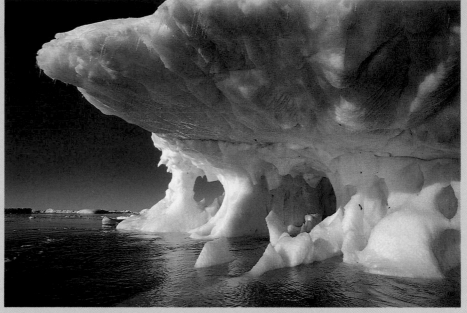

Sculptured ice

Above: An iceberg grounded near Petermann Island has been severely undercut by ocean currents and wave action. Had the top-heavy berg not grounded near the coast, it would have rolled over and probably split apart. Antarctic water is so clear that the "foot" of an iceberg often appears turquoise beneath the surface.

Left: In midsummer a considerable amount of melting takes place from glacier fronts and icebergs around the edge of the Southern Ocean. This Terre Adelie Land iceberg's ten-foot icicles are running with fresh water.

Right above: Pancake ice forms on the surface of the Ross Sea in March as the temperature drops with the onset of autumn. An oily coating of freezing sea water gradually solidifies to create "pancakes" with upturned edges. In turn, these eventually coalesce, merging to form a complete cover of sea ice. Antarctic sea ice reaches its maximum extent or thickness in early spring.

Right below: This blue pock-marked iceberg near Pleneau Island seen through a snowstorm creates an image reminiscent of the inside of a child's crystal ball that snows when it is shaken.

Far right: Light catches the edges of the flutings on the underside of an iceberg which has just turned over in Paradise Bay.

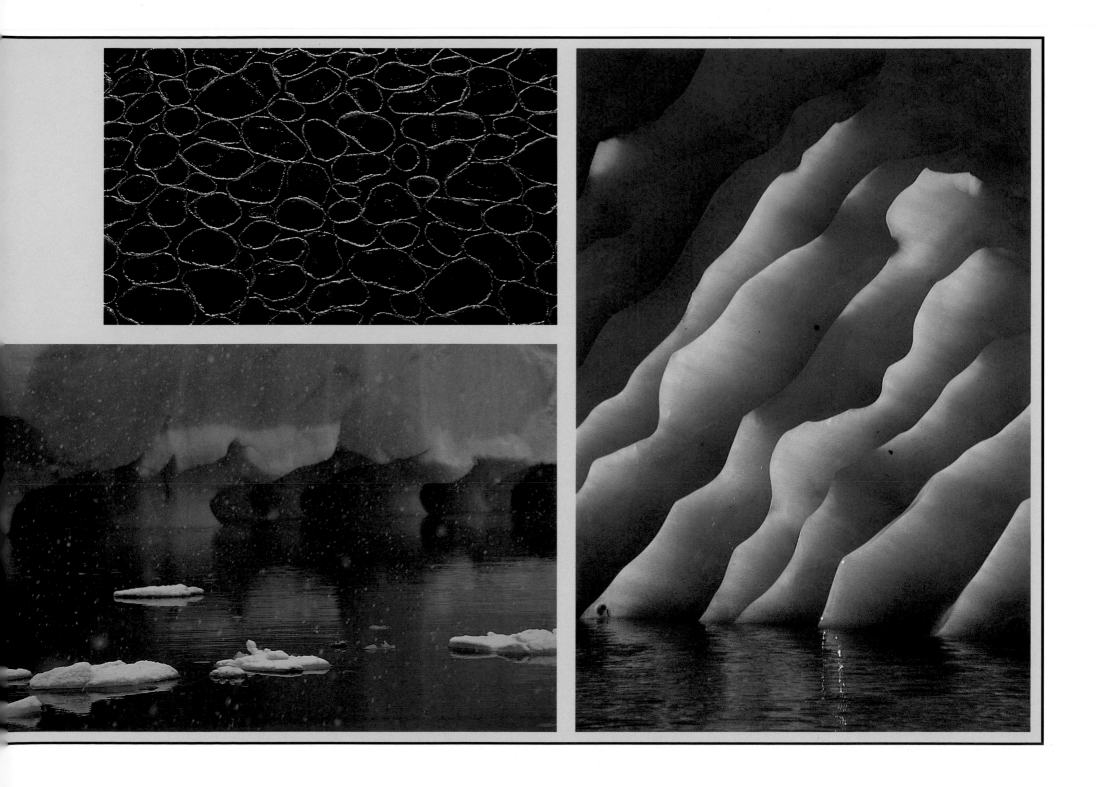

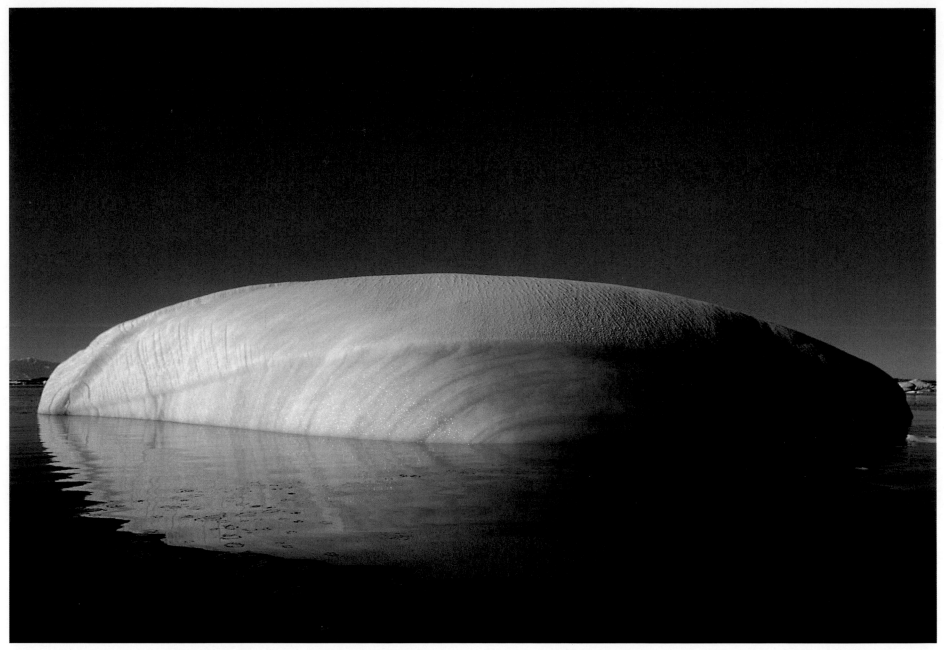

Above: This flying-saucer-shaped iceberg near Petermann Island has been perfectly smoothed by wave action before rolling over to reveal its underside. Endless shapes allow an active imagination to create all sorts of fantastic images.

Opposite: A vivid blue iceberg near the South Sandwich Islands shows how very old, highly compressed ice absorbs all wavelengths of light except blue.

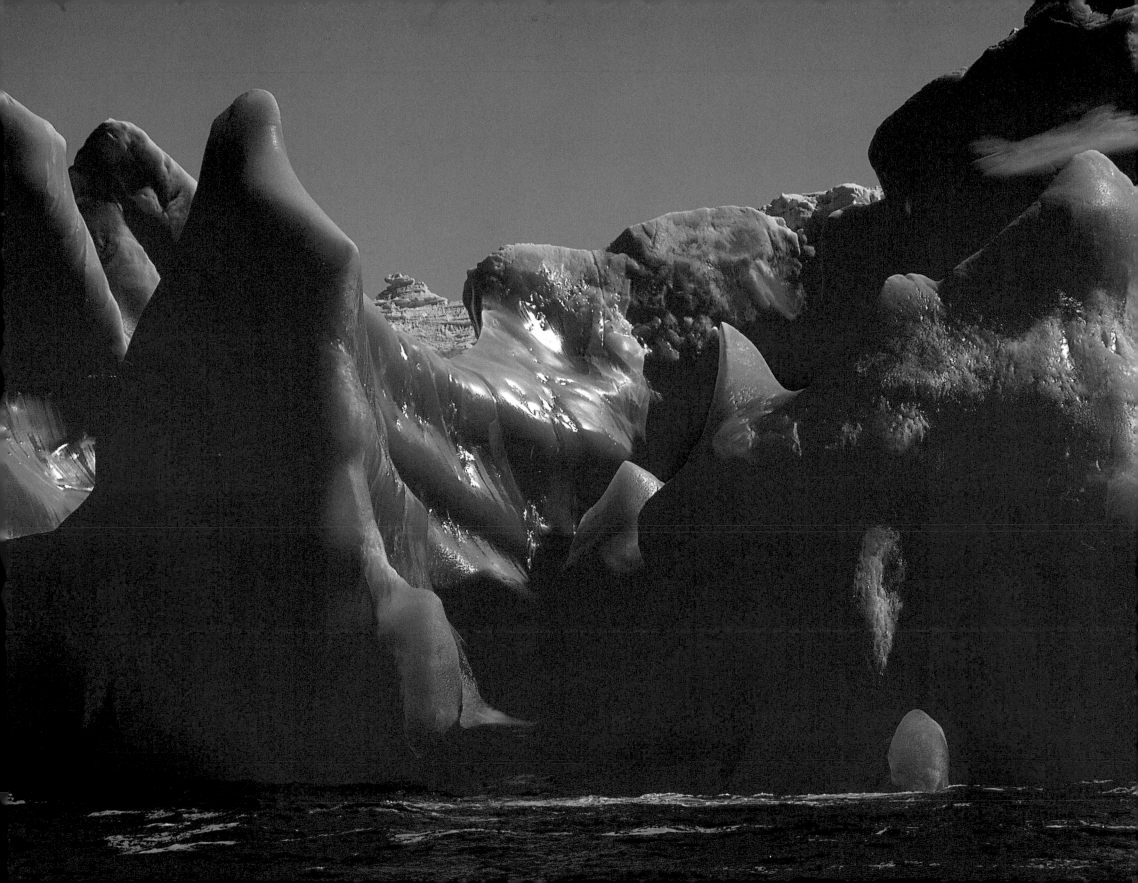

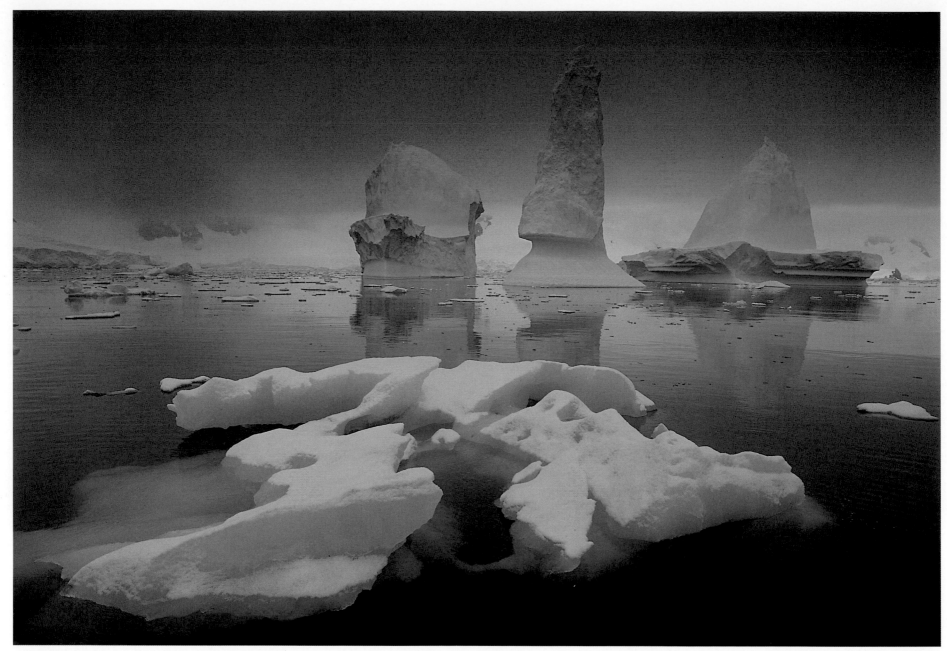

48

A windless foggy day in Paradise Bay on the Antarctic Peninsula is a perfect opportunity to create images of ice in very still water. The ice floe in the foreground is sea ice formed of frozen salt water whereas the iceberg spires behind originate from a glacier or ice shelf made of freshwater ice.

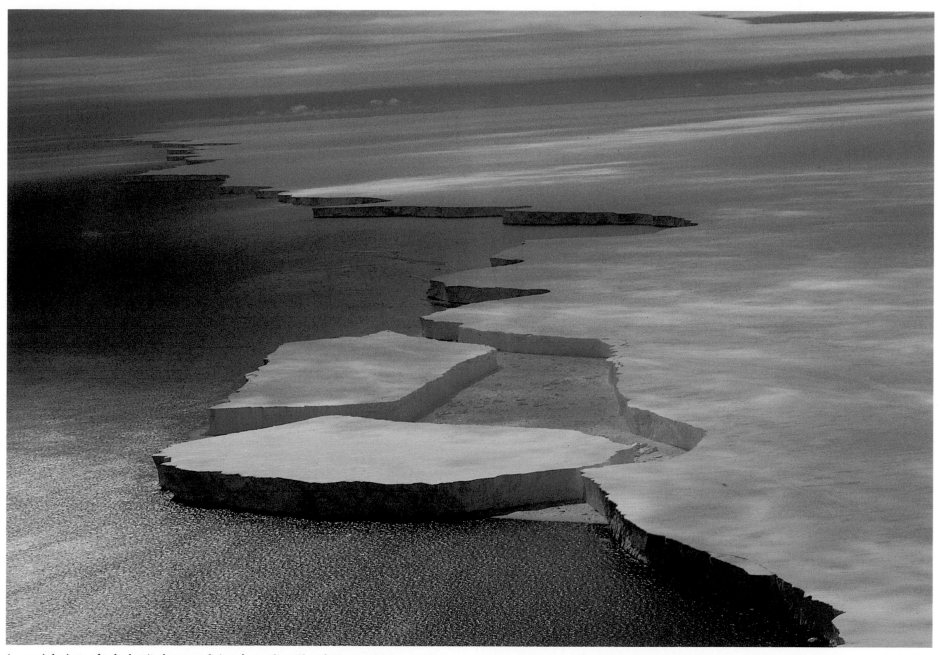

49

An aerial view of tabular icebergs calving from the side of Mertz Glacier on the George V Land Coast. As the glacier is pushed forward by the build-up of pressure created by ice flowing down from the East Antarctic Ice Sheet, it spreads out over the sea. Flexing caused by tidal action leads to the formation of new icebergs.

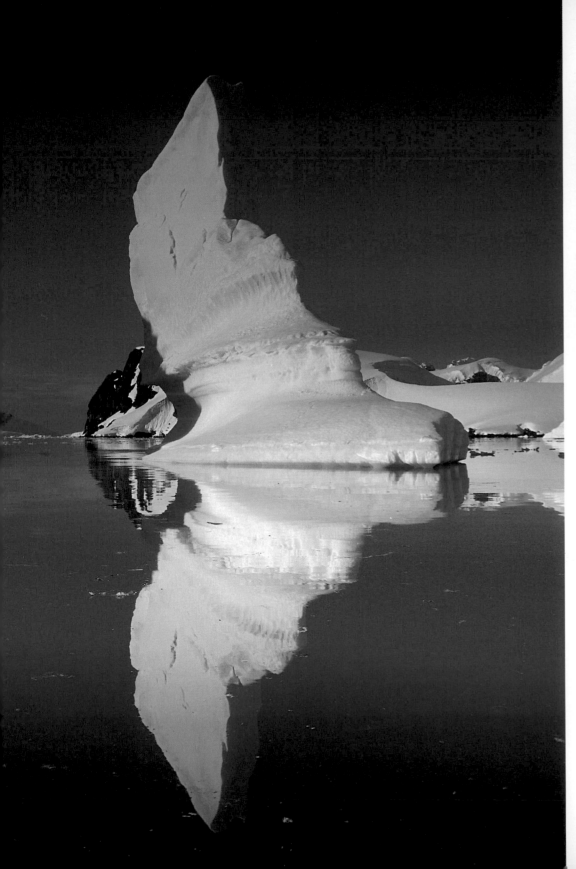

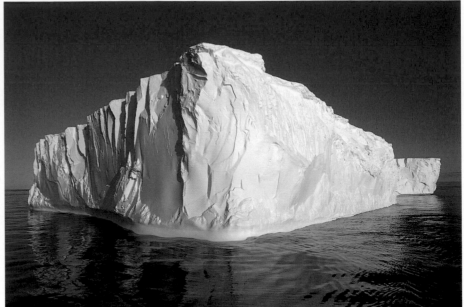

Above: A massive tabular iceberg shaped like an aircraft carrier floats through unusually calm water in the Ross Sea. Tabular bergs are so flat on top that fixed-wing aircraft have landed and taken off from them.

Left: A "batwing" iceberg has been created by a spire reflecting perfectly in the sheltered waters of Paradise Bay.

Right above: As if crafted by invisible chisels, wave action has eroded this iceberg on the Antarctic Peninsula to the surrealistic shape of a marble sculpture.

Far right: Icebergs take on a ghostly quality in the fog of Paradise Bay.

Right below: During Arctic blizzards, dry powder snow on Greenland's ice cap is blown and compressed into hard "sastrugi" ridges similar to those found on the Antarctic ice sheets.

    Unlike Antarctica, the Arctic surrounding the geographic North Pole is a frozen ocean of ever-shifting sea-ice floes, home for predators such as polar bears that are unique to the region.

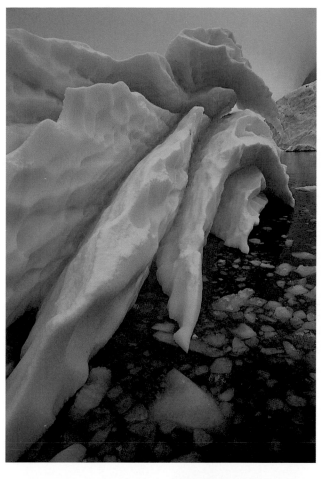

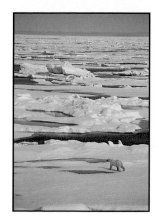

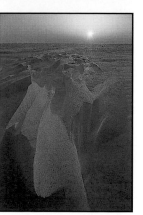

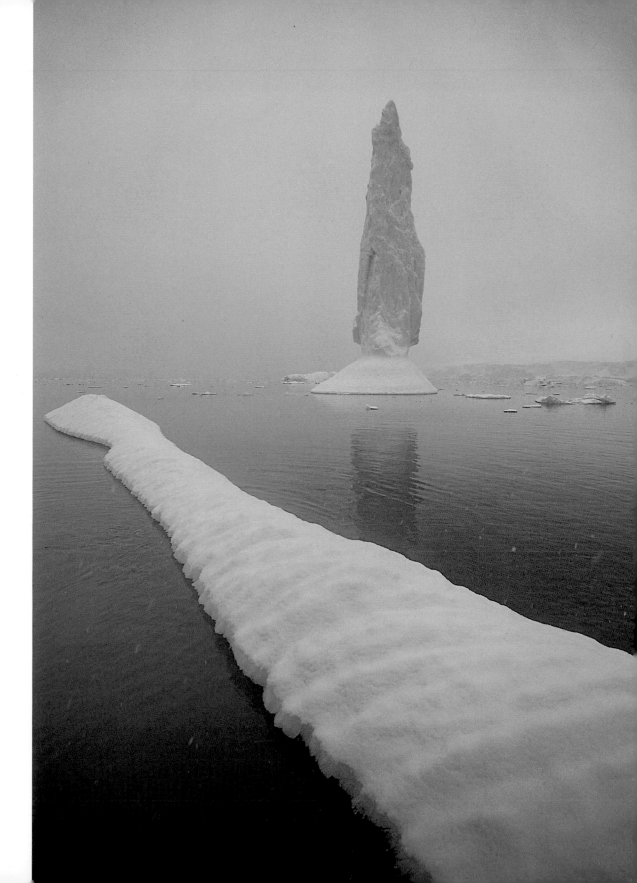

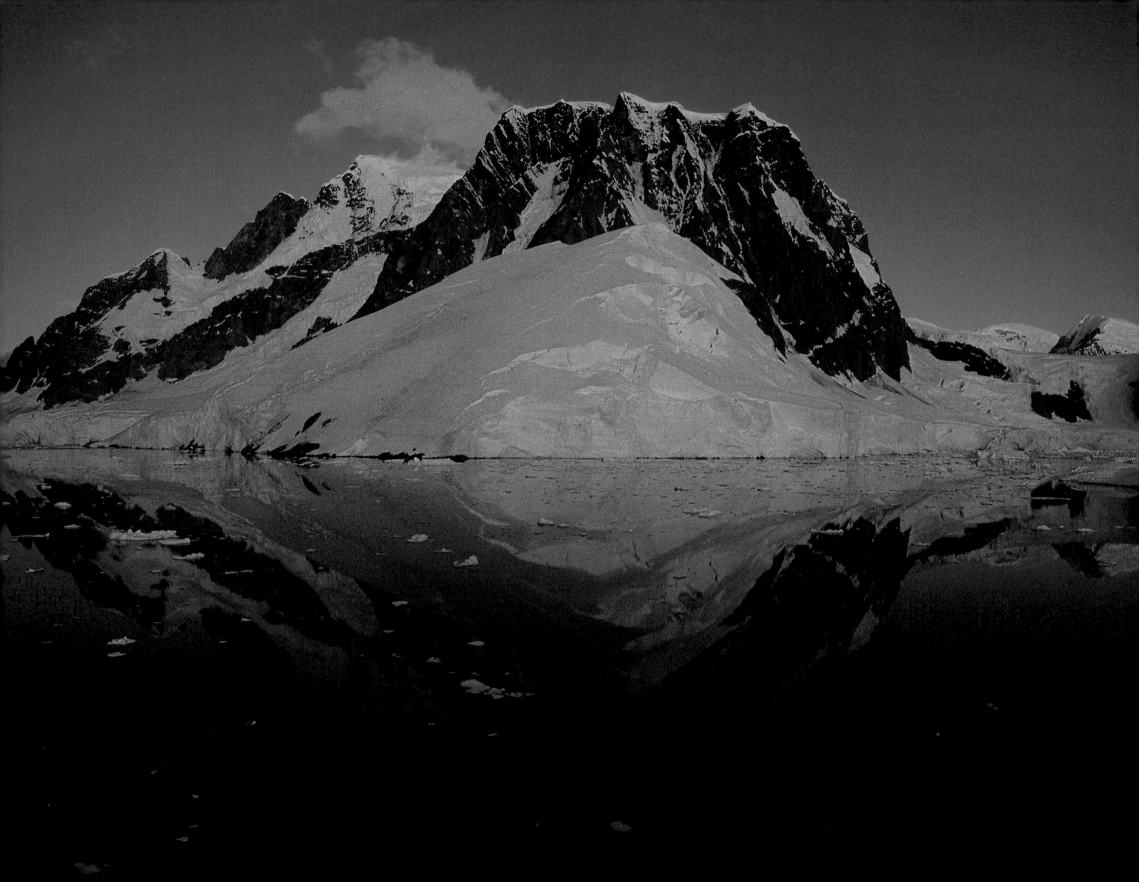

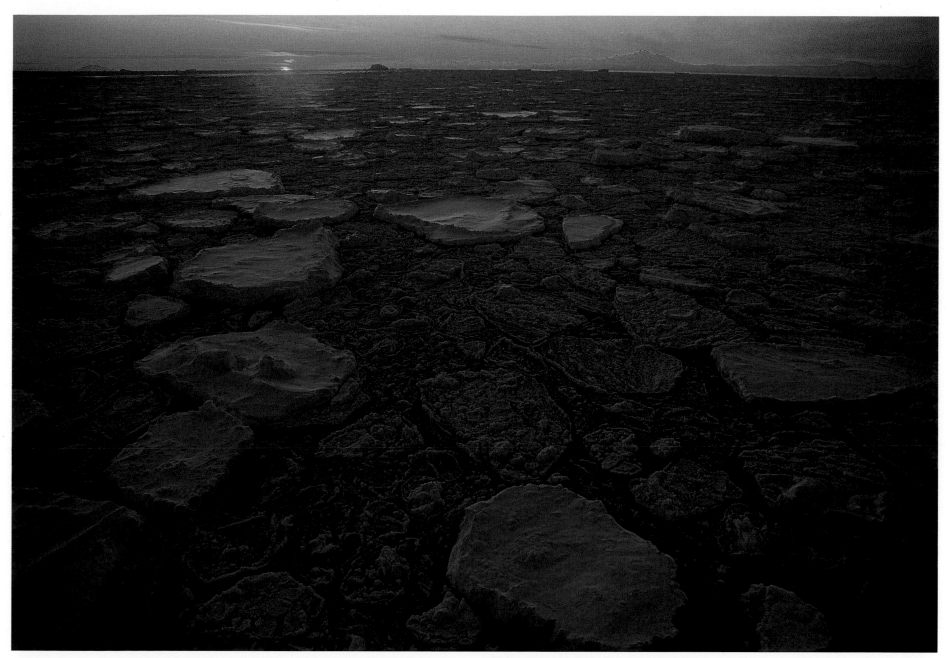

53

Above: The southern hemisphere's autumn month of March in the Ross Sea is always a time of rapid change. The air temperature drops on average nearly two degrees Fahrenheit each day and the sea starts to freeze. Pancake ice forms, gradually coalescing into bigger floes.

Opposite: Lemaire Channel reflections, Antarctic Peninsula.

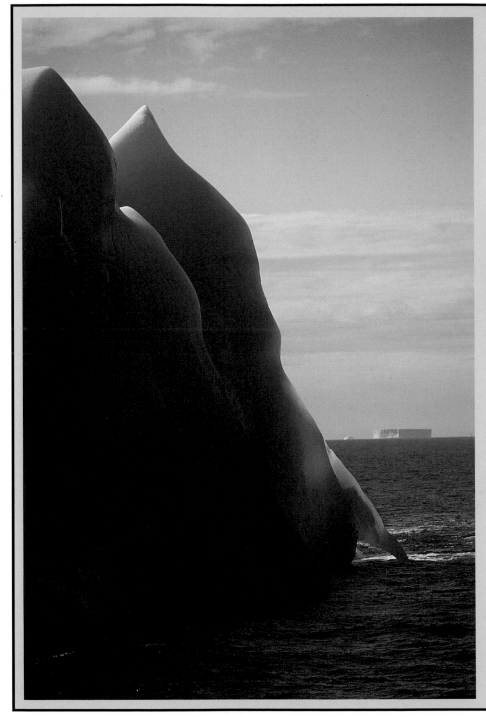

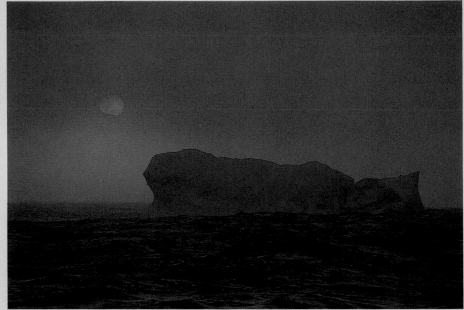

The changing face of icebergs

Above: A feeble sun tries to burn through fog as a small iceberg drifts northward in the Drake Passage. Icebergs can last for years if they are grounded off the coast, but most that move beyond the Antarctic Convergence quickly break up and melt.

Left: The delicate pale blue tips of an iceberg drifting between South Georgia and the South Sandwich Islands form a striking contrast with a dark Southern Ocean.

Right above: Driven by strong ocean currents in Antarctic Sound, icebergs can move at three or four knots even against the wind of a storm. Ships' officers maintain a healthy respect for the power and potential danger of fast-moving bergs.

Right below: Impregnated with moraine debris gouged out by a glacier, this iceberg off the Terre Adelie Coast looks more like a chocolate cake the size of a large house.

Far right: The eroded flutings of a recently overturned iceberg in Paradise Bay resemble the ridges of the loftiest summits in the Himalayas.

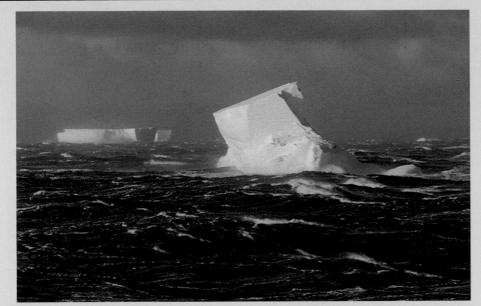

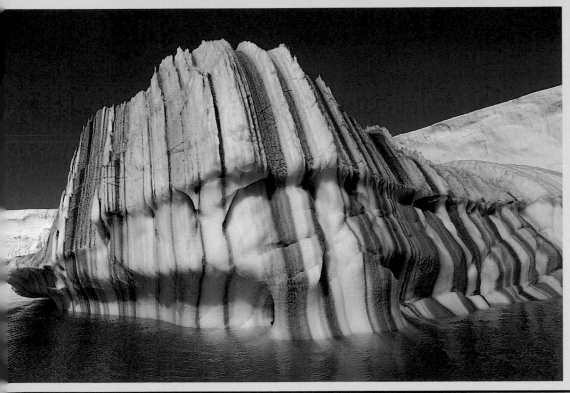

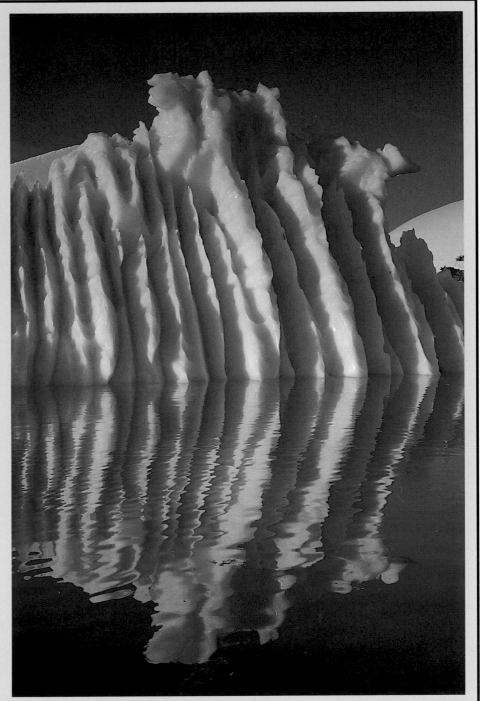

55

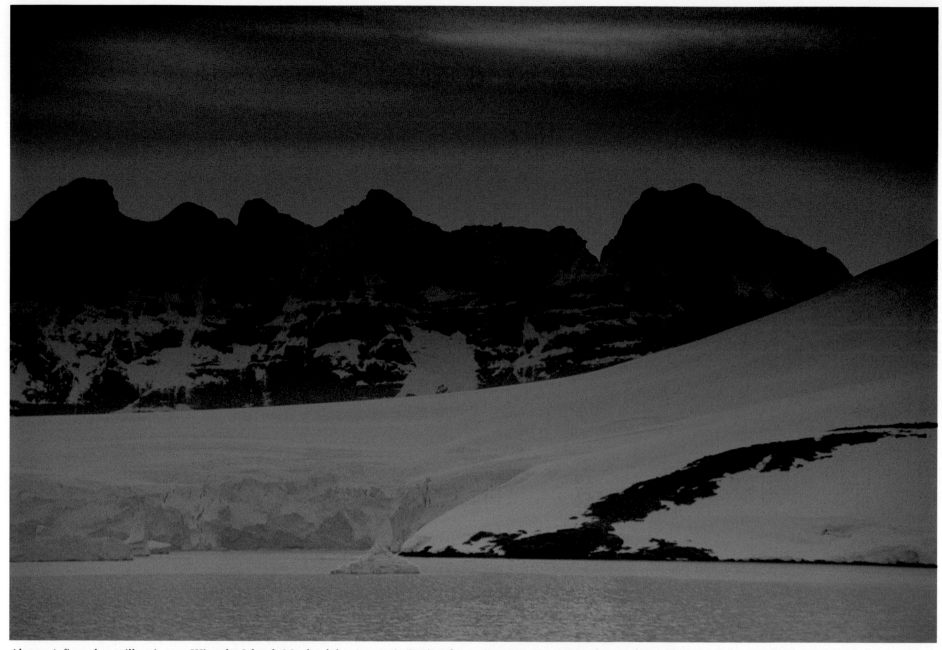

Above: A fiery dawn illuminates Wiencke Island. Much of the Antarctic Peninsula is north of the Antarctic Circle yet is truly polar compared to the equivalent latitudes in the Arctic.

Opposite: Sunset in the northern Ross Sea lights up Coulman Island, home of one of the largest emperor penguin colonies.

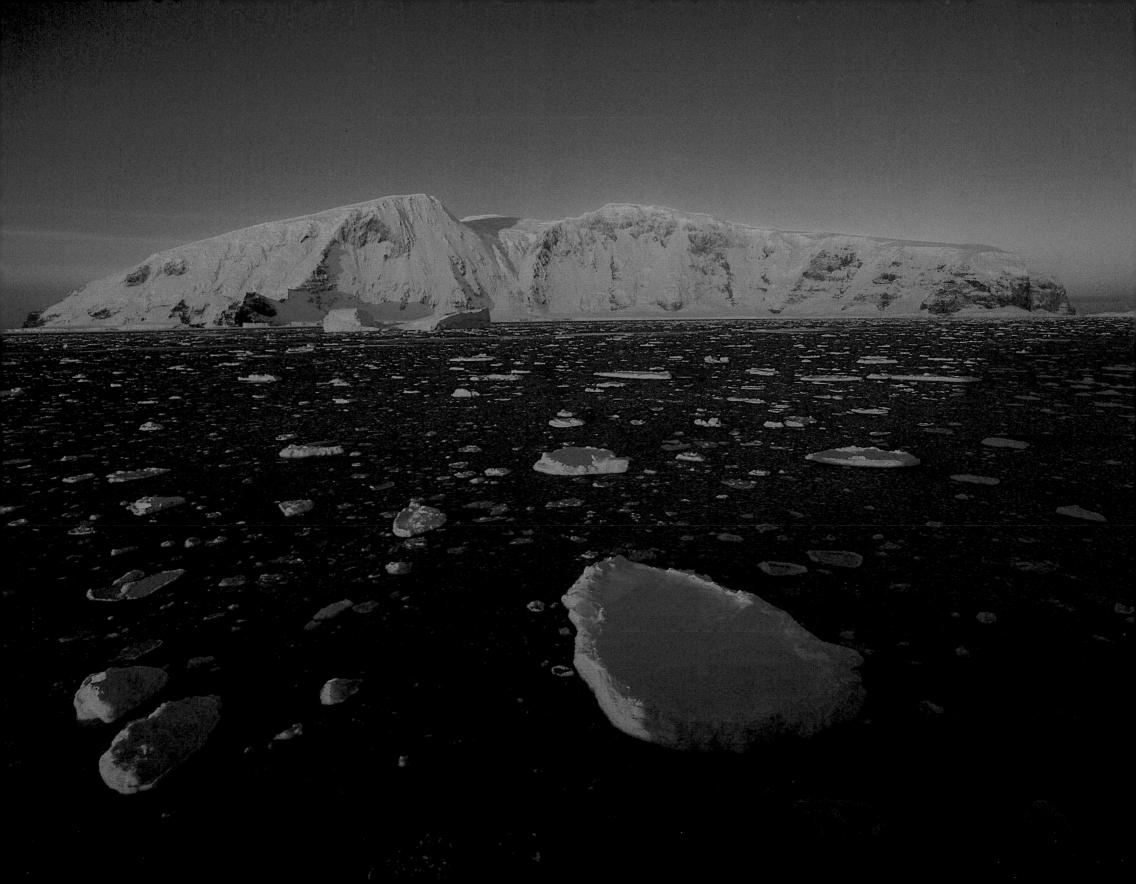

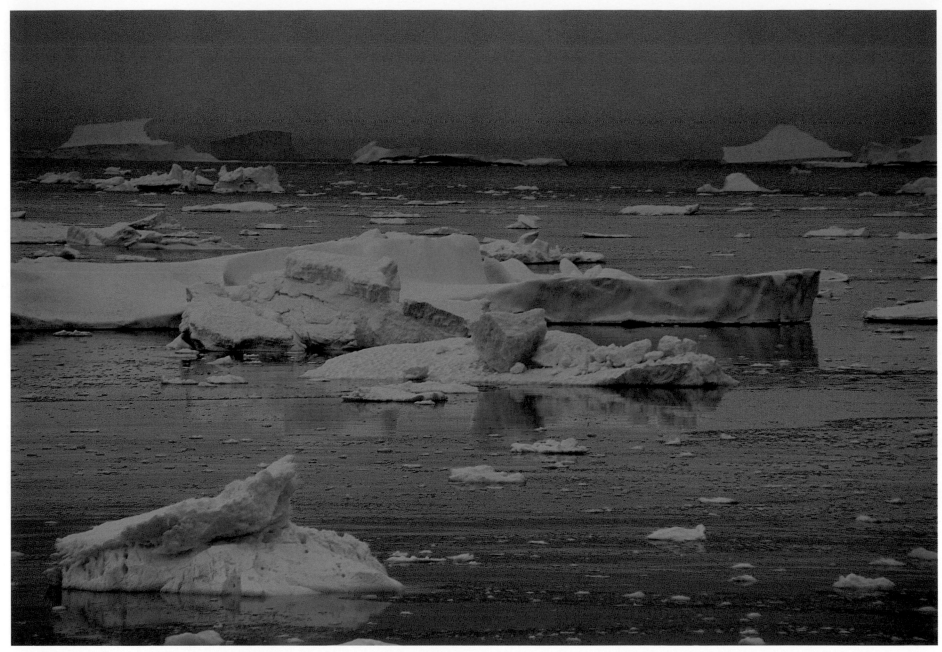

Seen from Mt. Scott, south of the Lemaire Channel, the soft sunset colors on pack ice and icebergs near Pleneau Island add a restful touch to the end of another great day on the Antarctic Peninsula.

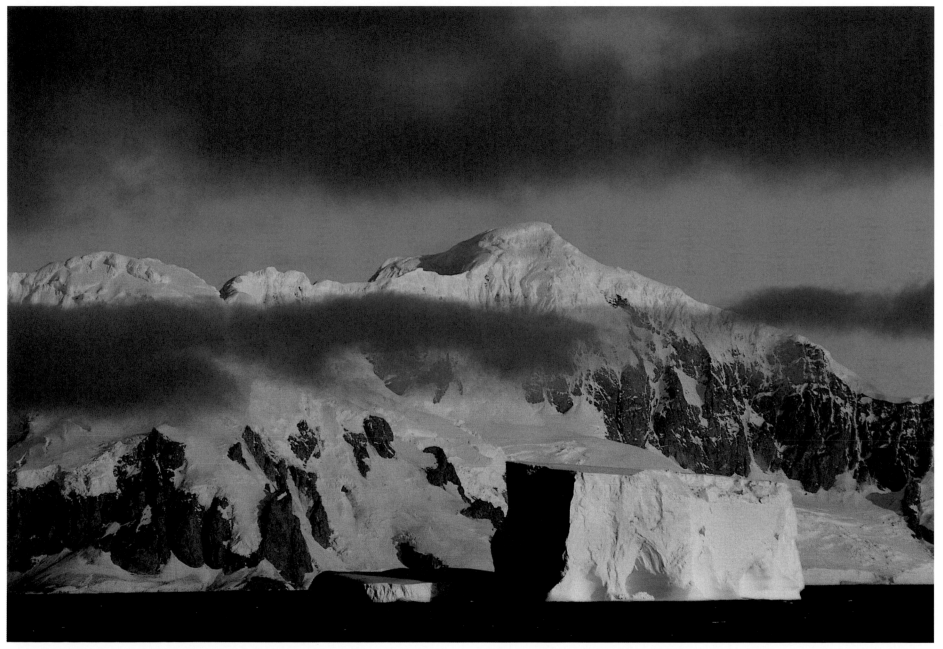

A small tabular iceberg drifts through Bransfield Strait. The 6,600-foot peaks of Livingston Island in the South Shetland Island group emerge as the morning cloud burns off. Although the South Shetland Islands are heavily glaciated, they do have significant vegetation zones rich in moss, lichens, and the Antarctic grass *Deschampsia*. The islands lie off the northern tip of the Antarctic Peninsula.

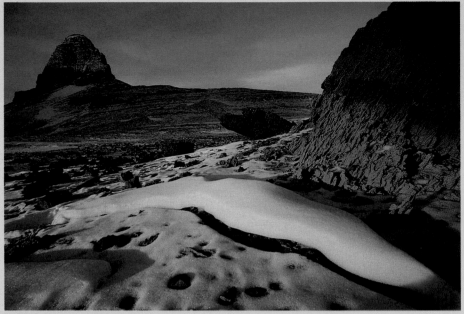

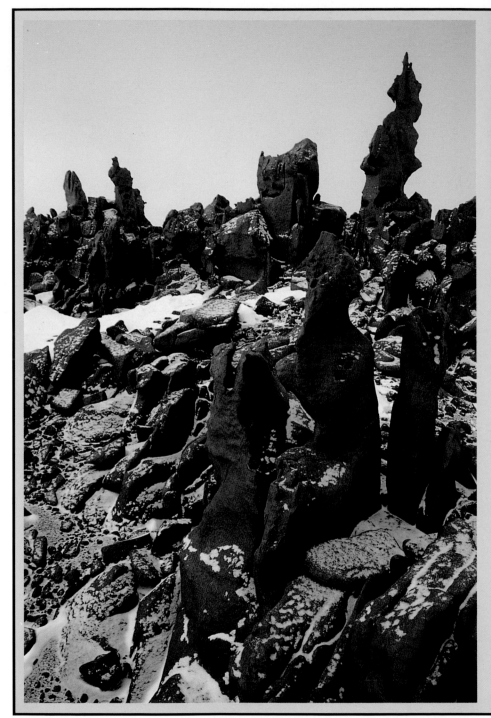

Victoria Land's Dry Valleys

Above: Soft evening light in the Olympus Range above the Wright Dry Valley catches the edge of a patch of drifted snow. The wind-blasted sandstone tower of Mt. Dido lies behind.

Left: Dry Valley "ventifacts," carved by wind and salt erosion, take on amazing shapes like trees from a Tolkien novel. Lightly dusted with fresh snow, this "forest" of ventifacts lies between Mt. Shapeless and the Olympus range above the Wright Dry Valley.

Right above: Pouring over the escarpment of sandstone and dolerite rocks at the head of the Wright Dry Valley, an icefall spills from the plateau of the Antarctic Ice Sheet onto the Upper Wright Glacier.

Right below: An icefall in the Taylor Glacier near Finger Mountain has been polished by scouring winds that sweep down from the Antarctic Ice Sheet. These powerful katabatic winds help desiccate the Dry Valley system so that lower down, closer to the coast, the Taylor Valley is like a moonscape.

Far right: Like the layers of a wedding cake, the sedimentary Beacon sandstone of the Asgaard Range straddling the Taylor and Wright Dry Valleys provides fossil evidence of a period when Antarctica was much warmer. Coal beds are also commonly found throughout the Transantarctic Mountains. A climber can be seen ascending the snow ridge.

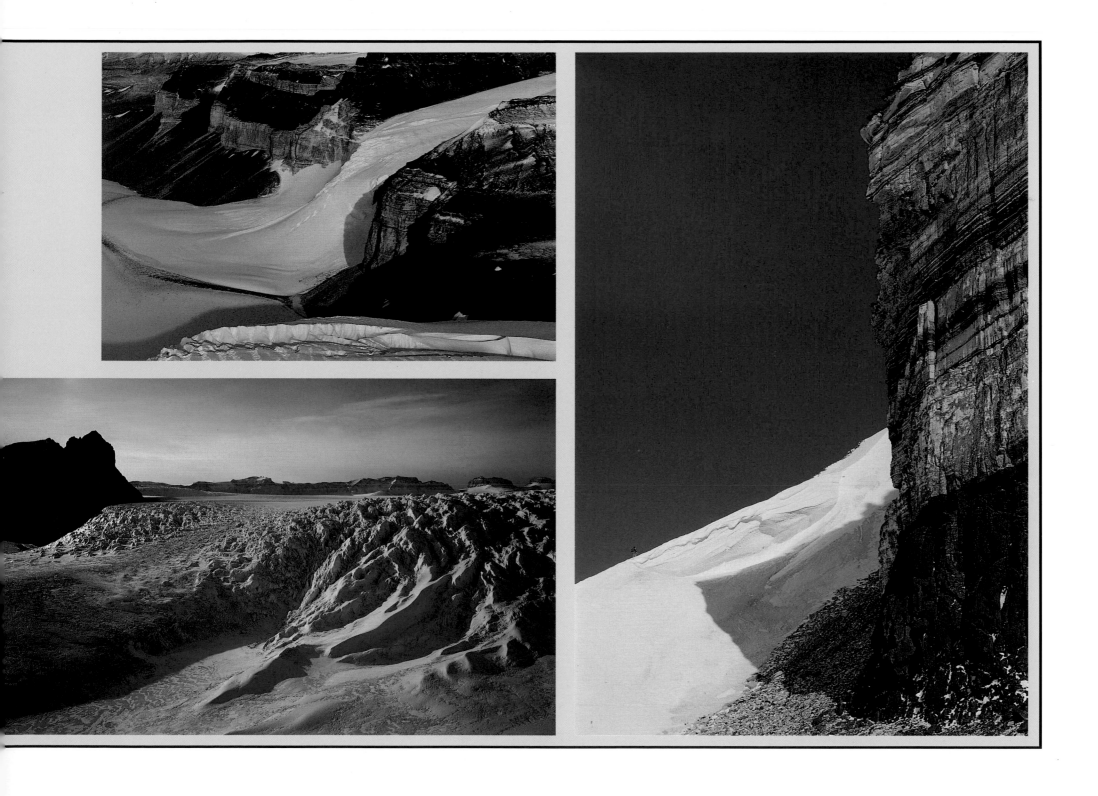

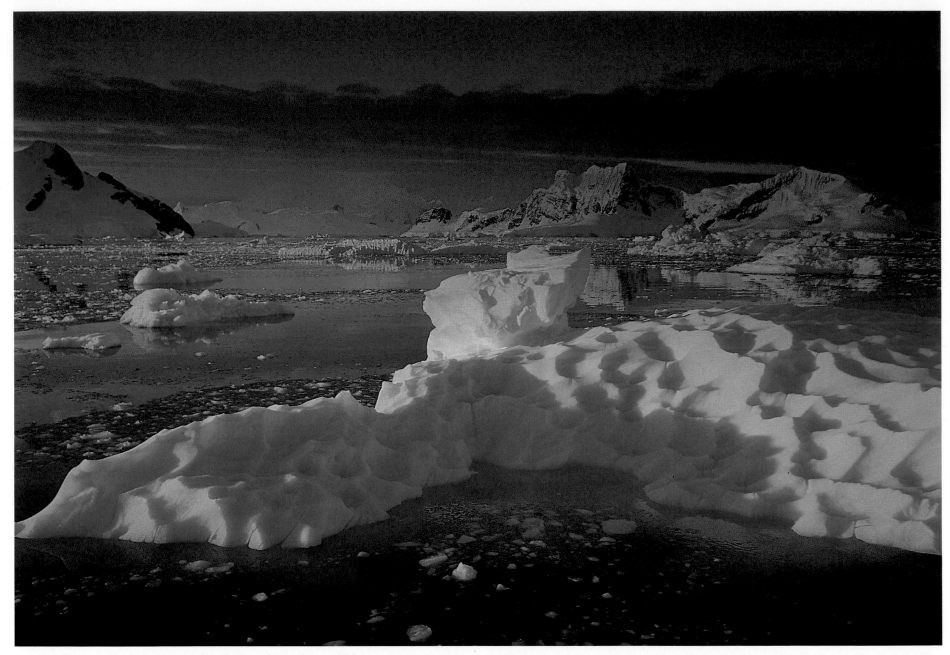

62

Paradise Bay on the Antarctic Peninsula is a place of incredible mountain scenery and tranquility. The entire bay is lined by glacier fronts which come right down to the water, often calving massive amounts of ice debris and small icebergs . At sunset the whole bay lights up like a Chinese lantern.

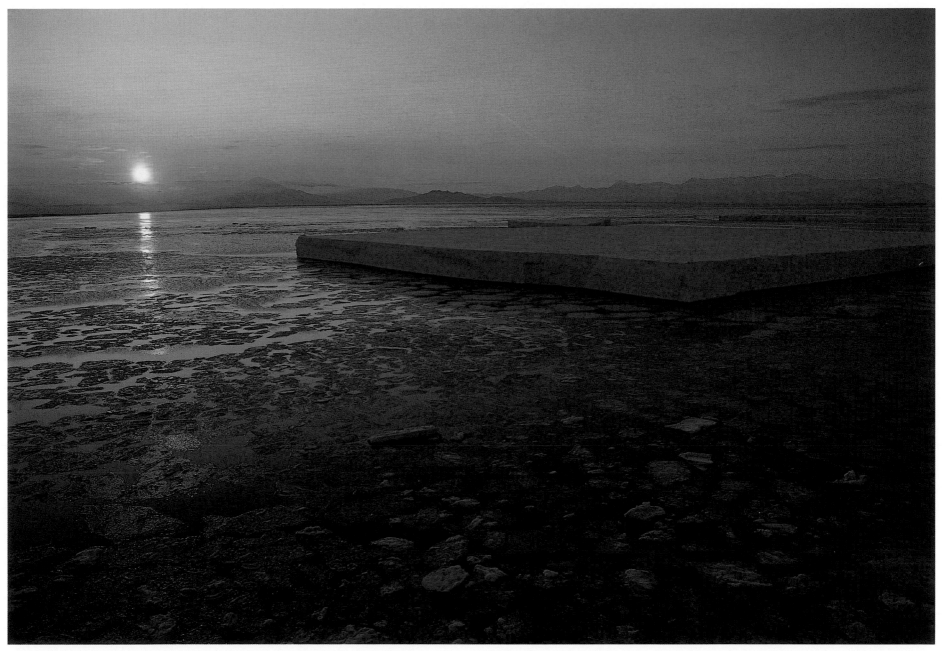

The March sun sets in McMurdo Sound near the 9,800-foot volcano Mt. Discovery as small chunks of the Ross Ice Shelf float northward into the Ross Sea. The New Zealand and American science communities at nearby Scott Base and McMurdo Station on Ross Island are now isolated for the winter until the new season begins in October.

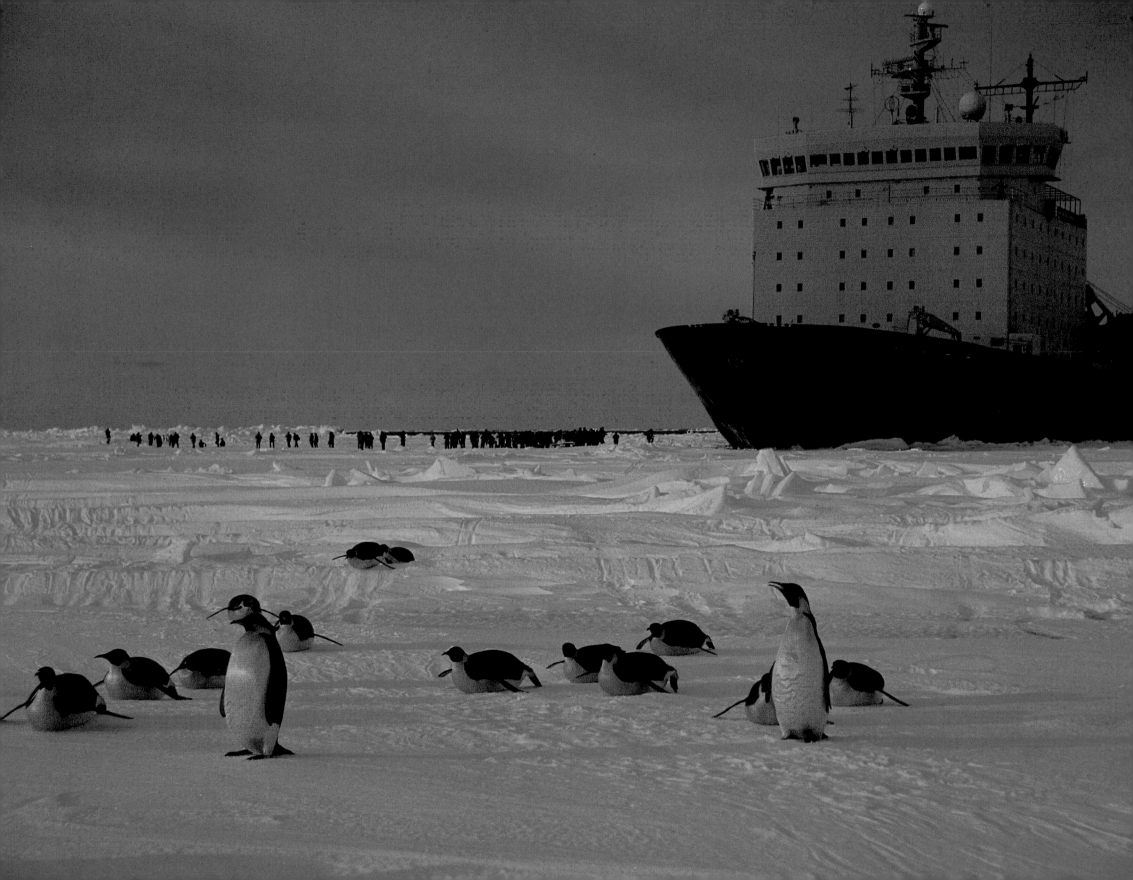

A SLIPPERY PATH

We shall not cease from exploration
And the end of all our exploring
Will be to arrive where we started
And to know the place for the first time.

T.S. Eliot.

An intangible yet profound fascination with Antarctica has us firmly in its grip. The drive to immerse ourselves in the aura and romance of this alien environment is unstoppable. An insatiable quest to gather scientific data also runs deep in our psyche. We crave knowledge, wealth, political kudos, or simply the experience of absorbing unfettered wildness as an antidote to the frenzy of life in lower latitudes. It is not human nature to leave things alone. And so, in the 1990s, there are cracks appearing in Antarctica's ability to cope with the indelible marks of concerted human endeavor. Increasing numbers are coming to Antarctica to study, to holiday, to dream of exploitation, and even to colonize. Despite warning signs of lasting impact, we continue to be inexorably drawn to this land of haunting beauty and hidden wealth.

As the turn of the century draws near, it is time to take stock, not just of our wayward manner in temperate regions but in the higher latitudes too. In Antarctica the era is long gone when surveyors with basic instruments had to endure windworn epics to make sense of bleak terrain and uncharted fogbound coasts. Gone too are the dog-driving geologists who sledged through unknown mountain ranges to unravel our geological past, piecing together the early steps of Gondwana's dance of the continents. Nostalgia

Opposite: Emperor penguins on Weddell Sea pack ice welcome Quark Expeditions' passengers from the icebreaker *Kapitan Khlebnikov.*

for those days lingers in clubs of men in tweed jackets and crested ties.

This is a time of powerful transportation, satellite communication, and refined management concepts such as "specially protected areas" and environmental impact statements. Scientists can ponder the most subtle nuance of their speciality, at times cocooned in large institutional bases. Despite modern facilities and equipment, there is still a great need for practical skills to live and travel efficiently in the field. It is exciting though, that both senior and junior academics, often from different countries, can now fly to a remote location and argue over the hard evidence laid bare before them. The benefits of modern logistics greatly facilitate the asking of good questions and hence produce good science. Antarctica has proven to be a vital laboratory for assembling information to solve issues of global interest and concern.

Largely unhindered by the bureaucratic restrictions of the 1970s, well-organized recreationalists are now able to enact their private adventures by utilizing commercial air or sea transport. Though costly, air access to the peaks of Antarctica's interior has opened up a vast alpine playground of limitless mountaineering potential. Many of the hostile barriers guarding interior Antarctica have been swept aside by modern attitudes and technology. While the benefits may be debatable, it is no longer essential to winter over on the continent to put in motion an extended journey. Every year, worldwide awareness of Antarctica's recreation potential grows. It is definitely an exciting time for avid polar travelers. Seemingly impossible dreams no longer need shimmer beyond the horizon, unrealized. Perhaps the age of recreational adventure in Antarctica is just beginning.

Once unthinkable, it is now routine for charter yachts and cruise vessels to roam the Southern Ocean and allow their passengers to savor Antarctica's coastal delights. Some come to observe and film wildlife, while others are dropped off to kayak, climb, and parapente around rocky spires which rise spectacularly above glacier-lined fiords. Summer cruises to Antarctica have now been in operation for over thirty years. Winter cruises may take place in the future. By utilizing powerful Russian icebreakers, Quark Expeditions, the most innovative company presently in the game, is able to link together unusual voyages to the remotest subantarctic islands or even the ice-choked Weddell Sea. It is now reality to charter helicopter-supported icebreakers with an extended capability. While Antarctic tour ships have run aground on rocks, it is to the credit of the industry that no one has died during Zodiac landings in spite of frequently operating in marginal conditions.

The overall impact of seaborne tourism remains low, provided groups stay on the move in self-contained units on small ice-strengthened vessels. There are, however, a few worrying trends starting to emerge. The number of vessels operating on the Antarctic Peninsula alone has risen alarmingly to about twelve with a total of 9,000 visitors arriving each season. This figure is perhaps double the number of government-supported personnel in Antarctica and yet, the total amount of the time ashore by tourists is but a small percentage of the time spent on the continent by scientists and their support staff. However, the potential for impact on easily damaged environments resulting from repeated tour visits to the same location is increasing. Sometimes, penguin colonies, seabird breeding grounds, and scenic spots with delicate vegetation cover can be visited by tour ships three times in one day.

Because of increased cruise traffic, there is a mentality evolving whereby it is acceptable that ships actually line up so they can disgorge passengers at key locations at an appointed hour. If this continues, the very essence of adventure cruising will be seriously eroded. Some may argue this is a good thing as it restricts visits to certain places and leaves others totally unfrequented. Should overly bureaucratic restrictions occur, through industry self-regulation, the spirit fostered by having a schedule flexible enough to take advantage of unexpected opportunities will be lost. There is a long-established tradition of generating a sense of discovery by nosing the ship into the myriad of bays and islands that never appear in brochures.

Large, relatively unmaneuverable vessels with inadequate ice-strengthening and the capacity to carry 400-plus passengers are also appearing on the scene. Although they abide by industry rules of only taking a hundred passengers ashore at a time, the resultant protracted operation inevitably destroys the very ambience they purport to seek. It is intensely refreshing to sit quietly observing wildlife and be regarded as a curio instead of an object of terror. It is also important to appreciate that silence is one of Antarctica's greatest gifts. Seaborne ventures with small vessels carrying fewer than a hundred passengers can achieve such intimacy with the environment only by retaining a flexible schedule and making deft use of weather and ice conditions to move everyone quickly.

There is no shortage of mountaineers who wish to climb Antarctica's highest peak, 16,400-foot Vinson Massif in the Ellsworth Mountains. Recreationalists, too, are clambering to reach the interior of the continent, hellbent on the South Pole. Supporting adventurers and at times, their entourage of film crews and journalists, is UK-based Adventure Network International (ANI), the only private company flying aircraft to Antarctica.

Operating from Punta Arenas, Chile, ANI pilots pioneered the daunting concept of landing DC4 and DC6 wheeled aircraft on natural runways of wind-polished ice. ANI now charters a South African pressurized Hercules aircraft which has increased the safety and reliability of the operation. From a tent camp at Patriot Hills, ANI flies Twin Otter ski-equipped aircraft anywhere on the continent, including "flying safaris" to emperor penguin colonies. Competently dealing with frightful logistical headaches over the years, ANI has now celebrated ten years of accident-free flying in Antarctica.

It is widely recognized that there is no room for poorly planned private expeditions. Self-sufficiency must be maintained so as to minimize the chance of impinging on the already stretched infrastructure of others. Thinking persists, however, that the line should be drawn at expeditions that are seen as contrived and seemingly pointless. Some feel a need to prejudge those who plan to climb yet another mountain or those who hope to carve another notch in history, in part simply to satisfy sponsors and the expectations of the media. Others look askance at egos bent on fabricating another "famous first" at any cost. On another tack, questions are asked whether visitors with an air ticket should have a legitimate, inalienable right to spend a few chilly minutes at the geographic South Pole. While the pressure on Antarctica has changed since the early 1900s, Amundsen simply dismissed the stay-at-home doubters and polar pundits of the day as people with "small minds."

With sightseeing overflights recommencing from Australia, have sufficient lessons been learned from the government-supported Air New Zealand DC10 operation which ended in tragedy at the base of Ross Island in 1979? In another incident, an aircraft laden with tourists crashed during landing procedures near King George Island, again killing all aboard. Commercial operators are exploring the questionable idea of flying clients to places such as Chile's Marsh base. Marsh's military aircrew dormitory is often labeled Antarctica's first "hotel," as it has been possible for casual visitors in the past to pay for a bed. From here, having saved the two-day voyage across Drake Passage and assuming King George Island's diabolical weather hasn't played havoc with timing, clients would be transferred to an awaiting cruise ship. Antarctica is also attracting individuals who are negotiating with cash-strapped governments to buy an unwanted base for their own use. Is this a prelude to a large hotel chain developing facilities on Antarctica's limited icefree land? Inevitably, like government bases, the operation and resupply of commercial land-based accommodation, if allowed to proceed, would have a major impact.

Should there be more rules? If so, who will enforce them? Are some of the present activities beyond the limit, creating needless or unacceptable impact and degradation of Antarctica's environment and spiritual quality? Thankfully, Antarctica's exclusivity to the science community is over, but with the new-found freedom and access for anyone, with the drive and the means, come obligations.

Are we also overstepping the mark in our quest for scientific knowledge? With the building of yet more government bases in Antarctica, the number of year-round science facilities run by seventeen different nations has risen in 1996 to forty-four. The pyramid of imported supplies necessary to support such permanent operations is enormous. Should governments reevaluate the installation of automated equipment to record scientific data throughout winter months so as to cut down on the necessity for a year-round staffed program? Despite stricter environmental guidelines for every facet of a station's program, the potential for significant impact remains high. At least Antarctic administrators have moved on from the attitude prevalent in the 1960s and 1970s when entire bases were simply abandoned, complete with chemicals, batteries, explosives, and fuel which subsequently leaked into the surroundings. Thankfully, much of the day-to-day garbage generated at bases is now exported from the continent instead of being casually discarded in the sea or in a bulldozed snowpit.

As the cost and complexity of ship operations increase, there will be mounting pressure to construct sealed runways for wheeled aircraft on icefree land near major bases. The UK has recently completed a runway at Rothera on Adelaide Island. The French, too, at Dumont d'Urville, constructed a large runway but only after severely affecting petrel and penguin breeding grounds by dynamiting and bulldozing entire islands. Despite concerted private protest, Antarctic Treaty nations remained silent on the French abuses.

A few of the summer-only bases on the Antarctic Peninsula are a sham, producing little, if any, worthwhile science. Poorly informed, uncaring military or construction personnel at these bases can, at times, impact heavily on the ecology. For example, Chinese at Great Wall Station raided penguin nests for eggs, and bored off-duty Chileans drove tracked vehicles indiscriminately through extensive moss beds. They also happily stoned seals.

Some governments no longer find a military logistic structure cost-effective to support Antarctic science. Others still use their military as an adjunct to overt political maneuvering. The concept of experienced commercial air and sea charter operators replacing the military to play a safe, efficient role in Antarctic science is already underway. Since 1978, the importation of pregnant women and now whole families from Chile and Argentina to colonize military-run "villages" is a particularly virulent brand of flagwaving in a region that has overlapping territorial claims.

The quality and scope of future Antarctic science need increased scrutiny by national committees to cut out needless duplication of effort and to ensure that entry to specially protected sites, the removal of fossils, and the handling of animals is strictly ethical. More credence needs to be given to The Netherlands' policy. As newcomers in the Antarctic, they have refused to build their own base and currently operate by paying their way on other nations' science programs. While joint-nation logistic support has been a healthy part of Antarctic programs in the past, this needs to be extended even further in the future.

Government-owned huskies were finally removed from Antarctica in 1994 — the end of a colorful era. It is now stated that no expedition can bring dogs to the continent for fear of introducing viruses to endemic fauna. And yet, all three private groups that did import huskies in the past decade journeyed inland away from any possible contact with animals. I hope future generations of spirited adventurers challenge this flawed thinking. The rationale is illogical when it is well known and apparently countenanced that the French Antarctic program continues to breed pet parakeets at Dumont d'Urville in close proximity to petrel breeding grounds.

The Antarctic ecosystem has the formidable defenses of low temperature and isolation. It is far from fragile and seems to have a resilience relative to its inherent simplicity. And yet, human endeavor increasingly has the ability to tamper with the balance. As the pressure of human visits mounts, we are charged with sensible and sustainable management. And yet, for future generations lured by Antarctica, be they scientists or recreationalists, it is vital that a sense of mystery and freedom of expression is not crushed by overregulation. As we embark on a new century we must acknowledge our responsibility for vigilance and self-regulation to ensure that activities are in harmony with the nature of this special place.

Opposite: A Zodiac full of seaborne visitors batters through heavy brash ice in an iceberg-filled Curtiss Bay, Antarctic Peninsula.

68

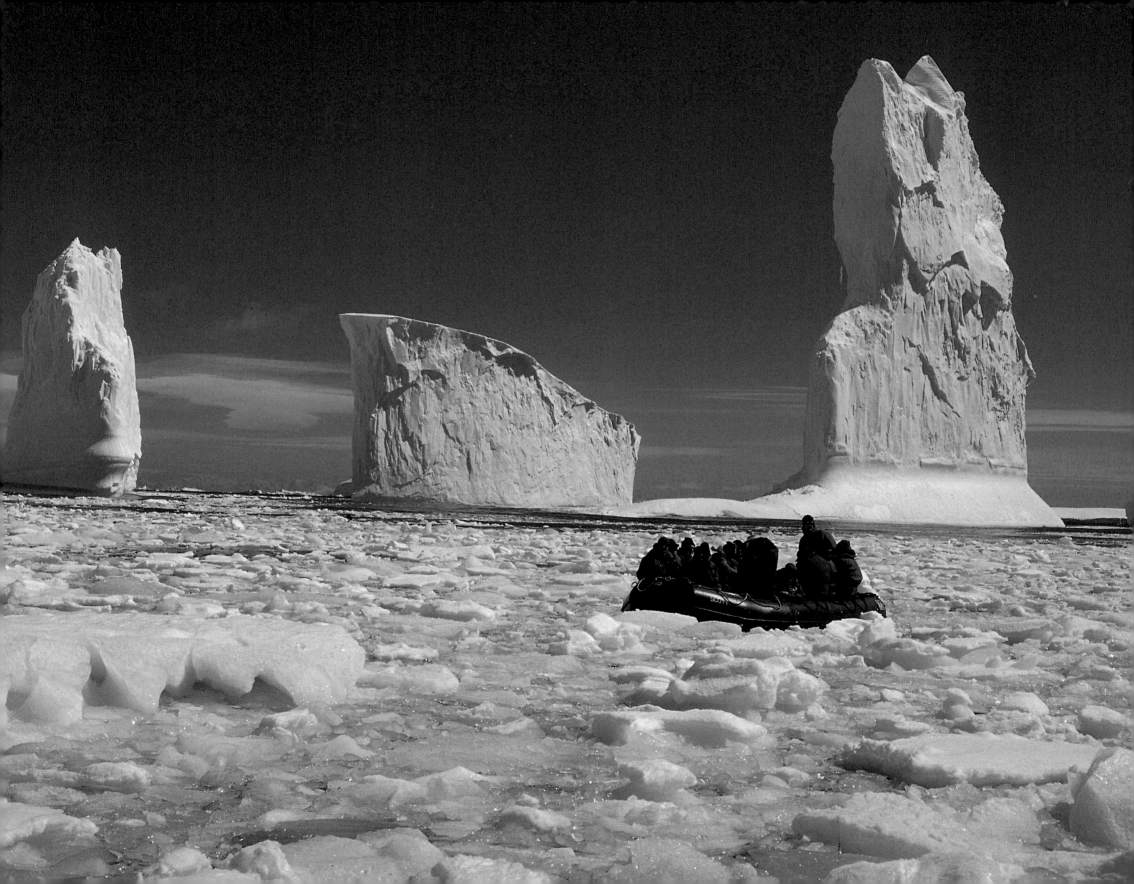

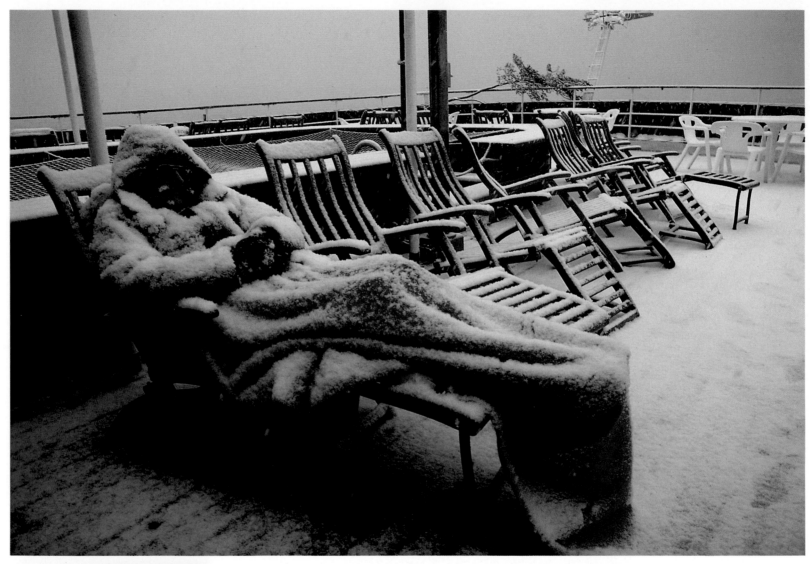

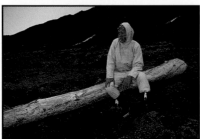

Above: Dedicated Antarctic tourist Alan Graham-Collier dozes on MV *World Discoverer* even after a snowstorm in the Amundsen Sea. While needing to obey a "code of conduct," tourists can play a valuable watchdog role by creating an awareness of the need for vigilant environmental management.

Left: Using dogs, Englishman Wally Herbert led the first crossing of the Arctic Ocean via the North Pole in 1968–9. Here he visits the bivouac site on Franz Josef Land where Nansen and Johansen wintered after their abortive attempt on the North Pole in 1894–95.

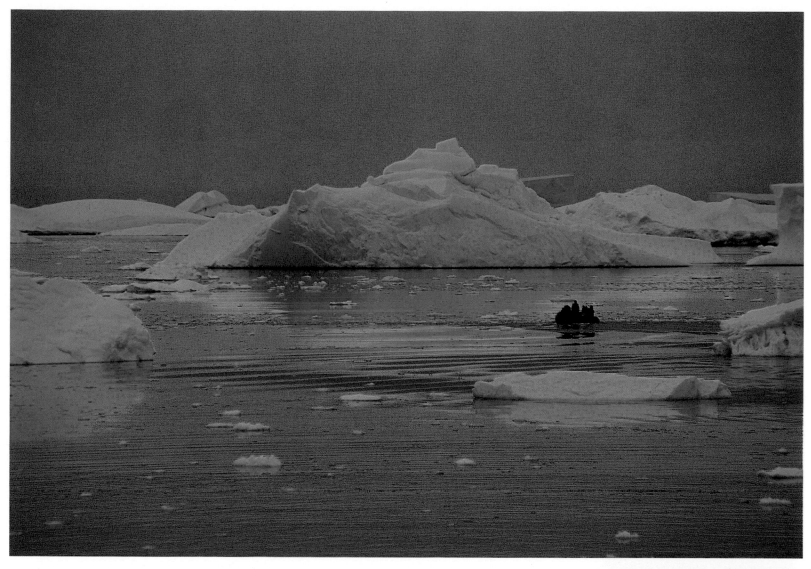

Above: Seaborne tourists enjoy a Zodiac cruise among icebergs near the southern end of Lemaire Channel. Turning the engine off and allowing the senses to open up to Antarctica's great gift of silence is always a highlight of seaborne cruising.

Right: In 1991, the nuclear-powered Soviet icebreaker *Sovetskiy Soyuz* utilizes helicopter reconnaissance to make the first surface-vessel transit of the Arctic Ocean via the North Pole. At the time, only three other surface vessels, all nuclear-powered, had reached the North Pole.

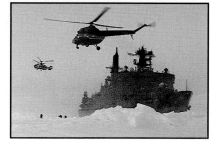

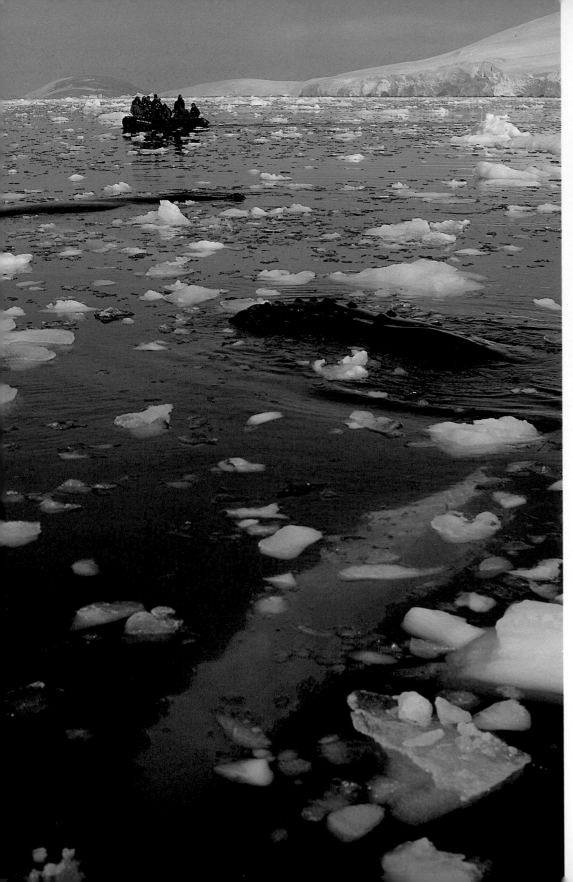

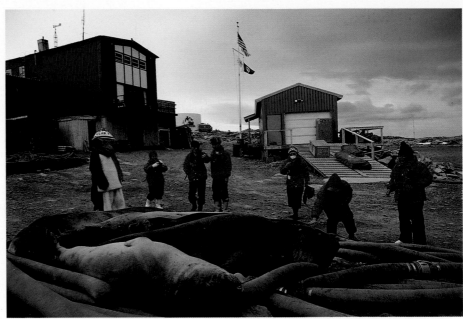

Above: Elephant seals delight in snoozing on the warm fuel hoses at the American biology station Palmer on Anvers Island. Disguised as a penguin, an American scientist conducts a tour party around the base. Visits to government bases need to be well coordinated in advance to minimize disruption to base routine.

Left: It is a very special experience to cruise beside humpback whales in the Antarctic. These two humpbacks were playing together among loose brash ice near Pleneau Island. The humpback's long white-sided flipper is visible under the clear water.

Opposite: Cruising beside humpback whales near the Melchior Islands on the Antarctic Peninsula, it is a delight to observe the whale's playful habits. Fortunately, humpbacks are making a strong recovery with increasing numbers seen each summer in the Southern Ocean as they migrate south to Antarctica to feed. The recent creation of a Southern Ocean Whale Sanctuary will provide long-awaited protection for cetaceans in the southern hemisphere.

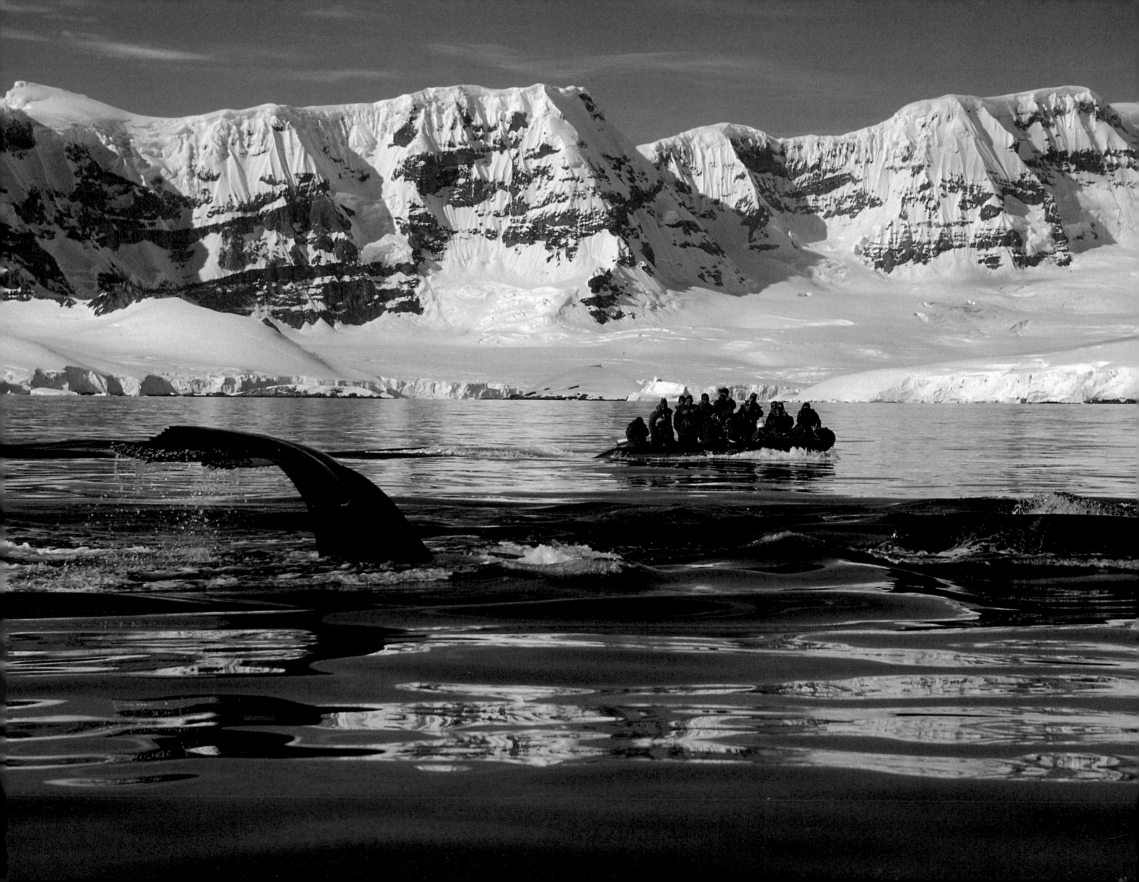

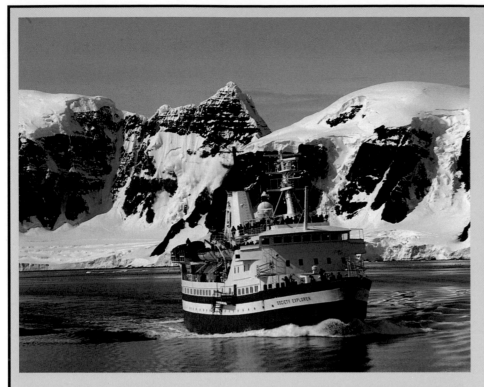

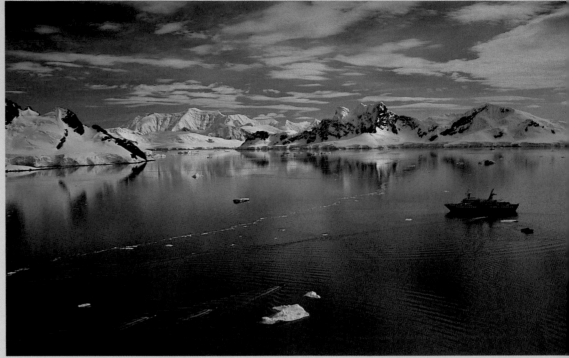

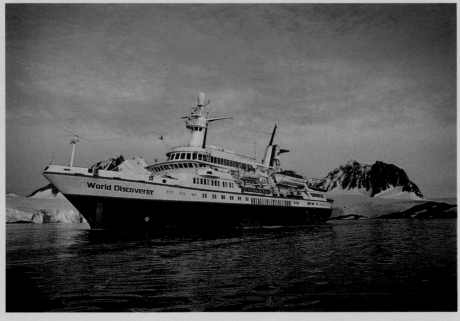

Antarctica's stalwart ships

Above and bottom left: Inflatable Zodiacs with 10–12 passengers are the key to seaborne adventure tourism. The ice-strengthened MV *World Discoverer*, seen here in Paradise Bay, was launched in 1975 and carries about 100 passengers.

Top left: The *Society Explorer* (formerly *Lindblad Explorer*), seen here in Neumeyer Channel, is the most famous vessel in Antarctic tourism. Launched in 1969, it has been to more environments on Earth than any ship ever built.

Right above: MS *Lindblad Explorer* is moored under a glacier at Cape Hallett in North Victoria Land. For years the *Explorer* has completed semi-circumnavigation voyages from South America to New Zealand via the Ross Sea. The *Explorer* has run aground twice in its career.

Right below: Quark Expeditions' Russian icebreaker *Kapitan Khlebnikov* cuts a path through pack ice in the Weddell Sea for the beleaguered British Antarctic Survey ship *Bransfield*.

Far right: The wooden RV *Hero*, seen here flying the Jolly Roger in Bransfield Strait, was a valuable part of the U.S. Antarctic Research Program until its retirement in 1984. American biologists conducted early krill research from the partly sail-powered vessel.

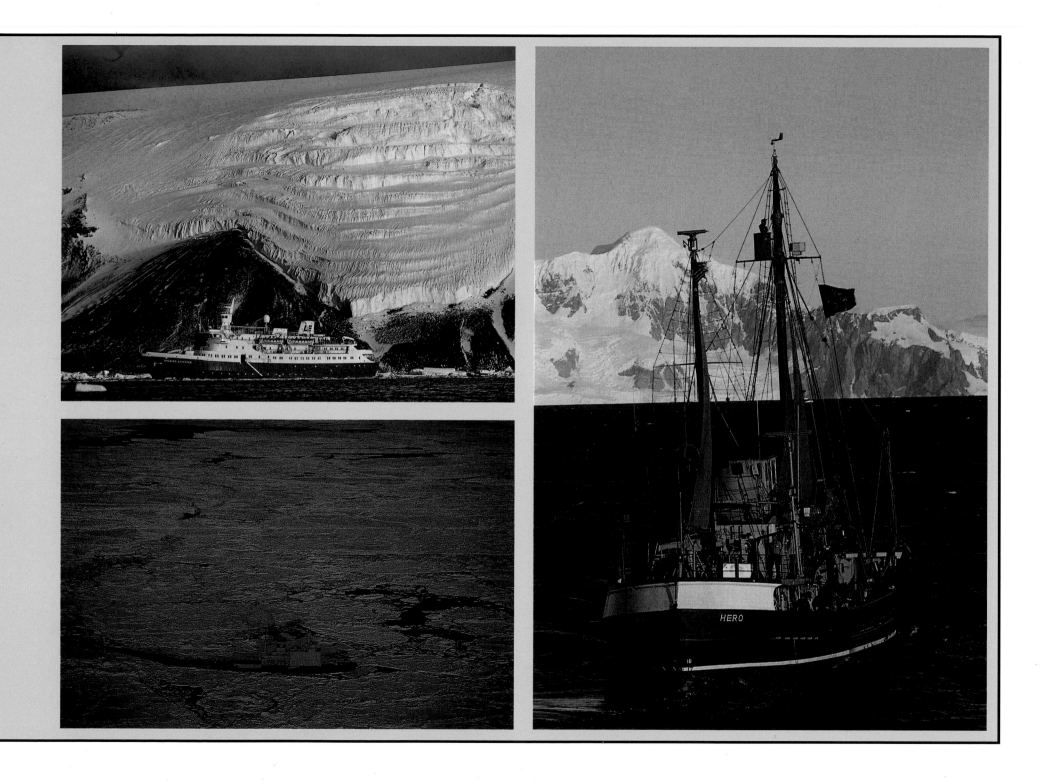

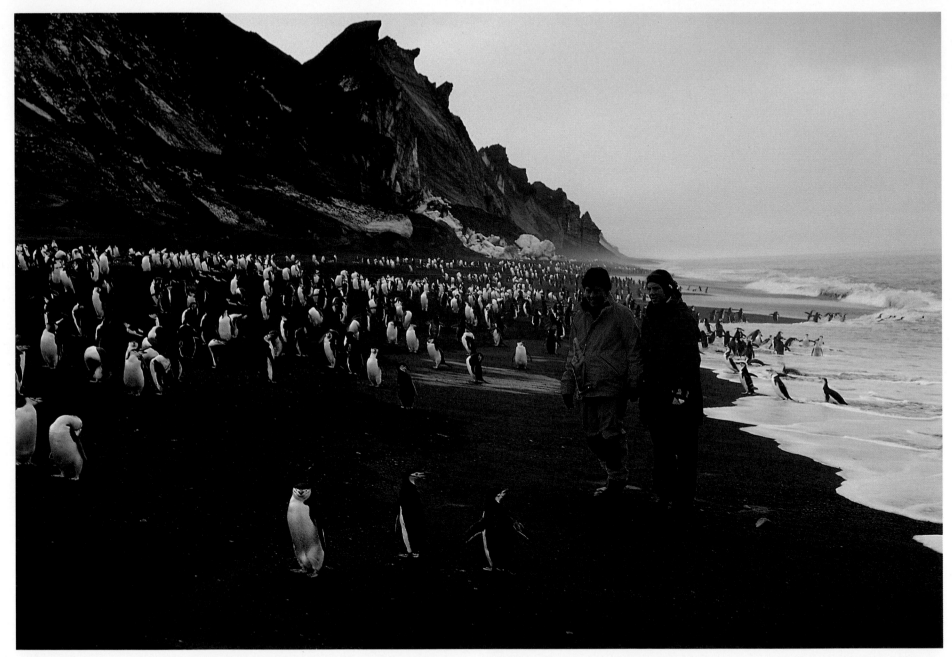

Above: A mother and daughter stroll along the black volcanic sand beach at Bailey Head, Deception Island, surrounded by hundreds of chinstrap penguins. Behind the beach, 200,000 chinstraps breed in an amphitheater of nesting sites.

Opposite: The view from Bailey Head down to the long beach and glacier front is spectacular. Quark's ship *Professor Khromov* can be seen at anchor.

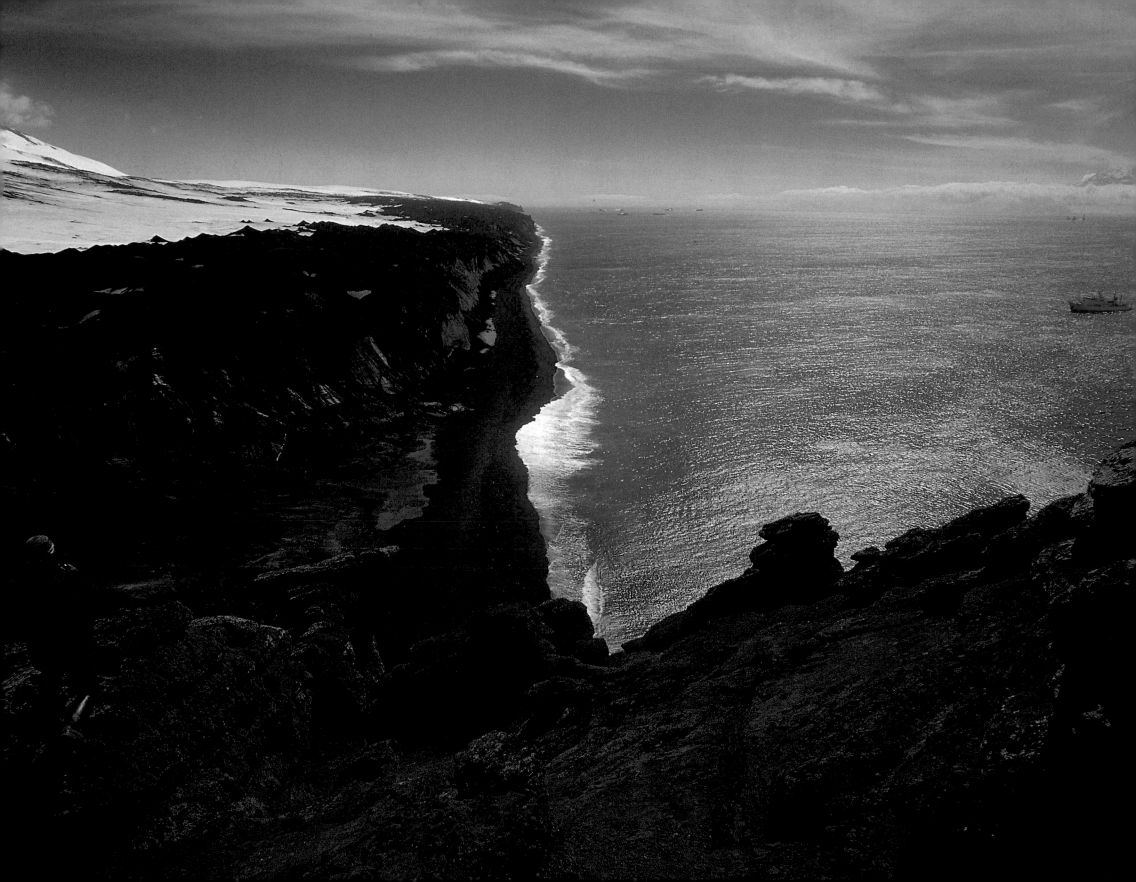

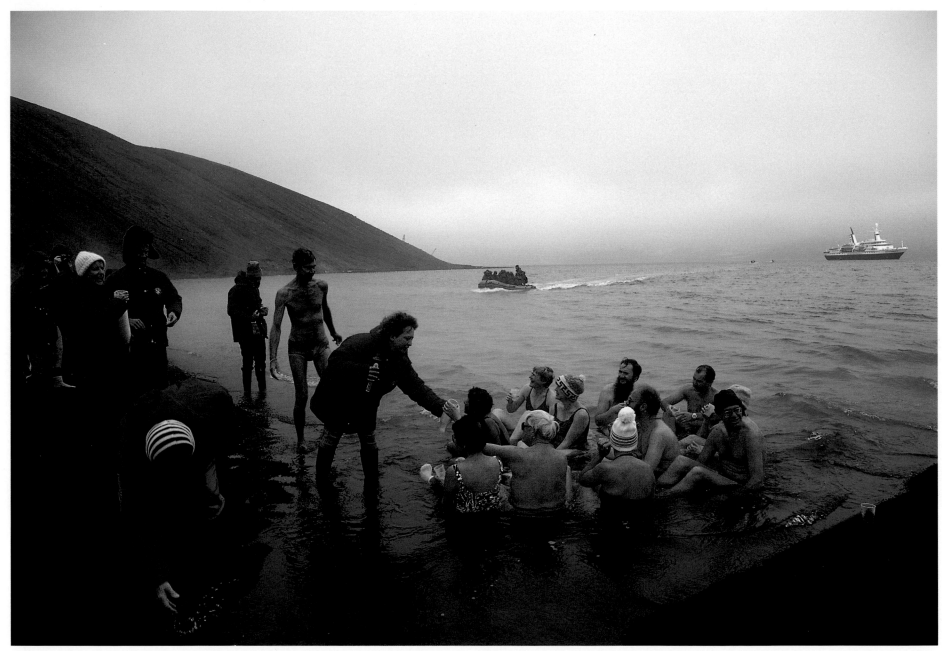

Frolicking in the volcanically heated sea water inside Deception Island's main caldera has become a regular light-hearted part of seaborne tourism on the Antarctic Peninsula. Sometimes seals and penguins emerge on the beach to view this strange ritual. Deception Island, in the South Shetland Island group, is a very active volcano with major eruptions as recent as 1969–70.

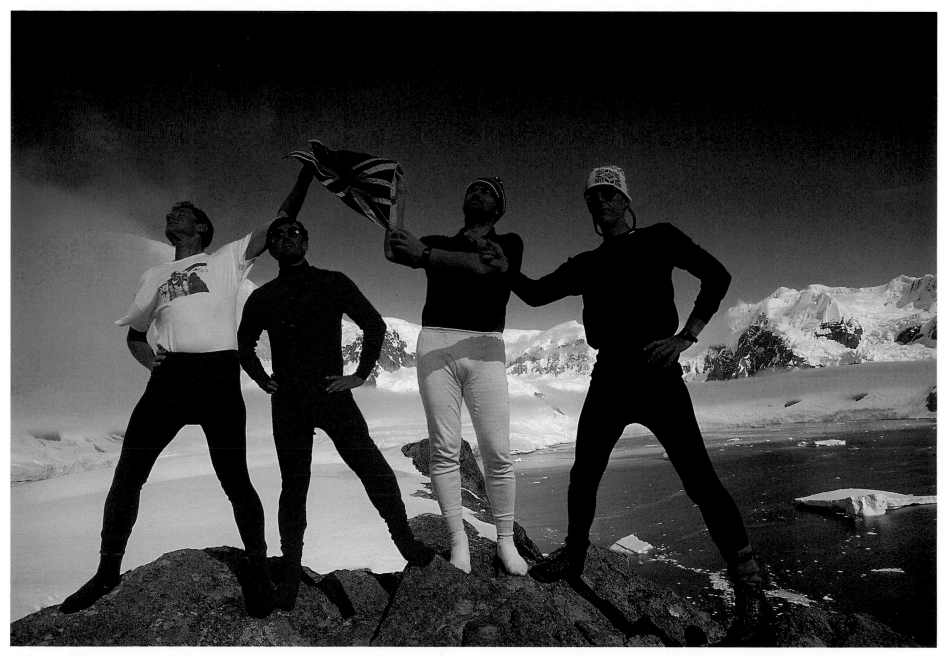

Feeling as if they have just climbed Mt. Everest, these British lads ham it up after "conquering" yet another Antarctic summit, this time in their longjohns! Even on a short vacation, seeing something of the uncluttered horizons of wilderness Antarctica is, for many people, an inspiring experience far removed from everyday city routine.

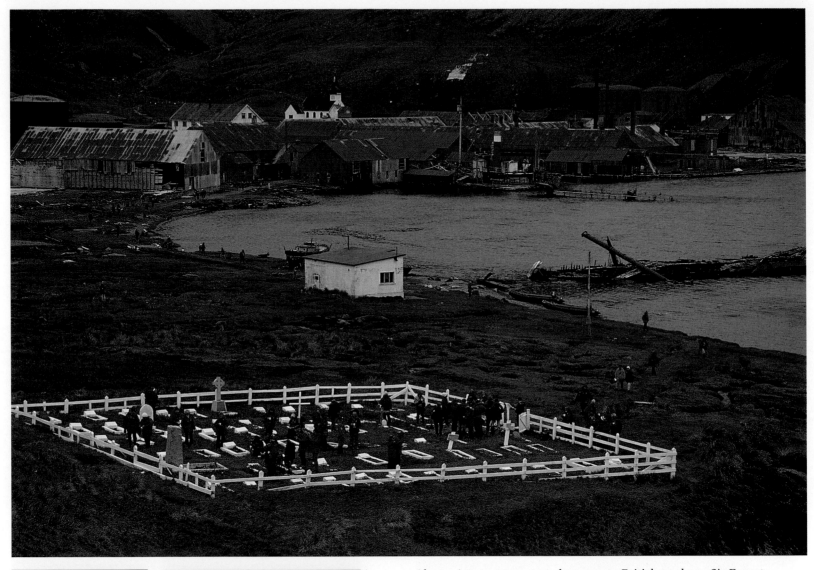

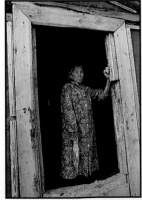

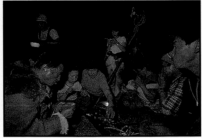

Above: A tour group pays homage to British explorer Sir Ernest Shackleton buried in the South Georgia cemetery at Grytviken.

Left: A Chukchi woman stands in her porch after brushing it with a bird wing. At 72 °N, on the Siberian coast, the walrus-ivory carving villagers of Uelen face a harsh Arctic life.

Chukchi nomads lunch on freshly killed reindeer meat inside their yurt-like skin tent pitched on Siberian tundra.

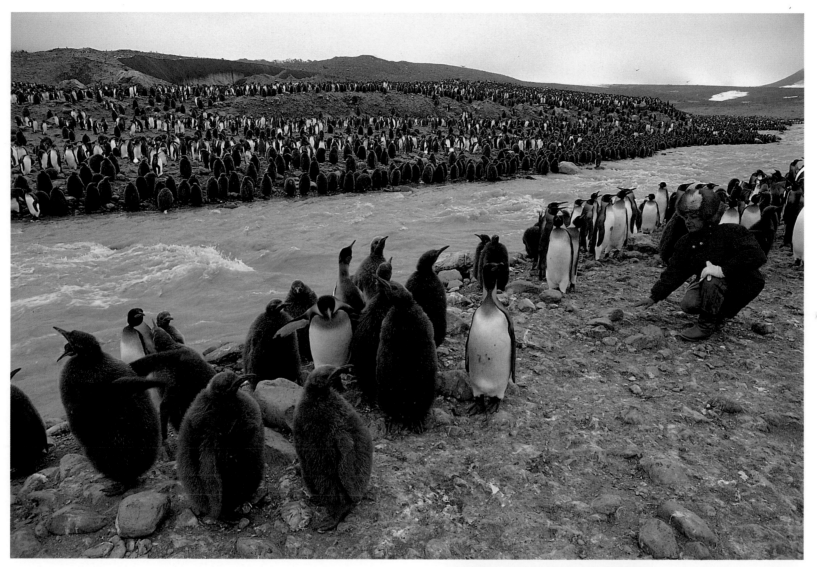

Above: A Russian woman quietly squats beside king penguins at St. Andrew's Bay on South Georgia. Intrigued by her fox-fur hat, fuzzy-feathered brown chicks soon surround her.

Right: Weak reindeer are brought down and killed for winter food supplies by Siberian Chukchi nomads using leather lassos.

Chukchi women skin a reindeer. Every part of the animal is utilized for food, clothing, tents, and sleds.

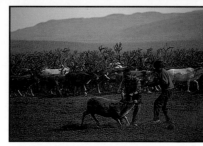

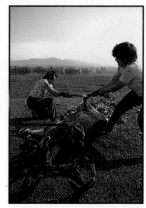

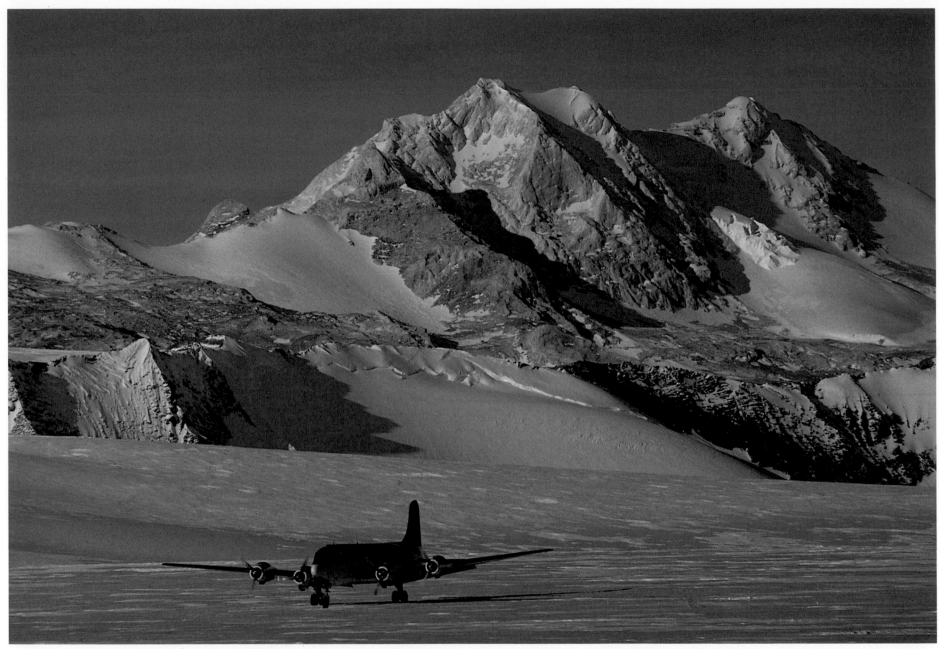

Adventure Network International pioneered the concept of landing wheeled aircraft in Antarctica on natural runways of wind-polished ice. In 1989, ANI used a DC4 to fly from Chile to Patriot Hills at 80°S near the Ellsworth Mountains.

Now they use much larger pressurized Hercules aircraft to carry an extra payload of equipment and passengers on a safer, more routine schedule.

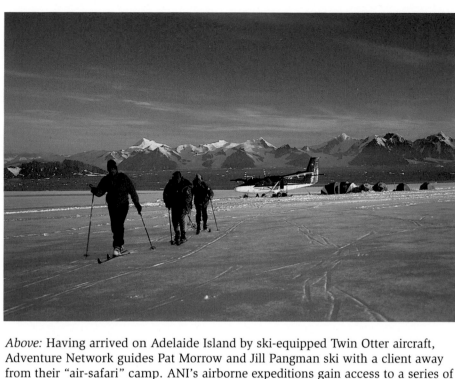

Above: Having arrived on Adelaide Island by ski-equipped Twin Otter aircraft, Adventure Network guides Pat Morrow and Jill Pangman ski with a client away from their "air-safari" camp. ANI's airborne expeditions gain access to a series of campsites close to Antarctic Peninsula peaks or areas of wildlife interest.

Right: ANI's DC4 unloads climbers and supplies after landing on wheels at the Patriot Hills ice runway. Operating out of Punta Arenas in Chile, ANI is the only commercial aircraft operator taking private expeditions to Antarctica.

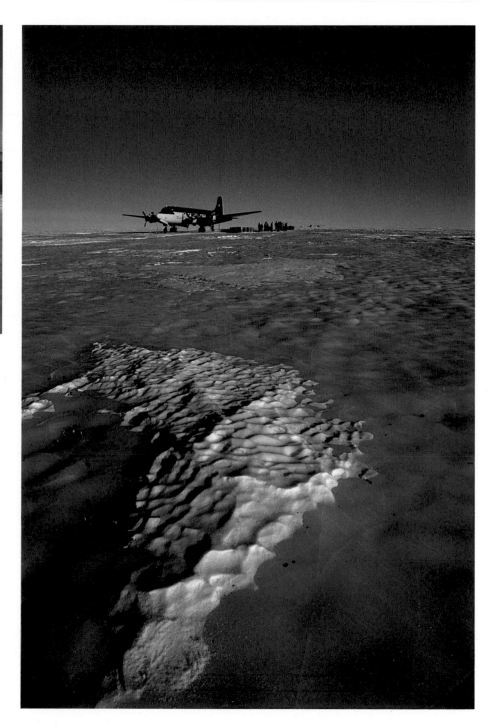

83

83

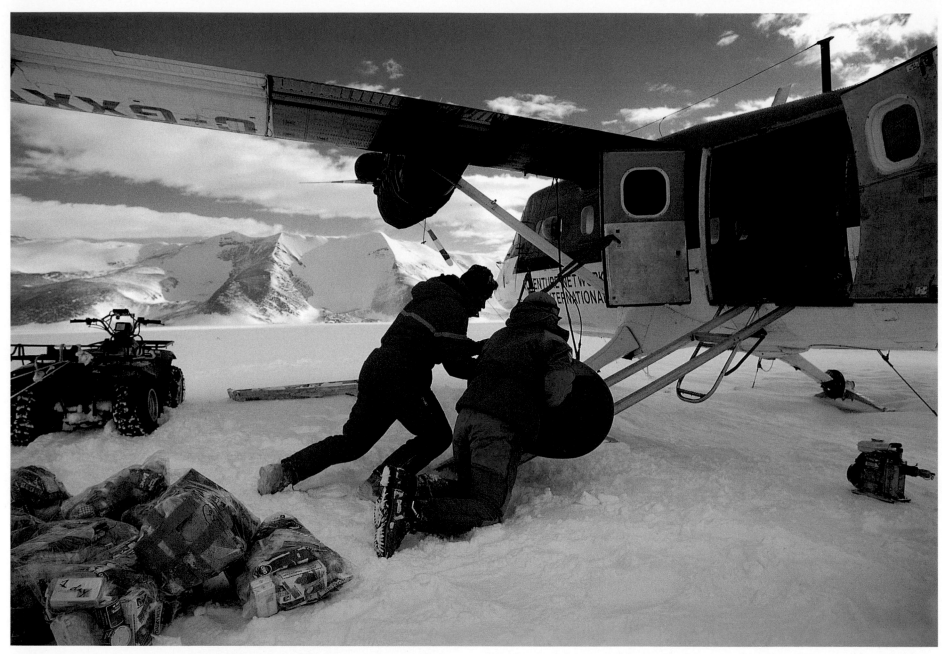

84

Above: Adventure Network International guide Vern Tejas and pilot Henry Perk load supplies onto a Twin Otter for a flight to 86°S in support of an ANI guided expedition which skied to the South Pole in 1989.

Opposite: ANI doctor and base-camp manager Lisa Densmore carries a pair of skis past precious fuel barrels during a surface blizzard in the Patriot Hills.

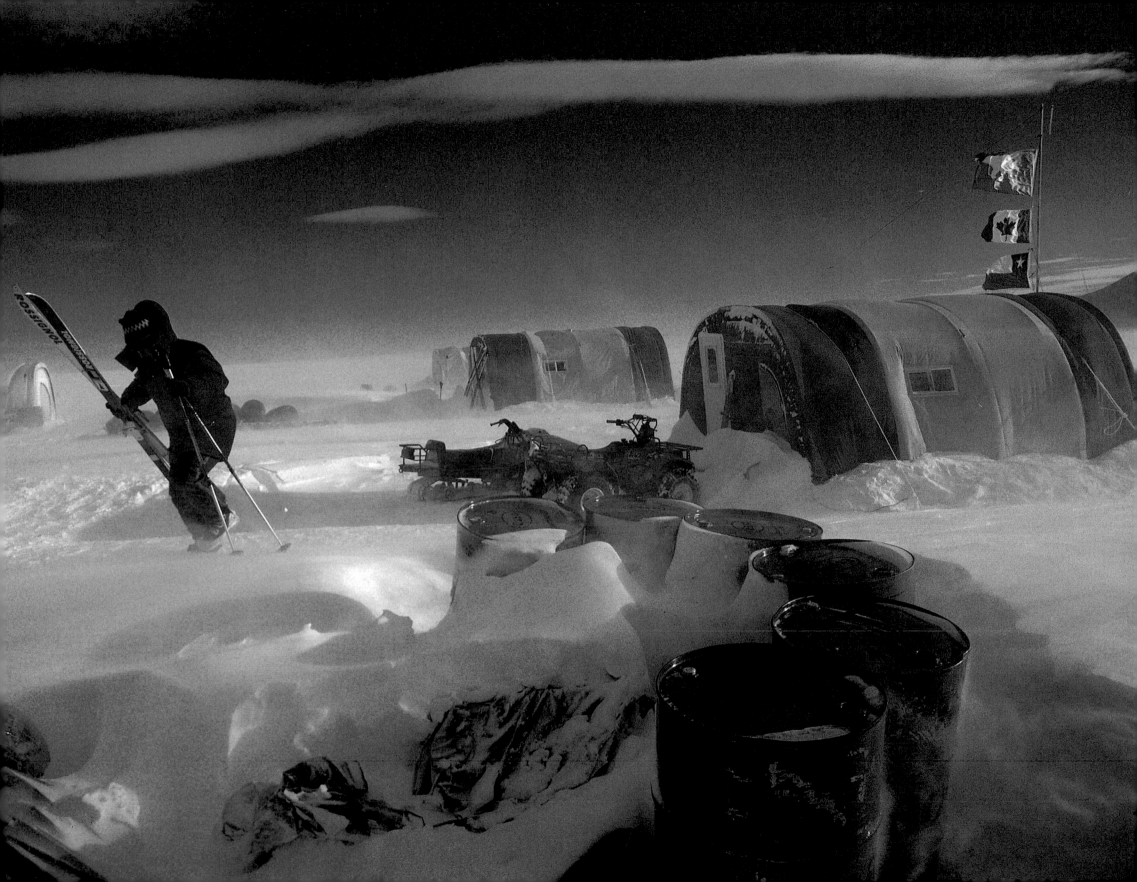

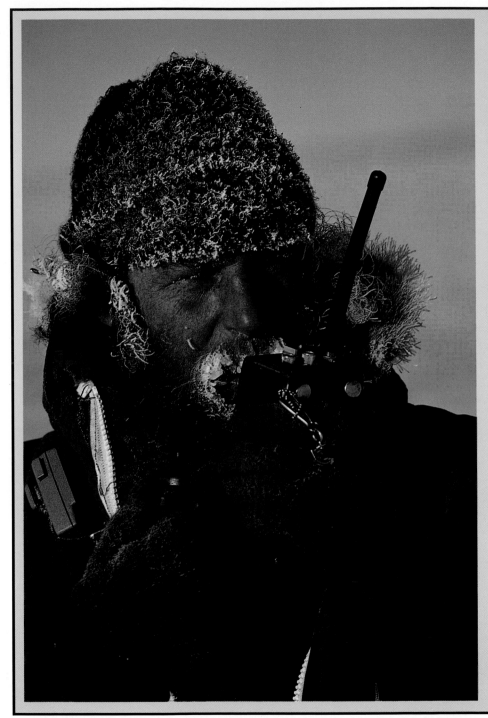

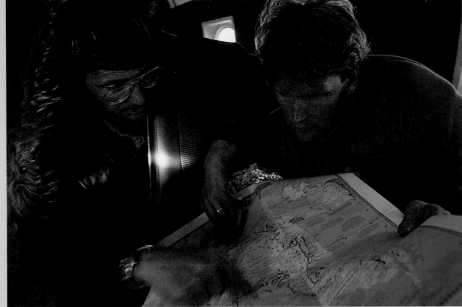

Tribute to Antarctic characters

Above: Flying over the Ellsworth Mountains in a DC4, veteran polar pilot Giles Kershaw (left) and geologist Greg Mortimer discuss Antarctic expeditions. Giles' flying exploits for British Antarctic Survey and his own company Adventure Network International are legendary. Giles died in a gyrocopter crash in Antarctica in 1990. Greg was the first Australian to climb Vinson Massif, Antarctica's highest peak.

Left: New Zealand winter-over dog handler Gary Bowcock radios Scott Base on Ross Island while driving a husky team across McMurdo Sound.

Right above: Scott Base dog handler Bill Eaton is proud of the model sled crafted as a midwinter present.

Right center: An Argentine marine biologist in a snowstorm near Almirante Brown Station on the Antarctic Peninsula sips maté, a herbal drink.

Right below: Andrew Brown (right) and the late Gary Ball, two mountaineers with the New Zealand Antarctic Research Programme, give each other a hug outside Scott Base.

Far right: Garth Varcoe died in a helicopter crash on Ross Island in 1992 after many selfless years working for the New Zealand Antarctic Research Programme. Ever ready to do difficult, dirty, and cold tasks, Garth coordinated the rebuilding of Scott Base in the late 1970s.

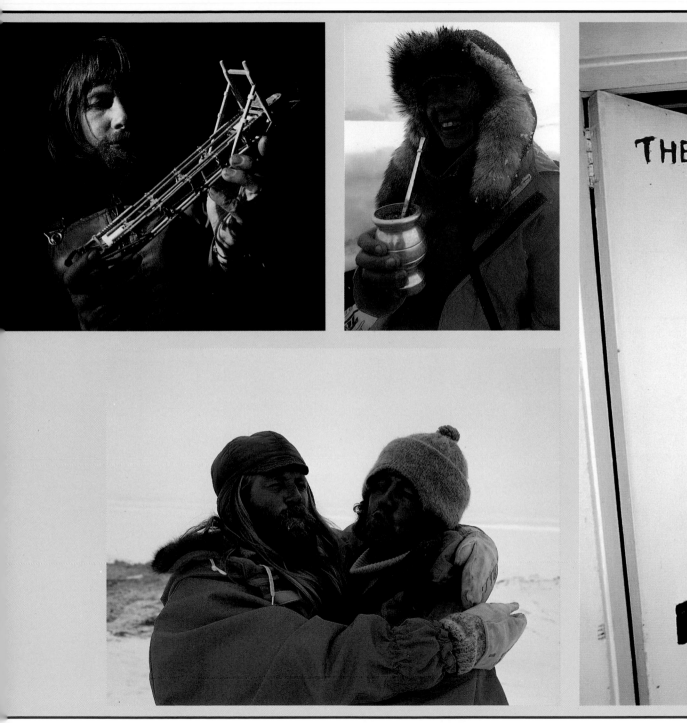
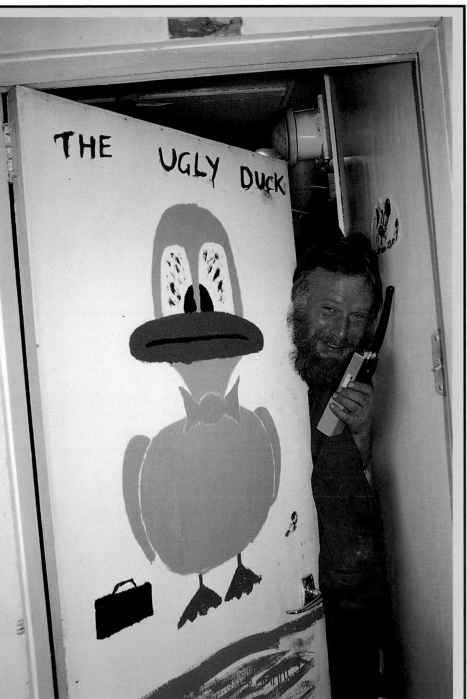

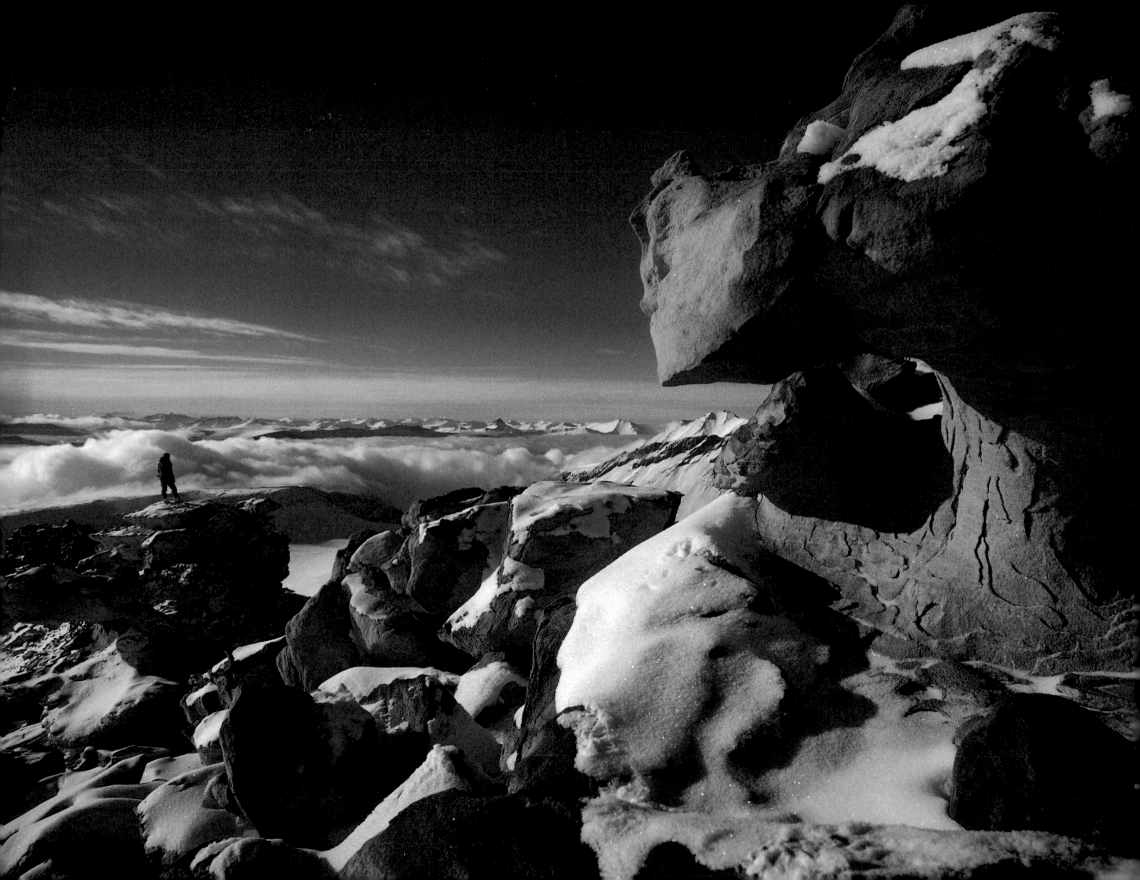

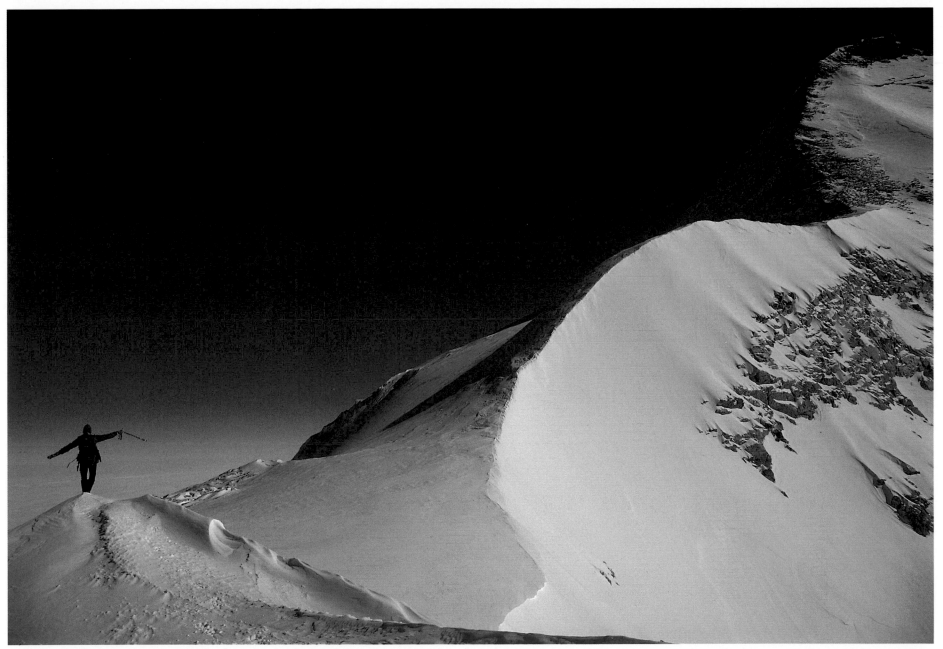

Above: Greg Mortimer climbs a ridge during the 1989 ascent of a new route on Mt. Shinn, one of Antarctica's highest peaks in the Ellsworth Mountains. Greg now runs an adventure company, Polar Journeys.

Opposite: Australian Mike McDowell stands on weathered sandstone of Brunhilde Peak in the Dry Valleys. A driving force behind Quark Expeditions and Adventure Network International, he plays a pivotal role in modern Antarctic expeditions.

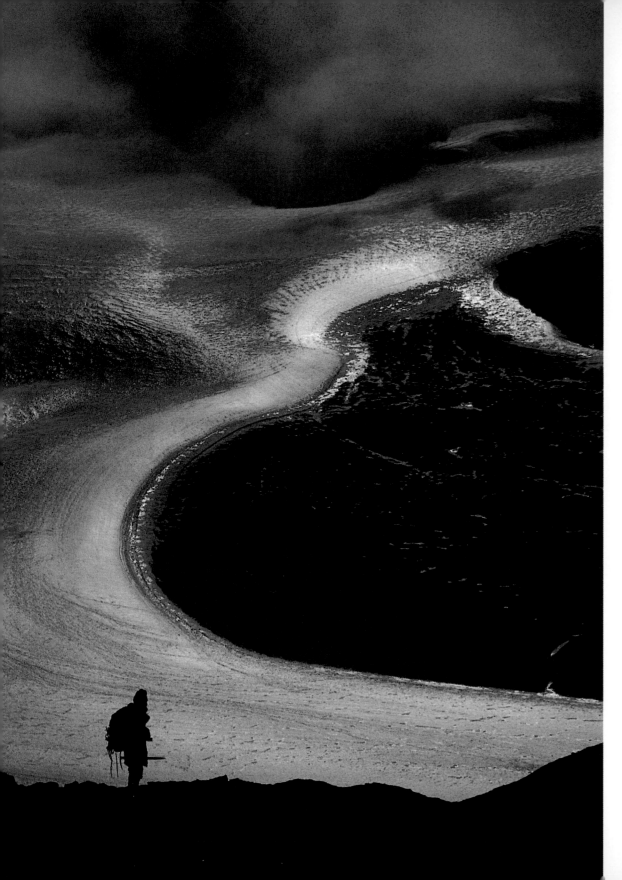

Left: A mountaineer is silhouetted against the Webb Glacier near Mt. Bastion as it flows from the East Antarctic Ice Sheet toward Victoria Land's Dry Valleys.

Below: 10,000-year-old mammoth tusks are discovered in the permafrost on the Arctic's remote New Siberian Islands. As for elephant and walrus ivory, human greed for mammoth ivory is insatiable.

At 80° N, Arctic poppies (*Papaver radicatum*) bloom on the Russian Arctic islands of Franz Josef Land. While the Antarctic does support two small flowering plants, they could not survive at 80° S. Most southern higher plants are found in the subantarctic latitudes 50–55° S.

Opposite: A climber nears the summit of Vinson Massif. At just over 16,400 feet Vinson is the highest peak in Antarctica. Expeditions to remote Antarctic ranges such as the Ellsworths require experienced team members and a carefully crafted logistic plan. Vinson Massif was not sighted until 1957 and received its first ascent in 1966 by American mountaineers with U.S. government backing.

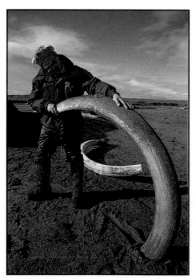

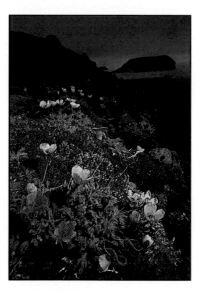

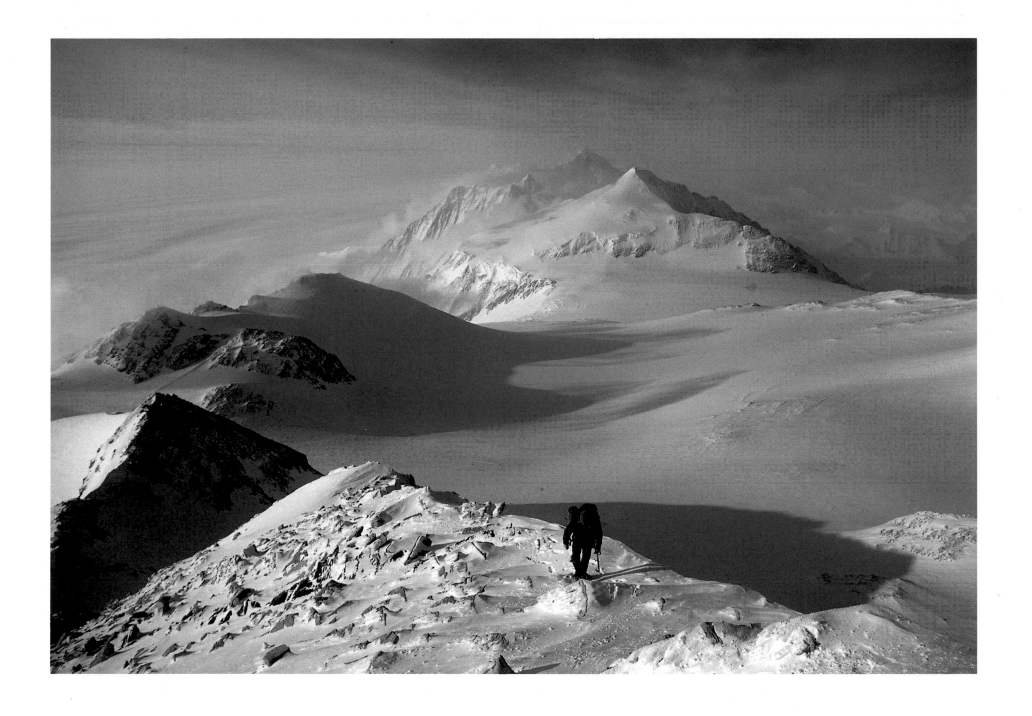

91

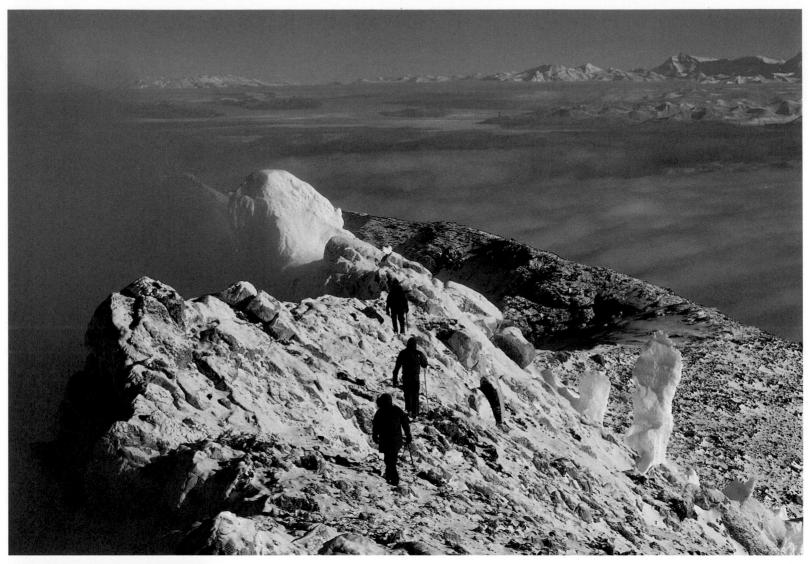

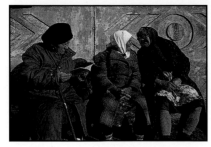

Above: Climbers on a private expedition based near Shackleton's hut at Cape Royds teamed up with members of the 1990 Greenpeace expedition from their base beside Scott's hut at Cape Evans to make an ascent of Mt Erebus. Here the climbers circle the summit caldera of the active volcano.

Left: Enjoying the Arctic summer sun, three women from the Siberian port of Providenya sit outside their apartment block.

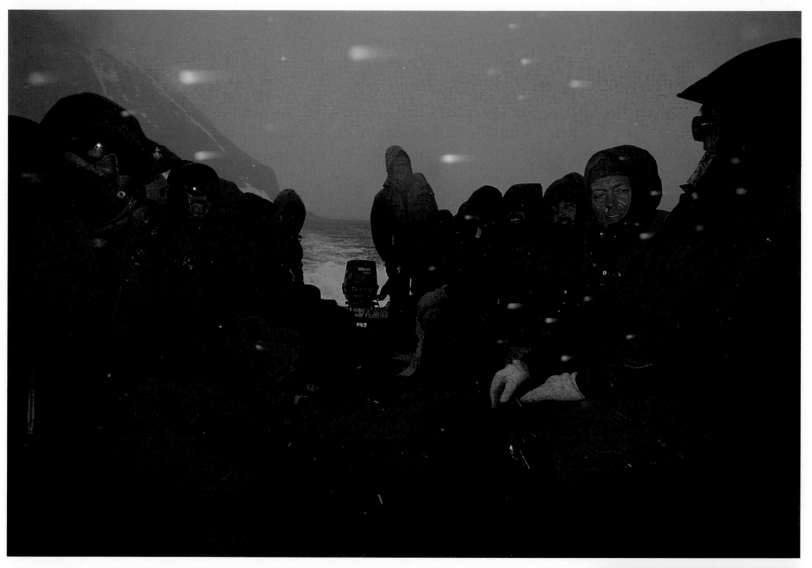

Above: Cold, wet, but thoroughly happy climbers in a Zodiac return to their ship in Errera Channel on the Antarctic Peninsula after the first ascent of Peon Peak on Ronge Island in 1996.

Right: Relishing another warm night wrapped in a reindeer skin clothing and sleeping chamber inside the yurt-shaped tent, this Chukchi nomad has perfected living off the land in the Siberian Arctic.

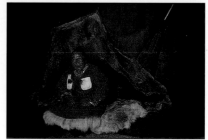

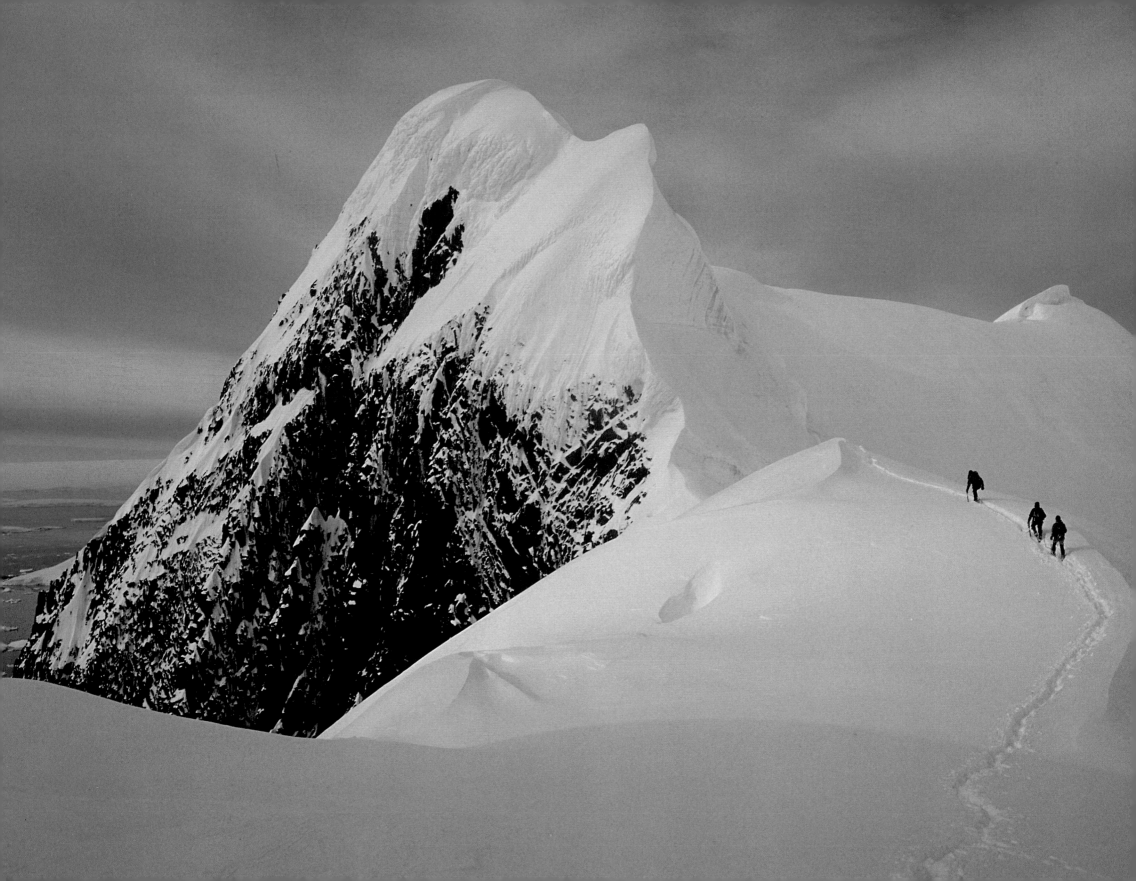

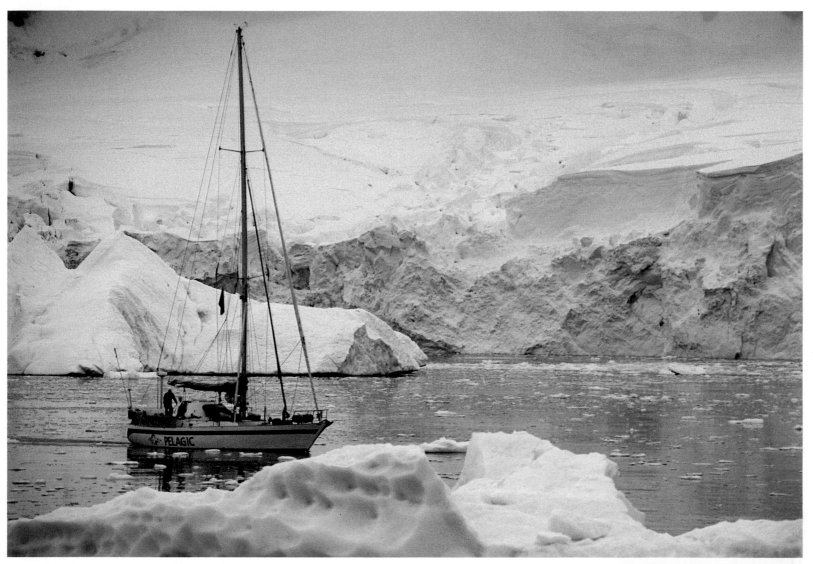

Above: Despite dismantling their year-round base at Cape Evans, Greenpeace has continued its presence in Antarctica by visiting Antarctic Peninsula bases on various vessels including the chartered yacht *Pelagic* skippered by Skip Novak.

Right: Siberian hunters have always shot walrus for meat and hide but now they often leave the carcass, merely chainsawing off the heads for valuable ivory tusks.

Opposite: Climbers descend the summit ridge on Mt. Scott, a prominent peak near the southern end of Lemaire Channel on the Antarctic Peninsula.

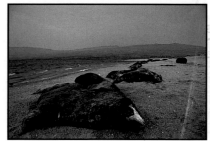

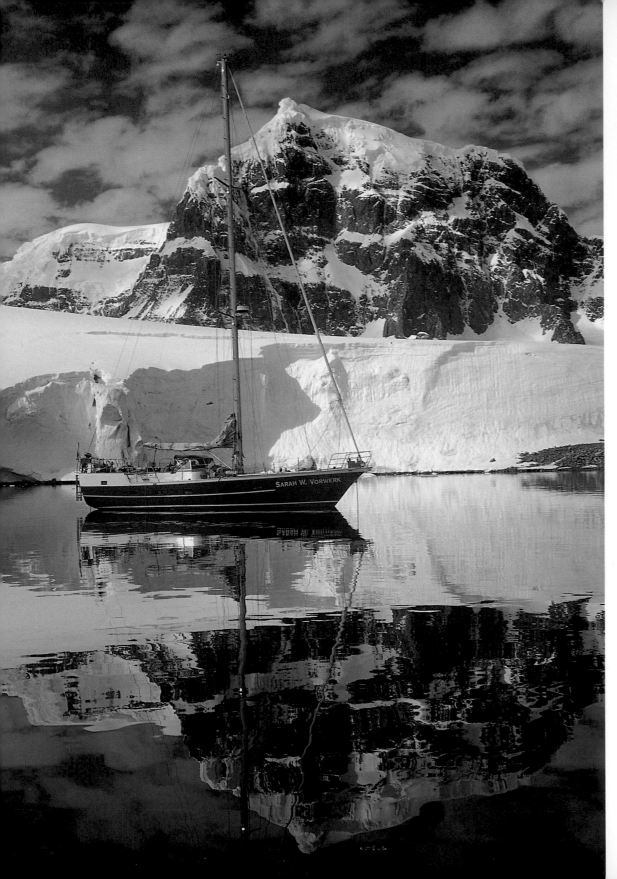

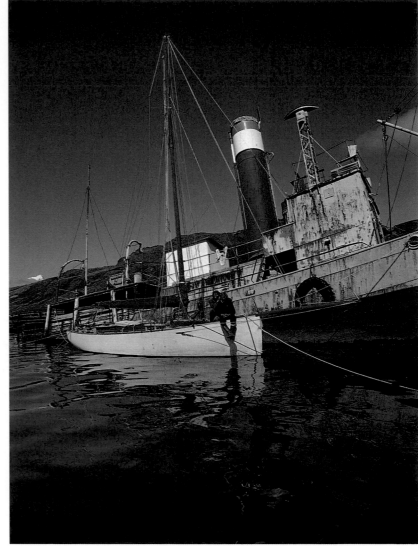

Above: Tim and Pauline Carr have lived for over two years on their tiny wooden yacht *Curlew* at Grytviken. They work on the late Nigel Bonner's dream — the South Georgia whaling museum. With no radio or engine, the Carrs have also sailed *Curlew* to the Antarctic Peninsula.

Left: Sarah Vorwerk at Port Lockroy, Wiencke Island. About 15 yachts each summer brave the Drake Passage for a cruising holiday on the Antarctic Peninsula. Some hail from Australian and New Zealand ports. Yachts can be chartered from Tierra del Fuego and the Falklands.

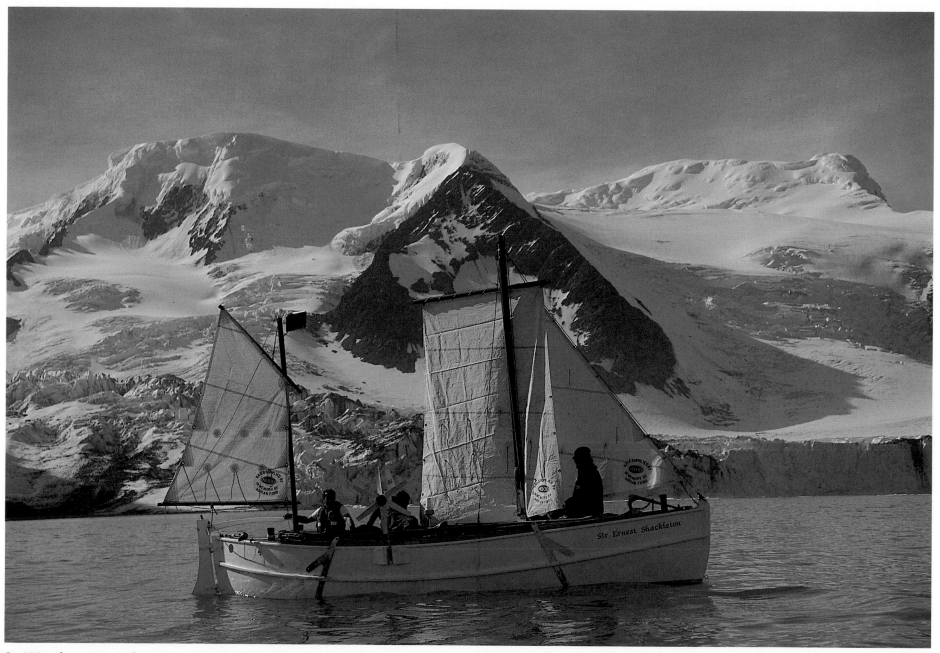

In 1994, three men and a woman repeated Shackleton's epic 800 nautical mile open-boat voyage from Elephant Island to South Georgia. The British expedition and their replica of Shackleton's *James Caird* were transported to Elephant Island by icebreaker. After a windless start pictured here, the team survived the arduous voyage to South Georgia. Unlike Shackleton, the foursome didn't cross the mountainous island.

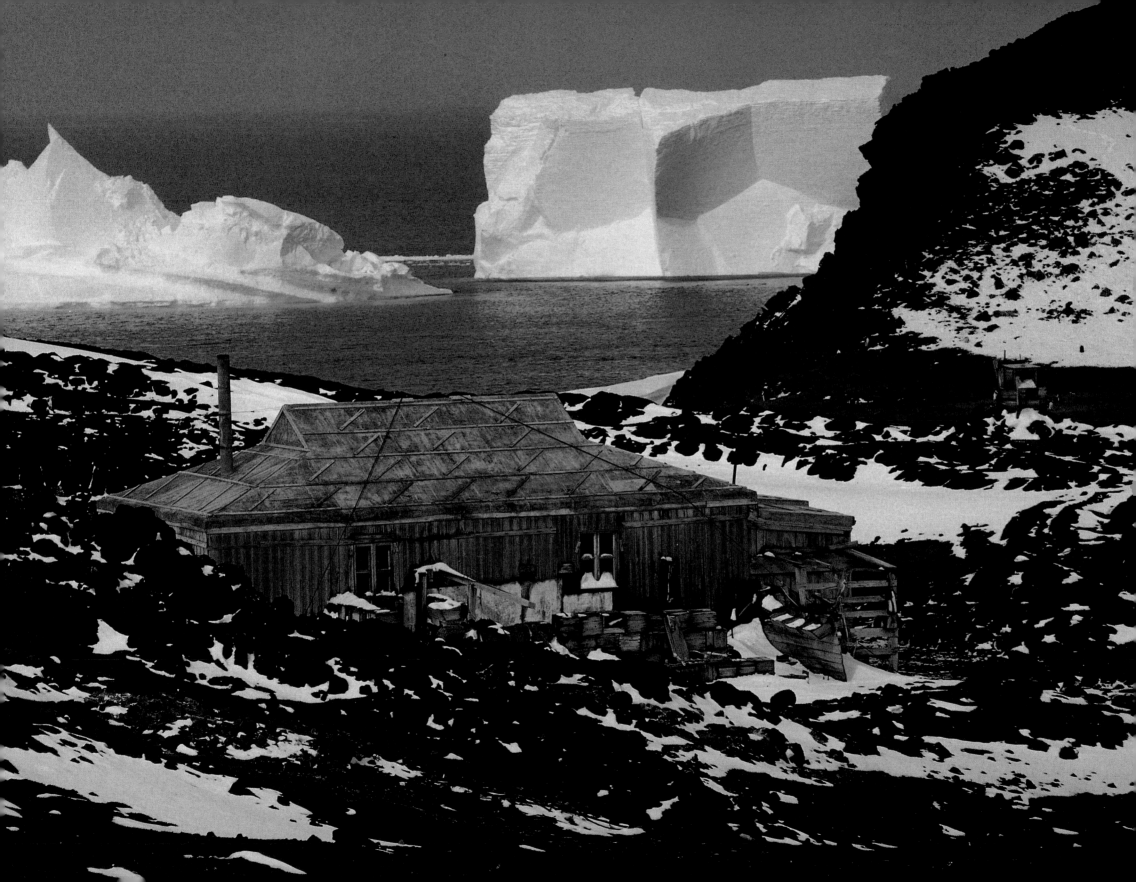

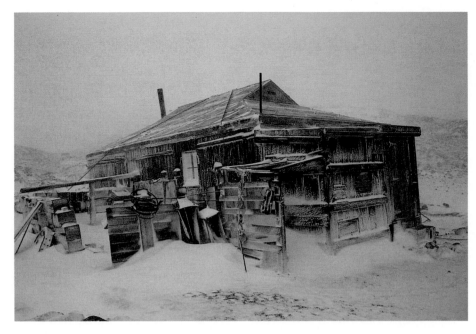

Above: The 1907–9 British Antarctic Expedition under Sir Ernest Shackleton lived in this hut at Cape Royds on Ross Island. From here, the explorers discovered the Beardmore Glacier — a gateway to the South Pole — reached the South Magnetic Pole, and made the first ascent of Mt. Erebus. Seen here in a blizzard, the building creaks and groans like a wooden ship in a storm. During winter darkness, Shackleton's men wrote, printed, and bound with packing case lids the *Aurora Australis*, the first book published in Antarctica.

Opposite: Shackleton's hut at Cape Royds is dwarfed by small icebergs grounded off the headland. Like the other historic buildings in the Ross Sea region, Shackleton's hut is maintained by the New Zealand Antarctic Heritage Trust.

Right: Australian geologist Douglas Mawson, who had also been a member of Shackleton's 1907–9 expedition, built this hut at Cape Denison in Commonwealth Bay to support his own 1911–14 expedition to George V Land. Mawson's "Home of the Blizzard" hut is now badly weathered by severe wind erosion and is filled with ice.

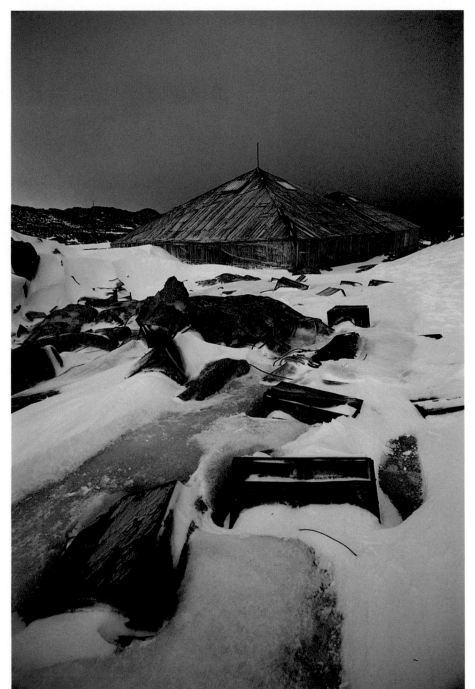

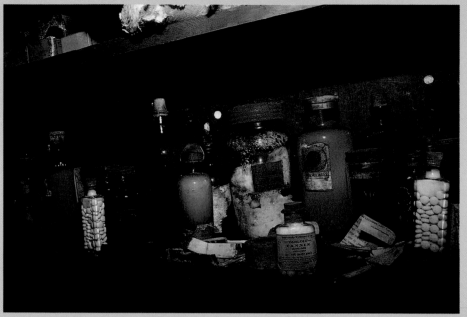

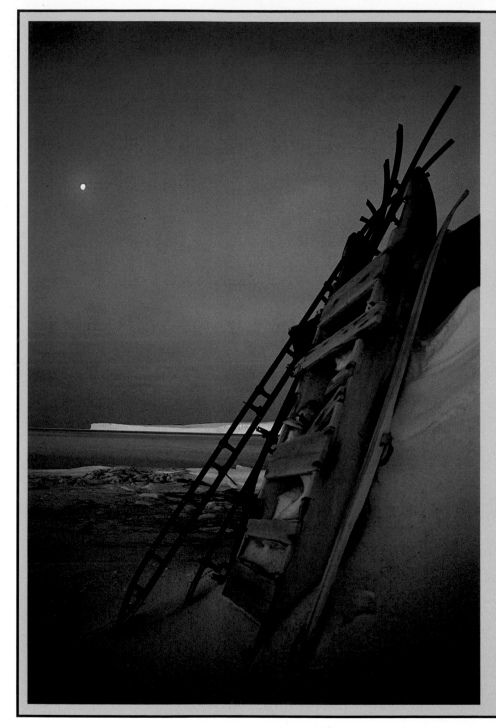

The heroic past lives on

Above: Drug supplies used by Edward Wilson, medical doctor, watercolor artist, and second in charge of Captain Scott's 1910–14 expedition. These supplies remain in Scott's hut at Cape Evans on Ross Island. Neither Scott nor Wilson returned from the journey from this hut to the South Pole.

Left: One of the old cargo sleds used at Scott's Cape Evans hut still stands against the wall. The Barne Glacier which juts out into McMurdo Sound is visible beyond the hut.

Right above: Food supplies and a cooking stove outside Scott's hut at Cape Evans. The kerosene Primus was the single most important item that made polar exploration possible. The design has not changed and very similar stoves are still in use in Antarctica today.

Right below: Herbert Ponting's darkroom inside Scott's Cape Evans hut is almost exactly as he left it at the end of the 1910–14 expedition. Ponting's remarkable black and white prints are, along with Frank Hurley's from Mawson and Shackleton expeditions, a beautiful and most graphic record of Antarctica's "Heroic Era."

Far right: A passenger from a visiting cruise vessel captures the mood inside Shackleton's hut at Cape Royds by sketching in her pad with charcoal.

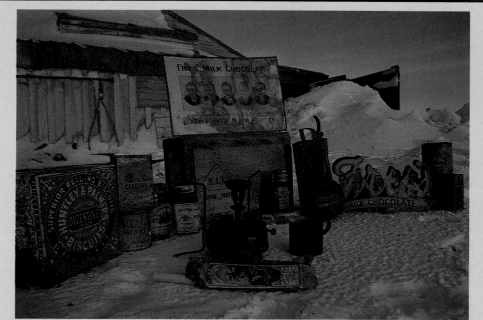

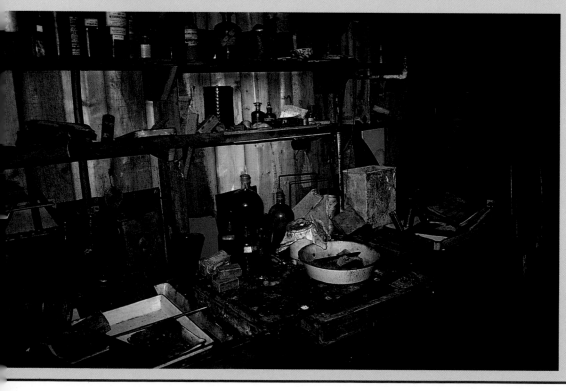

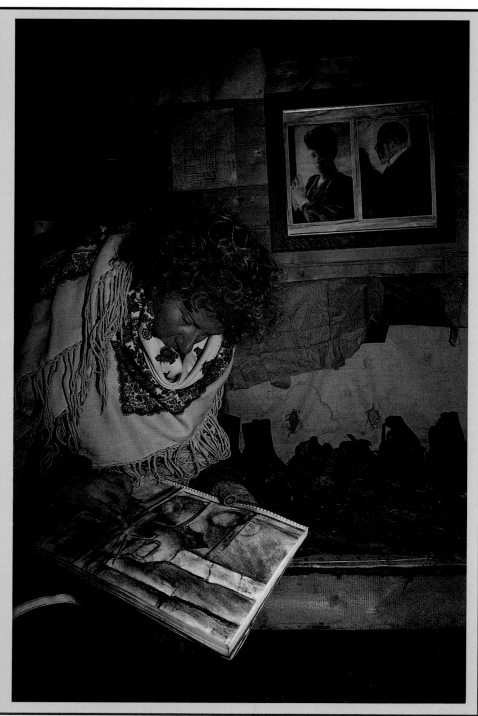

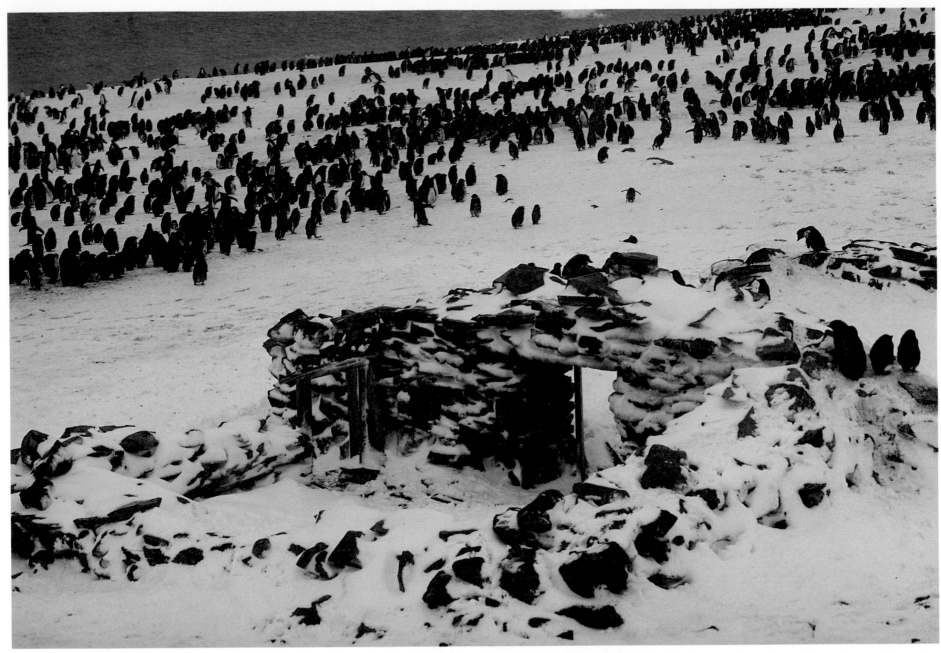

Above: Paulet Island is an important historic site for the stone wall remains of an emergency hut built by Captain Larsen and his crew after their ship supporting the Swedish Nordenskjold expedition was crushed by pack ice. Twenty men spent the miserable winter of 1903 here living on salvaged supplies and penguin meat.

Opposite: Winter snow blanketing Scott's hut at Cape Evans.

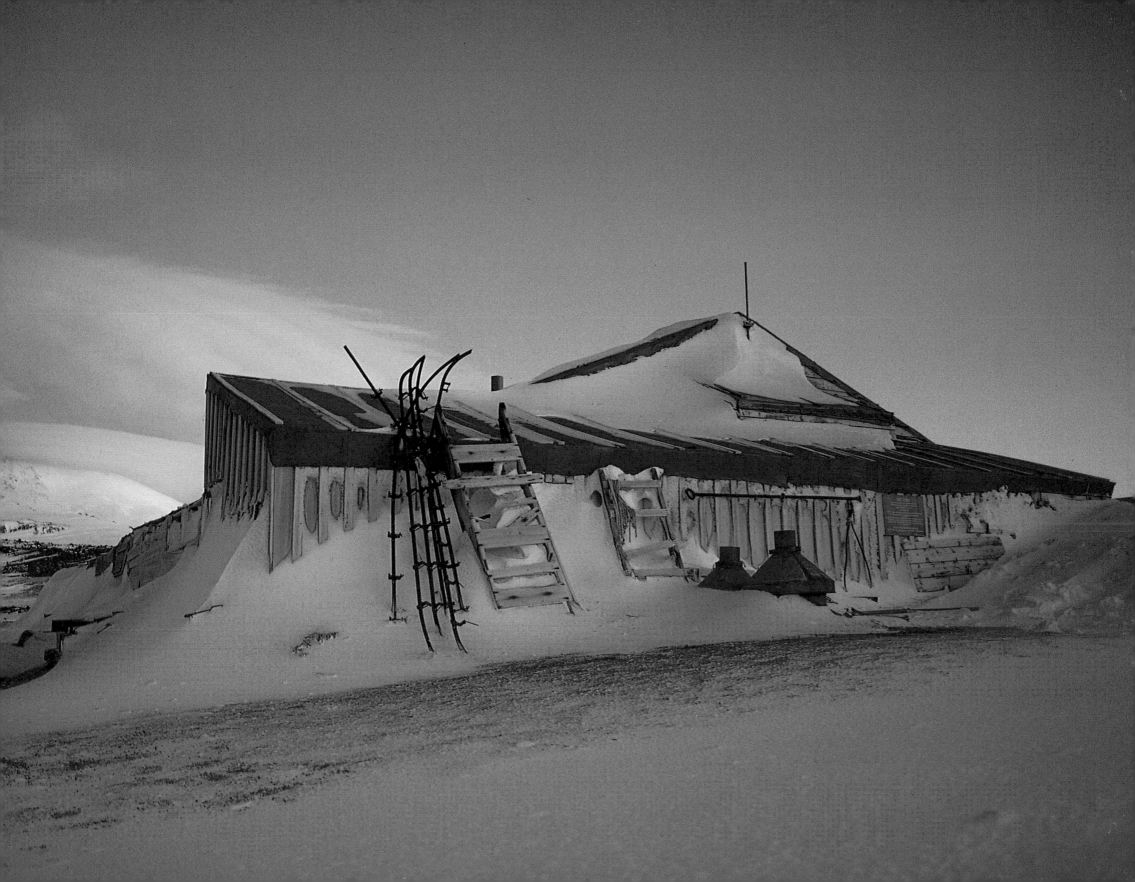

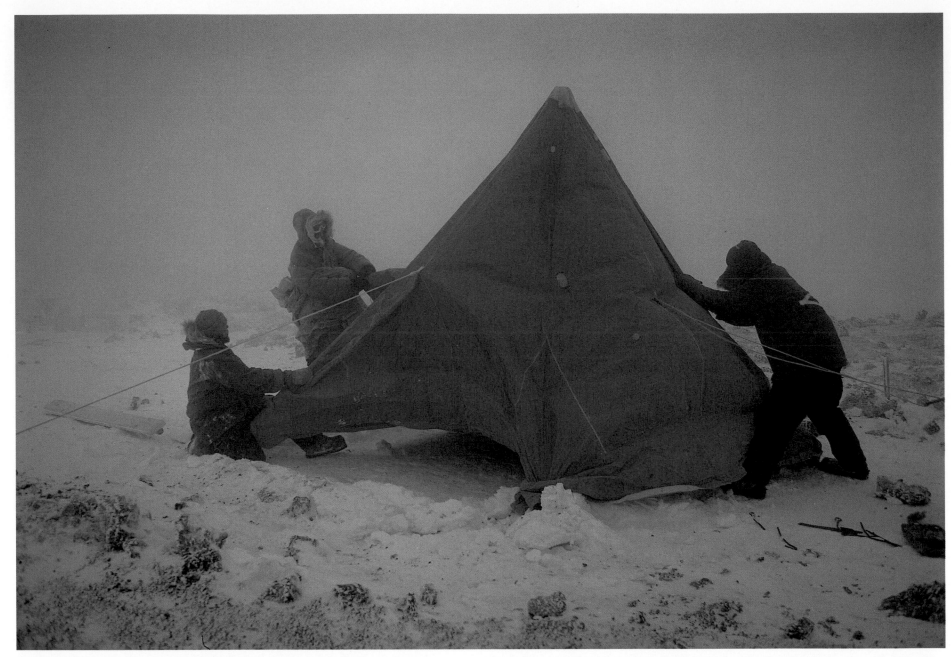

Scientists living on the summit of Mt. Erebus must endure high winds and temperatures ranging from 14 to −36° F. Here, three men are repitching a 66-pound polar tent which was blown away by the wind near the summit caldera of the volcano. Adjusting to the effects of high altitude, staying warm and properly hydrated remain difficult tasks to deal with before getting on with the job of research.

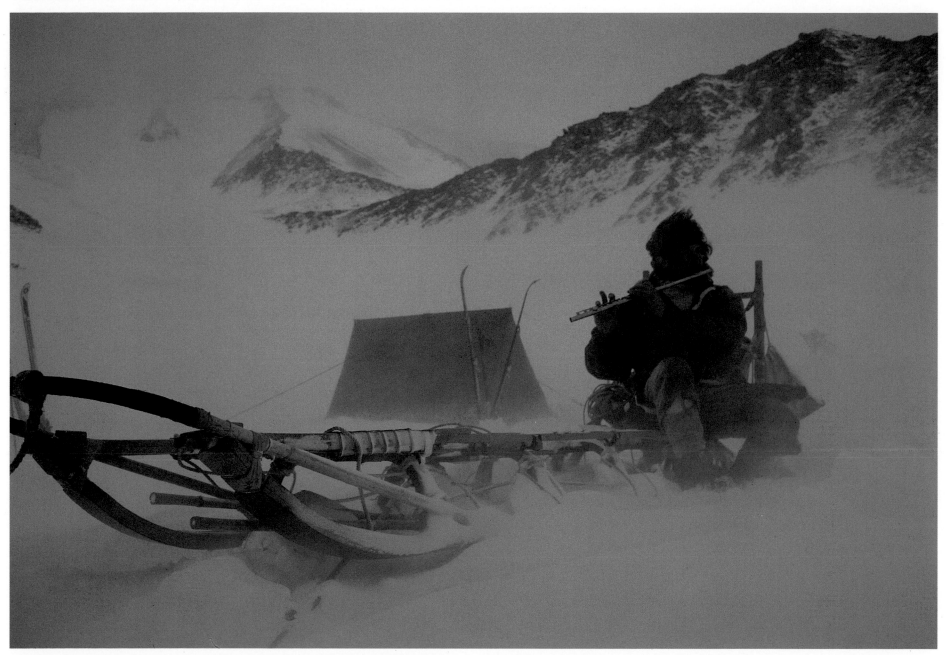

The New Zealand geologist Adrian Daly plays a flute in a blizzard while sitting on a wooden sled at the end of his day's field work. The campsite is at the head of the Blue Glacier under the Royal Society Range — 13,120-foot peaks in the Transantarctic Mountains. Adrian had some of his toes and parts of fingers amputated after this expedition due to frostbite.

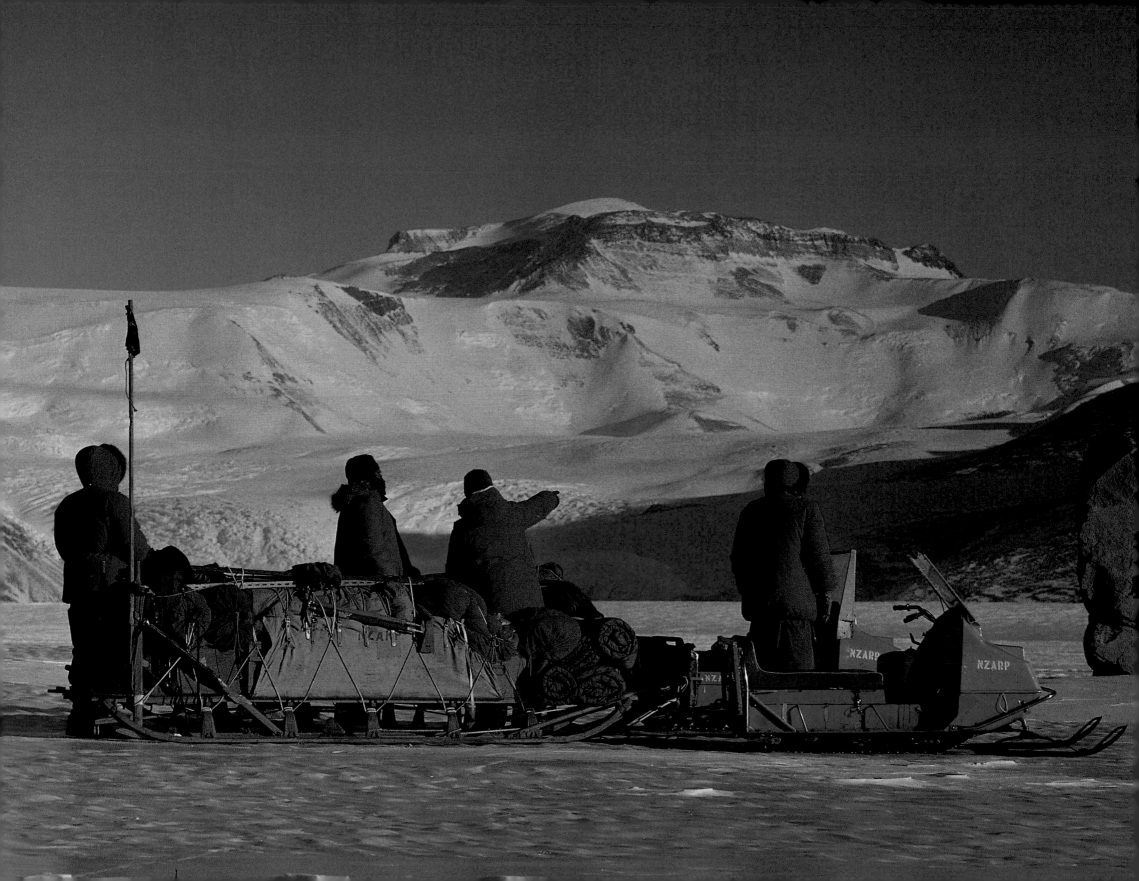

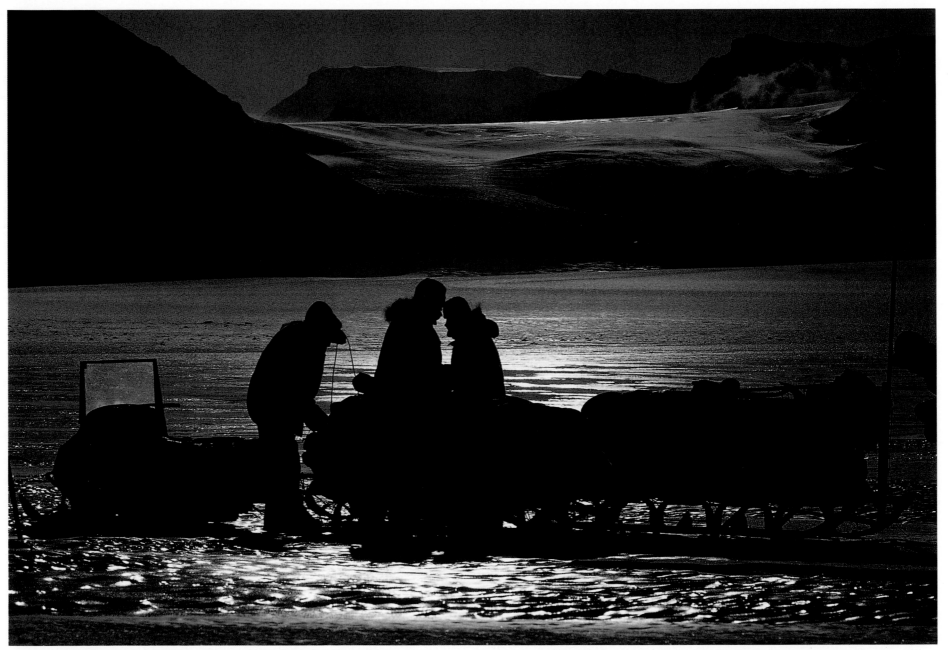

At the confluence of the Taylor and Ferrar Glaciers on the edge of the Dry Valleys, a team of New Zealand geologists unlash equipment from their sled. The ice is polished by strong wind, making travel and camping difficult.

Opposite: New Zealand geologists and glaciologists use motor toboggans and wooden sleds to travel up the Ferrar Glacier. This view was taken at midnight under the 13,120-foot Mt. Lister in the Royal Society Range.

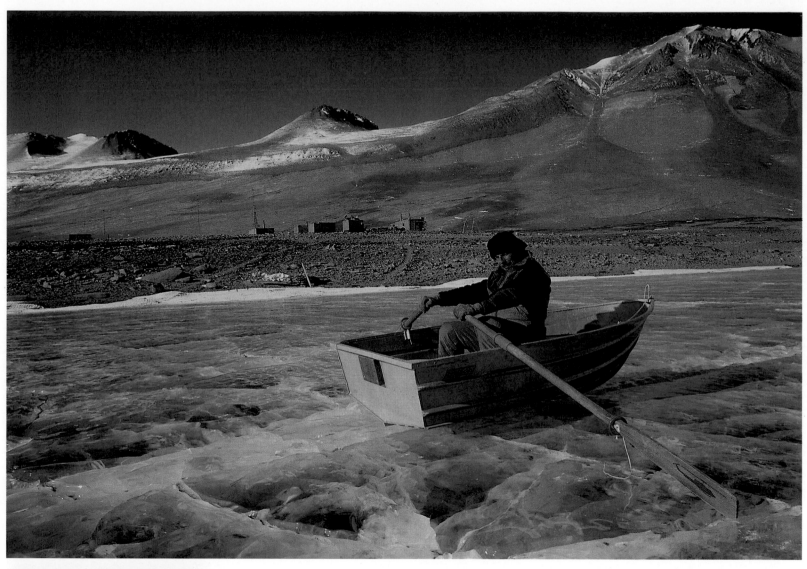

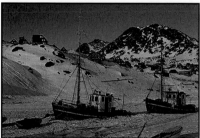

Above: Field assistant Peter Sampson "rows" New Zealand's only boat in the Antarctic across the frozen surface of Lake Vanda in the Dry Valleys. Vanda Station was once the center for science and logistical support in the Dry Valleys. It has now been removed due to rising lake levels.

Left: In early spring, fishing boats remain frozen into the sea ice at the village of Ammassalik on the east coast of Greenland.

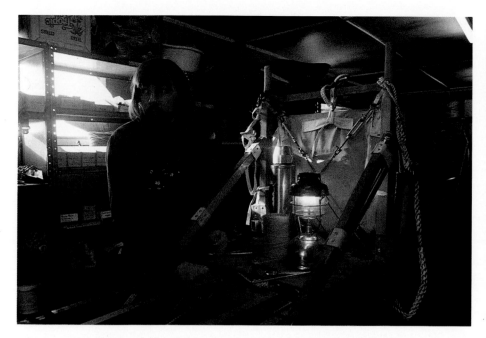

Above: Field assistant Bill Eaton spends the winter months at New Zealand's Scott Base repairing the wooden sleds with twine and leather thonging. Meticulous work on the sleds, polar tents, kitchen boxes, and other field equipment by the winter-over field assistant has proved vital for New Zealand to maintain its good safety record in the Antarctic.

Right: Using a theodolite to record a bearing from Cape Roberts to a distant peak, New Zealand surveyors establish essential ground work for a major international sea-floor drilling program in McMurdo Sound. Coring sediments laid down in the Ross Sea has proved crucial in developing an understanding of the age of various glacial periods as well as the uplift of the Transantarctic Mountains.

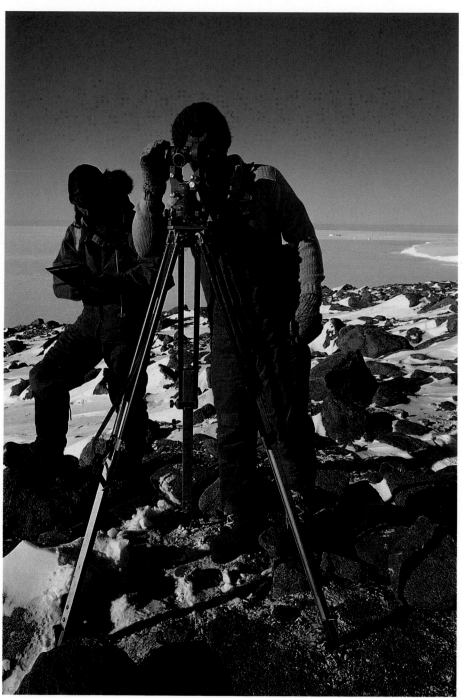

109

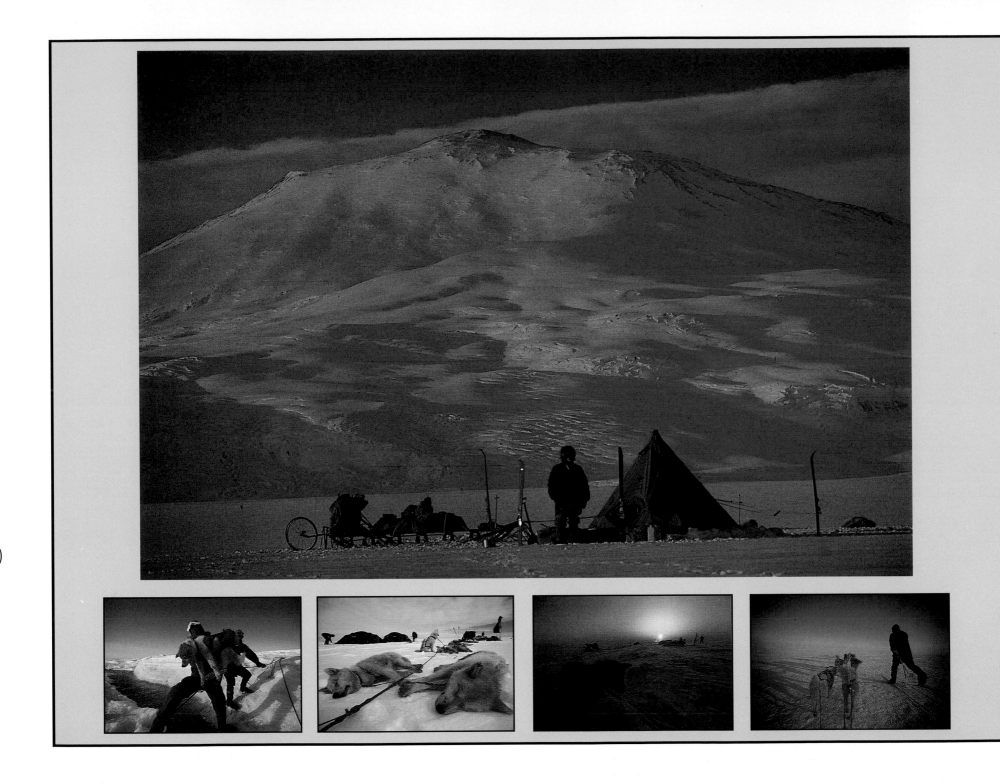

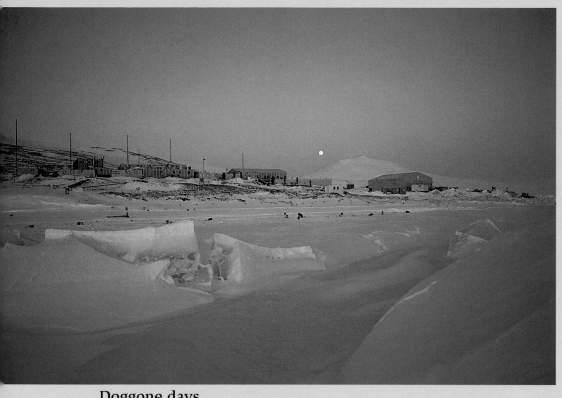

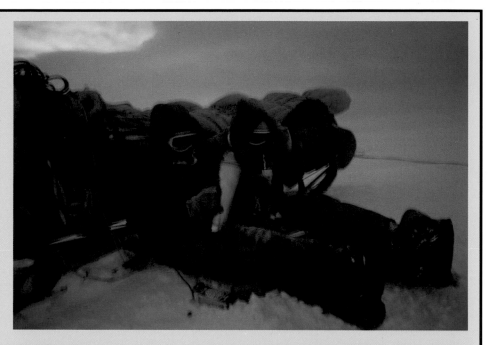

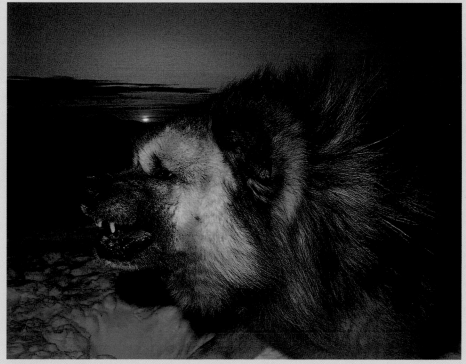

Doggone days

Above: New Zealand's huskies settle down on the sea ice in front of the old Scott Base. The furthest south of any Antarctic husky, the "Kiwi dogs" served New Zealand well for over thirty years, undertaking many arduous sledding journeys throughout the Transantarctic Mountains. The howl of a husky on Ross Island will long be remembered.

Above right: Driving dog teams is one of the hardest yet most satisfying ways of traveling in Antarctica. These two dog handlers are exhausted by a windstorm near Black Island on the Ross Ice Shelf and seek respite behind their sled.

Right below: An angry husky snarls at another dog. Huskies are friendly toward humans but can fight savagely with rival dogs.

Left: Under the imposing flank of Mt. Erebus, both huskies and their handler settle in for a night at Windless Bight during a journey to Cape Crozier. The last husky left Antarctica in 1994 — the sad end of a colorful era.

Left bottom: Dog travel in the polar regions lives on in the Arctic. These four images illustrate aspects of an expedition that crossed the 375-mile-wide Greenland icecap along the Arctic Circle in 1993.

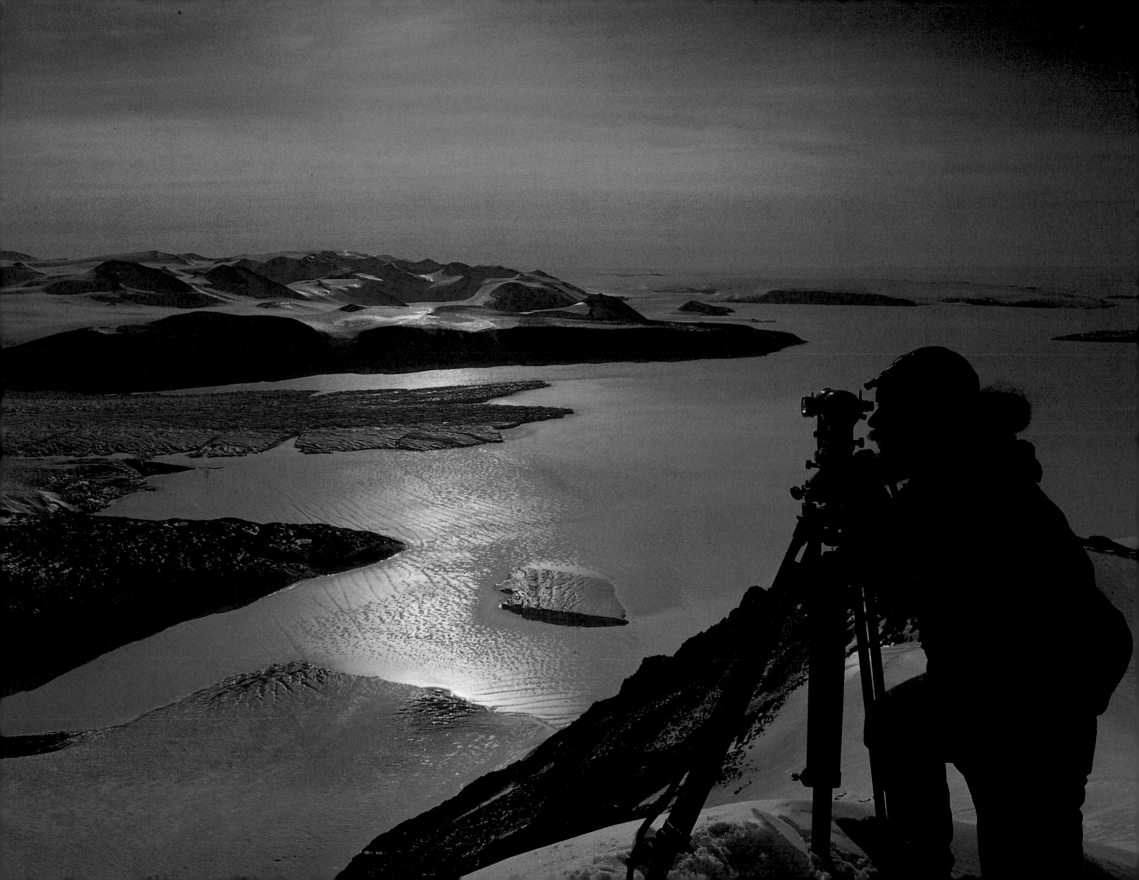

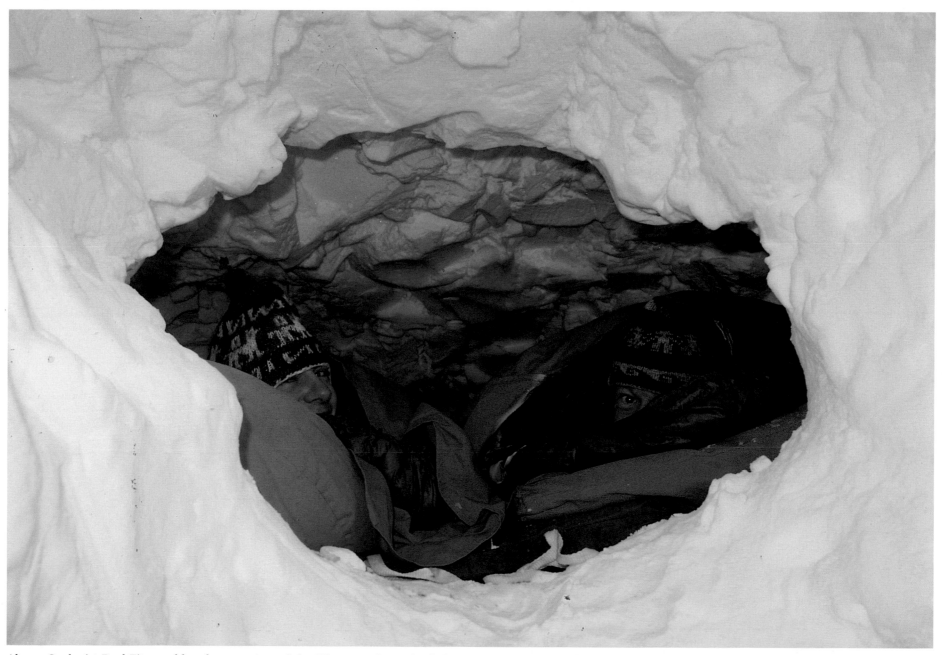

Above: Geologist Paul Fitzgerald and mountaineer John Watson wake up in their emergency snow shelter crafted during a pre-expedition course. Practicing the basics of survival have paid handsome dividends for New Zealand field parties.

Opposite: A New Zealand surveyor takes a bearing from Mt. England above the Mackay Glacier on the Victoria Land coast.

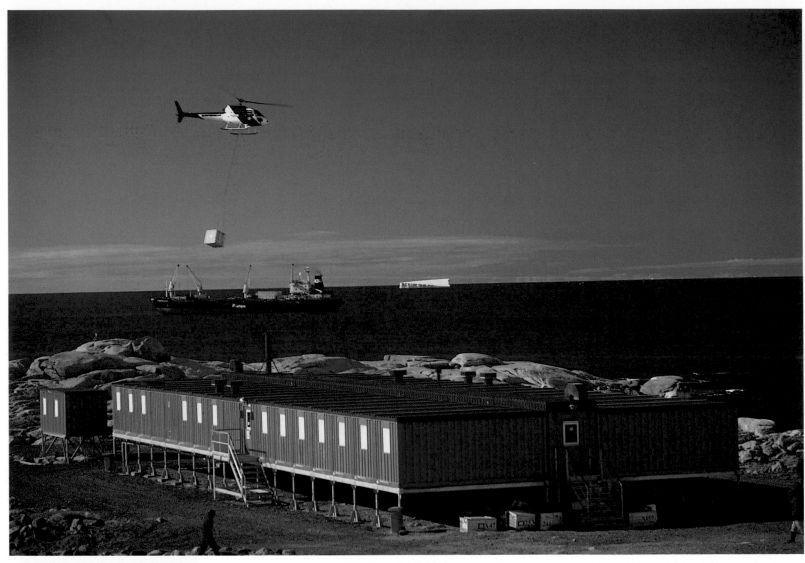

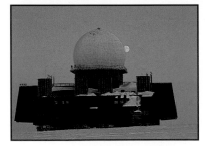

Above: A New Zealand helicopter shuttles supplies from a ship to the Italian base at Terra Nova Bay. This new science base was constructed in North Victoria Land in the 1980s.

Left: The moon sets over the dome of DYEII Dewline early-warning radar station perched on the Arctic Circle on Greenland's ice cap. With the Cold War tension of potential nuclear missile attack gone, all four similar military facilities in Greenland have been abandoned.

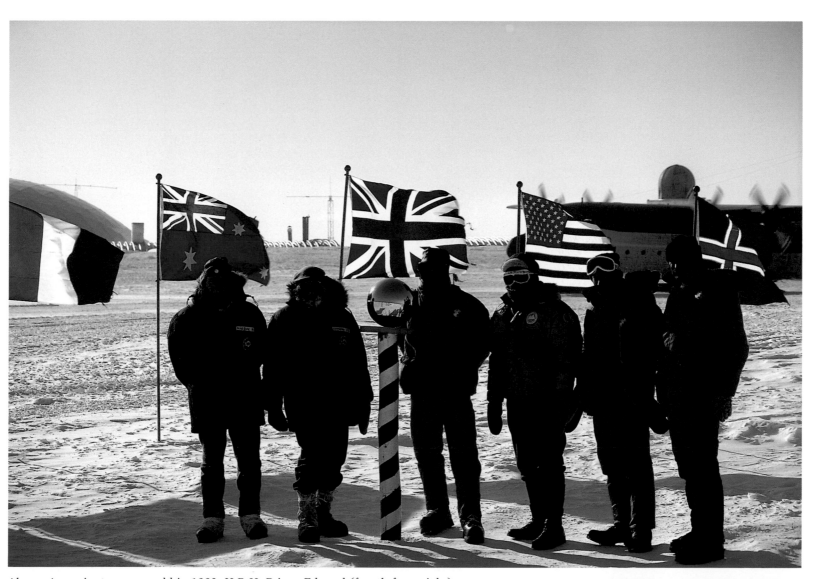

Above: As a nineteen-year-old in 1982, H.R.H. Prince Edward (fourth from right) pays a flying visit to the Amundsen-Scott South Pole Station. Behind the prince and his escorts are flags of the Antarctic Treaty signatories. Whether government VIP, scientist, fare-paying tourist, or recreational adventurer, all are visitors to Antarctica and must abide by the same code of conduct designed to minimize impact.

Right: In contrast to the South Pole at over 9,840 feet, the North Pole lies in the Arctic Ocean. American sax player Jesse Hill celebrates her arrival at 90° N in 1991 on the Soviet nuclear-powered icebreaker *Sovetskiy Soyuz*.

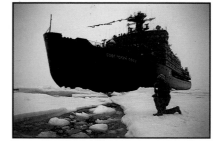

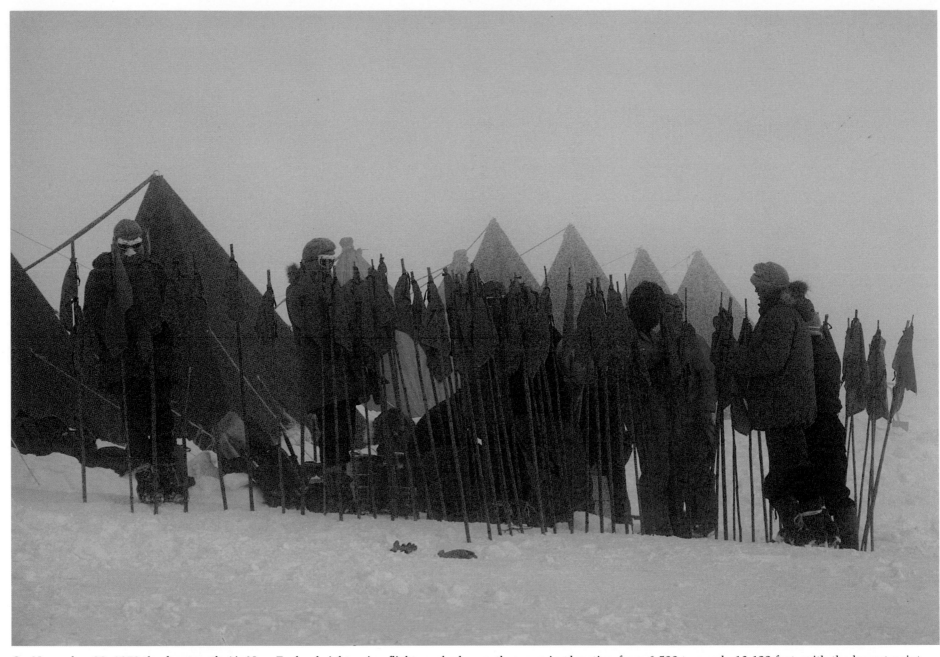

On November 28, 1979 the fourteenth Air New Zealand sightseeing flight crashed into the base of Ross Island only 1,440 feet above Lewis Bay. None of the 257 passengers and crew survived. Ross Island volcanoes, directly in the aircraft's path, range in elevation from 6,500 to nearly 13,100 feet, with the lowest point between them 5,250 feet. This view of the crash site shows the recovery team assembling flags to mark bodies before they were covered over with drifting snow.

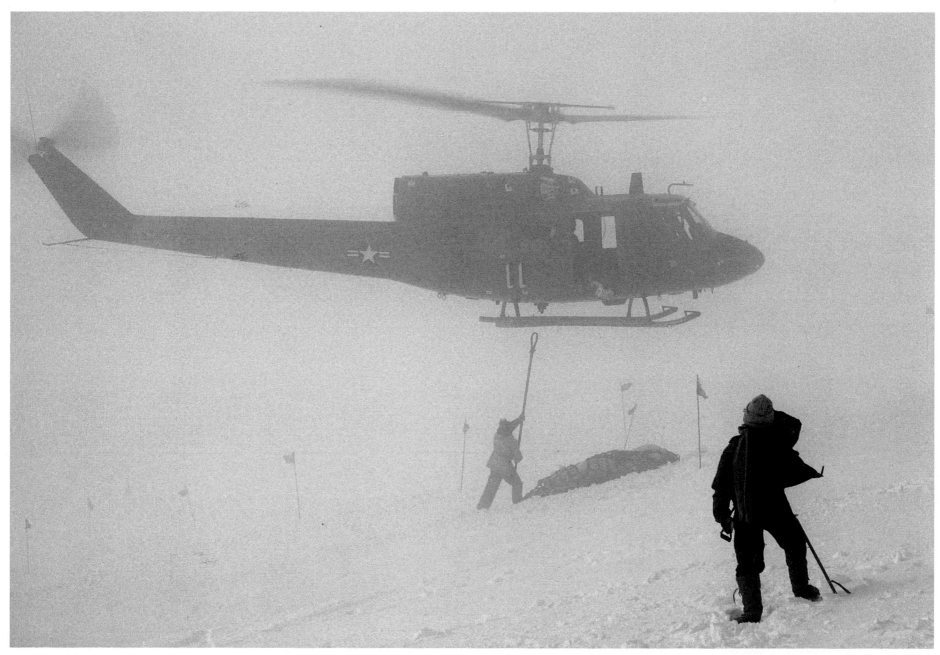

A combined American-New Zealand team assisted with the Air New Zealand DC10 crash recovery operation, which lasted ten days. Utilizing helicopters from nearby McMurdo Station, pilots often flew in poor visibility to make pickups from the crash site. Most of the 257 victims of the tragedy were returned to New Zealand for burial. Antarctic sightseeing flights from South America and Australia have since taken place in the 1990s.

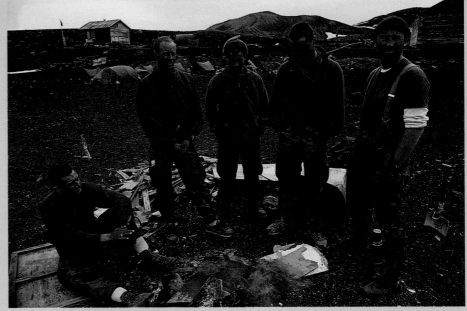

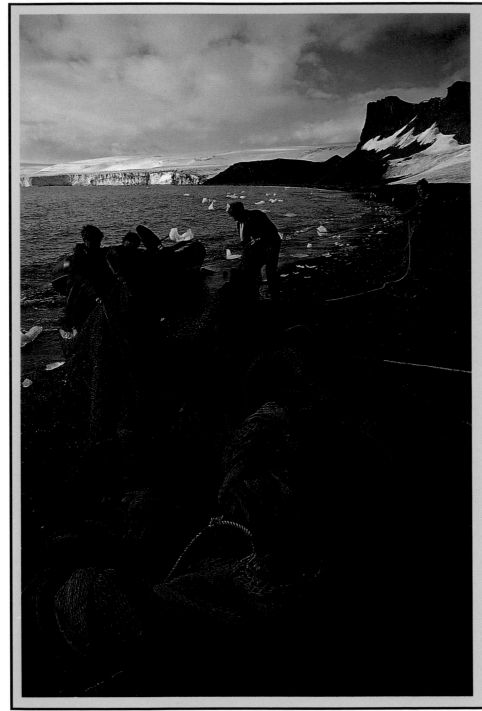

A heavy human hand in Antarctica

Above: British soldiers sent to the Antarctic on a training exercise show little regard for the environment during their stay on Deception Island. Old equipment and buildings are torn apart and burned. Should these buildings be preserved as historic relics, or should they be removed from Antarctica?

Left: Tourists help to remove a fishing net from Hannah Point in the South Shetland Islands. Antarctic wildlife is increasingly found trapped in nets and plastic garbage discarded by the fishing industry.

Right above: Chilean and Argentine bases in the Antarctic are staffed by military personnel. The infrastructure to support their families has also been established, in part to bolster territorial claims in the region. This Argentine family lives at Esperanza on the Antarctic Peninsula.

Right below: Despite considerable protest, France continued to use explosives on islands inhabited by breeding petrels and penguins to construct a hard-surface runway for large aircraft near their base, Dumont d'Urville. The airstrip has now been temporarily abandoned.

Far right: Thule Island in the South Sandwich Islands is just north of 60°S and so beyond protection by the Antarctic Treaty. In 1983, after the Argentine-British conflict, British forces returned to the Argentine base on Thule and, although surrounded by thousands of penguins, blew the entire base up, leaving a disgraceful mess.

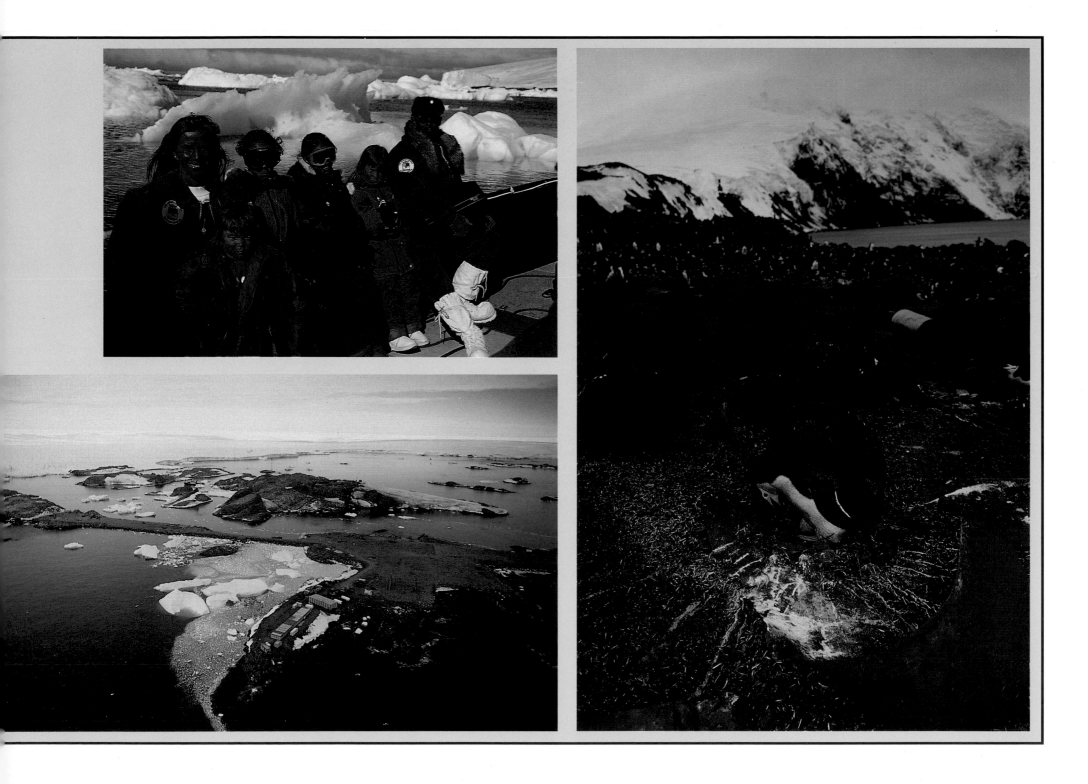

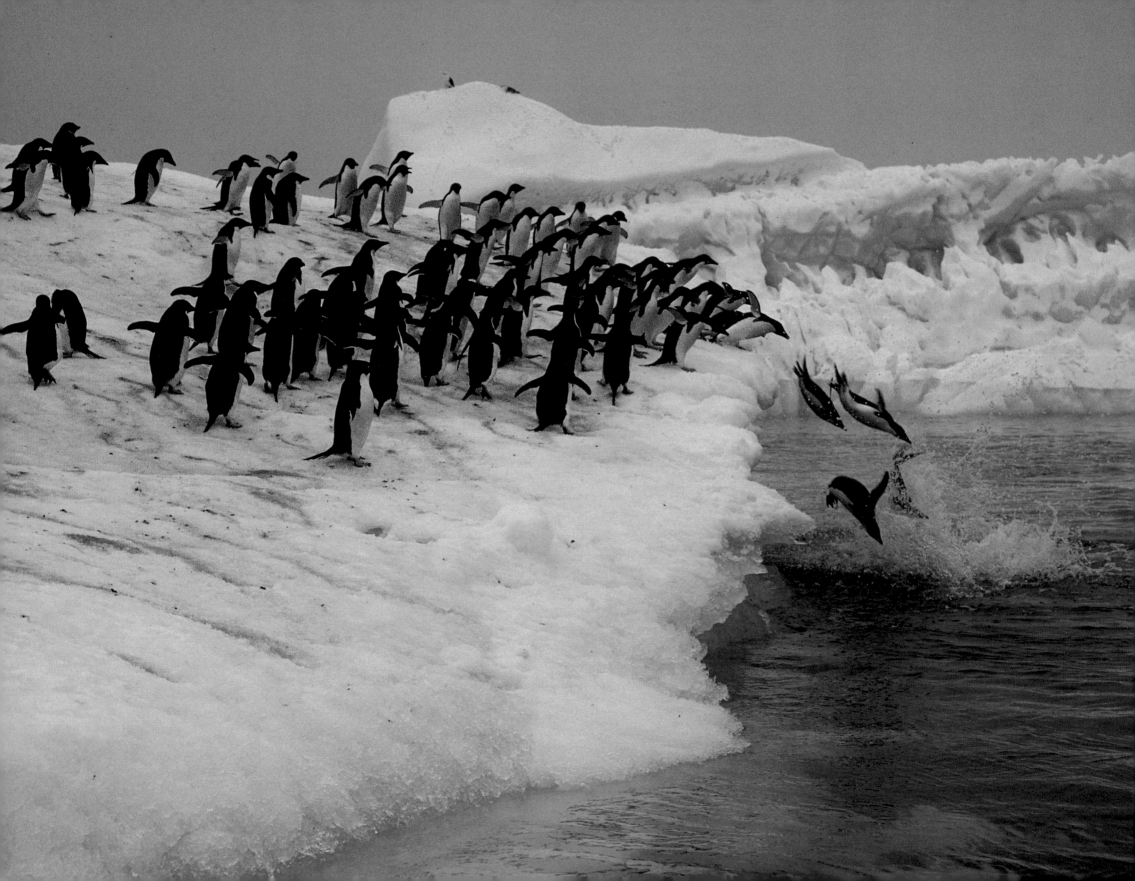

WILD AND FREE

In the slippery silence of a sombre new morning sky and water merge. The muted icescape is transformed into an embroidery of dappled magenta and mauve as we lower the boats for a chance encounter with feeding humpbacks. It is a brief yet intense meeting of two remote cultures — a fleeting sojourn, precious, never forgotten.

The whales, singly or at times in consort, spiral upward to create a dancing circle of bubbles. This cunning performance forces the frenzied krill to the surface, trapping the hapless prey in an impenetrable web of air. With trailing baleen plates the humpbacks explode skyward, mouths agape, their giant pleated rorquals bulging and overflowing with food. Then, with slow-sighing breaths, they blow a pungent fishy mist over us adding to the magic of the moment.

Way out here at this raw polar edge of ocean and ice, so far from the clutter we call civilisation, it is simply astounding that these barnacled leviathans are, like us, warm-blooded mammals exquisitely capable of emotion and sensitivity. And yet, the humpbacks are driven by a mighty migration for food, atuning themselves each summer to this frigid realm. They journey on in peace and perfect solitude, seeking nothing from us except perhaps an apology for our piracy and pillage which has rendered the cetacean empire confused and in ruin.

Diary excerpt January, 1996.
Gerlache Strait, Antarctic Peninsula

Of all the remarkable creatures in Antarctica, it is the whale that evokes the greatest sense of mystery and wonder. Their immense size alone is mesmerizing. Compared to the feeling of familiarity humans experience with pen-

Opposite: Adelie penguins (*Pygoscelis adeliae*) dive from an iceberg, Weddell Sea.

guins and seals that are so easily approached on land, whales are elusive, their number is small and their appearance, even to the sharpest observer, spasmodic and usually transient. Perhaps it is the unpredictability of whale encounters combined with their obvious intelligence that makes the meeting all the more memorable.

Baleen whales migrate to the Antarctic each summer from calving grounds in warmer waters. As they roam the Southern Ocean, sei, fin, minke, humpback and the 180-ton blue whales gorge themselves on masses of the shrimp-like zooplankton called krill. As filter feeders, they gulp mouthfuls of krill by skimming the surface or lunging upwards from below. They retain huge quantities of krill using fibrous baleen plates hanging from the roof of the mouth and their tongue to force out the water. The deep-diving sperm whale, the largest of the toothed whales, is another summer migrant. Sperms feed differently from baleen whales as they have a jaw full of peglike teeth designed to grip slippery squid.

Fast-swimming minkes, which prefer to stay close to pack ice, are the only whales that remain in the Antarctic year round. With a healthy population estimated to be 400,000, it is the most numerous whale in the Southern Ocean. At only twenty-six feet it is also the smallest. As there were plenty of large whales to catch from both shore-based and pelagic (ocean-going) whaling fleets during the first half of the century, the minke evaded the slaughter of its more valuable slower-swimming cousins. Ironically, the minke has been the only whale killed in the Antarctic in recent years by Japanese "scientific" whaling ships.

The Japanese were furious with the 1994 decision by the International Whaling Commission (IWC) to establish a Southern Ocean Whale Sanctuary. At a time when Iceland and Norway are recommencing whaling in the North

Sea, the sanctuary has been heralded around the world as a great step forward for cetacean conservation in the south. Given the grisly massacre of whales around Antarctica in the past, it is appropriate that the cetacean world should be allowed to regenerate its spirit and vigor in the Southern Ocean without human intervention. Thankfully, blue whales are now being spotted in the Southern Ocean, bringing hope that the largest creature ever to live on the planet may be journeying back from the brink of extinction.

There are more species in the Antarctic ecosystem than just the whales, penguins, and seals. Apart from tiny mites and springtails which live in mosses or under rocks, all of the other Antarctic animals derive their livelihood directly from the sea. The great albatrosses and the thirty species of "tubenose" petrels are all impressive foragers and navigators over vast distances. Hundreds of miles from the nearest land, it is astounding to watch tiny prions, storm petrels, and seemingly carefree snow petrels flit over the waves, buffeted by the wind like wayward silver paper. Flocks of cape petrels fly in unison beside ships, wheeling and turning as one. They are so silent on the wing yet so raucous around their nests on lichen-covered cliff tops. Other birds, too, have an important niche to fill. These include the gangly blue-eyed shag, scavenging skuas, and giant petrels as well as the scruffy chicken-like sheathbills which feed by dipping their scaly beaks into the most awful muck around penguin colonies. With a population totaling twenty million, however, the penguins are undoubtably Antarctica's trademark.

Many of us are stricken with an incurable passion for penguins. And rightly so. With comical movements and a hardy lifestyle, penguins in perky little dinner jackets have charmed their way into our hearts ever since the early sailors caught sight of them hitching rides on ice floes.

Penguins inhabit only the southern hemisphere, their northern limit being the Galapagos Islands. There are seventeen species of penguins ranging from the 5-foot, 88-pound emperor, found in the remotest corners of the Antarctic coastline, to the diminutive little blues from southern New Zealand and Australia.

Penguins are among the most captivating creatures in the animal kingdom. They are also highly skilled at surviving in a tough polar world. They need to be. With most penguin species inhabiting the subantarctic islands, only four species breed in the extreme climate of coastal Antarctica. The elusive five-foot-tall emperor symbolizes the hardiness of life around the rawest edge of the continent. Only half the size of the emperor are the three members of the *Pygoscelis* or bristle-tail genus — the gentoo, chinstrap, and Adelie. The bristle-tails are the most well known of penguins for their apparent mimicry of Laurel and Hardy buffoonery and Chaplinesque gait.

Penguins are remarkably resilient creatures. They have adapted to withstand the most extreme weather the Antarctic can hurl at them. To conserve heat, cold venous blood returning to the core from the extremities is prewarmed by running very close to outward-flowing arterial blood. With more densely packed, well-oiled feathers per unit area than any other bird, penguins have no problem staying warm and watertight in the water or even when facing the bitter sting of a blizzard. Strangely, penguins sometimes have trouble with overheating and can be seen panting or flapping their flippers to release heat from the least insulated parts of their body. With stiff, paddle-like flippers which are modified wings that can no longer fold, penguins have made the final perfect adaptation to a life primarily spent at sea. They may have forsaken the art of flight in the air, but the penguin's swift, graceful mastery of movement through clear Antarctic water is as impressive as the most spectacular aerobatics of an albatross.

The gentoo, chinstrap, and Adelie, like all penguins, only need to come ashore to breed, spending most of the year as truly pelagic creatures. They eat fish, squid, and importantly, krill. Consequently, a lot of time is spent seeking krill swarms whose patchy distribution is highly affected by the vagaries of Southern Ocean currents. Although satellite-tracking studies to monitor penguin movement at sea outside the short summer period are still in their infancy, the birds are known to return to the same breeding sites each spring. They usually pair with the same mate each season during most of a 12–15-year life span. When krill are scarce or the distance to reach the swarms great, penguin chicks can fall victim to severe stress from starvation or abandonment. If both adult birds are at sea, a single storm can wipe out an entire generation of chicks.

The life cycle of the emperor penguin is a fascinating study in itself. The emperor is the largest of penguins and so has big, relatively slow-growing chicks. Before going to sea, all penguin chicks must mature to the stage where they molt from down to adult plumage. The next largest penguin, the king, faces a similar development problem, but because they live much further south, emperors tackle the dilemma differently and start the breeding cycle earlier by laying eggs in midwinter.

It is intriguing to learn that when she has laid her egg, the female emperor departs to feed at sea. The male then commits himself to spending the remainder of the dark hostile months of winter alone or huddled with neighbors, incubating the single egg. Utilizing his own body reserves, he then shelters and feeds the vulnerable fluff-ball of a chick which is tucked between his scaly feet and a feathered skin flap under the abdomen. This is all done in temperatures as low as −49°F while shuffling about on the sea ice. Emperors are the only birds that do not breed on land.

While the male tends the chick, the female is at sea hunting food. Remarkably, she can dive to a depth of over 1,000 feet for up to twenty minutes in search of prey. Gorged on fish and squid after many weeks of effort, the female returns to the colony to relieve her emaciated mate. By midsummer, as chicks become independent, the emperor colonies start to disperse. The birds adopt a nomadic lifestyle on the pack ice for the remainder of the season.

If the most striking Antarctic bird is the emperor, then the most impressive marine mammal has to be the blotchy silver-grey Weddell seal. Even in the depths of winter when all other animals except the emperor have moved north into the Southern Ocean, the Weddell seal continues to enjoy its unique lifestyle. Not only is the Weddell an appealing, inquisitive seal, it is also a most remarkable diver and hunter in deep cold water.

At 78°S, McMurdo Sound freezes over with sea ice to a depth of many feet. Throughout the winter, Weddell seals maintain breathing holes by gnawing away at the ice with their ice-reaming canines and incisors. Come spring, in October, the females haul themselves out of these holes to give birth on the sea ice to sleek, charcoal-eyed pups.

Weddell pups grow quickly suckling fat-rich milk and weigh over 200 pounds by the time they are abandoned to fend for themselves, only fifty days old. Pups are encouraged or even forced into the water by the female in preparation for their first forays under the ice. Then they are left to learn the skills necessary to commence the life of a swift, silent hunter. From giving birth to weaning, the females have lost up to 330 pounds of their thousand-pound weight. They immediately embark on a series of dives for food to replenish their condition. And what incredible dives they are!

Unbelievably, over a period of thirty minutes (the longest recorded dive is ninety minutes!), Weddell seals can reach depths of up to 2,000 feet, traveling many miles horizontally away from their hole. How can Weddells possibly hold their breath for such a long time yet remain fully effective to echo-locate and catch bottom-dwelling 65–150 pound Antarctic cod?

Deep diving is possible for the Weddell by the storage of oxygen to a far greater capacity than humans in hemoglobin-rich blood and muscle tissue. During an extended dive, the seal's heart rate slows to a quarter of its surface rate. Significantly, while blood flow to the brain is maintained at a normal level, it is almost completely shut off to other organs such as the kidneys. Only by having highly collapsible respiratory systems and specially modified middle ears are Weddells able to withstand the high pressures experienced at depth. Collapsing the lungs also has the effect of eliminating the dangerous build-up of nitrogen levels in the blood.

For the Weddell, the problems of under-ice orientation and finding the right hole under a vast frozen surface vary dramatically between summer and winter. In summer there is plenty of light shining through "tide cracks" in the ice. The water is also the clearest in the world prior to December when clouding from phytoplankton bloom occurs. In good conditions, Weddells can find the breathing hole with apparent ease from up to 4 miles away. Large round eyes, three times the diameter of the human eye, certainly help. In winter gloom, the Weddell's ability to orient itself under the ice becomes extremely impressive even if the dives may be restricted to localized, relatively shallow 650-foot forays for food on well-rehearsed summer paths.

An accurate estimate of the Weddell seal population is difficult to achieve on a continent the size of Antarctica but numbers could be as high as 700,000. Weddell seals are found right around Antarctica, ranging as far north as South Georgia. Even more prolific than the Weddell, with a population numbering perhaps 15 million, is the fawn-colored crabeater seal. The crabeater spends all of its life at sea or, during summer, drifting sleepily hauled out on ice floes. Crabeaters feed on krill retained in the seal's dog-like snout after filtering out water through interlocking tricuspid teeth.

With the sheer dominance of the numbers of fur and elephant seals on the subantarctic islands and the Weddell and crabeater seals in the Antarctic, it is easy to overlook the other two main Antarctic seals. Neither leopard nor Ross seals are found in big numbers and prefer a solitary existence in the pack ice. The fierce leopard seal is a predator to be respected and is often found patrolling the offshore edge of a penguin colony. Not only does it feed voraciously on hapless penguins, but it also kills young seals. Leopards can lurch menacingly at unwary humans, at times with serious consequences. Chunky, squid-eating Ross seals, with their distinctive streaked necks, remain the least observed of Antarctic seals primarily because they inhabit the dense pack ice of the Weddell Sea and coastal eastern Antarctica where ships seldom penetrate.

Antarctica's seals and penguins are perhaps the last remaining really prolific and wide-ranging populations of unmanaged wild animals on the planet. By living outside the boundaries of artificial reserves, Antarctica's wildlife does not face the vagaries and inconsistencies of human control. For the scientist, Antarctica is the last chance to study extensive populations of large animals in their natural state. Equally, for visitors who journey across the Southern Ocean and for those who simply need to be assured great wilderness exists, Antarctica and its wildlife remain a vision of all that is sacred and untamed.

Opposite: Adelie penguins on icefloes, Paulet Island.

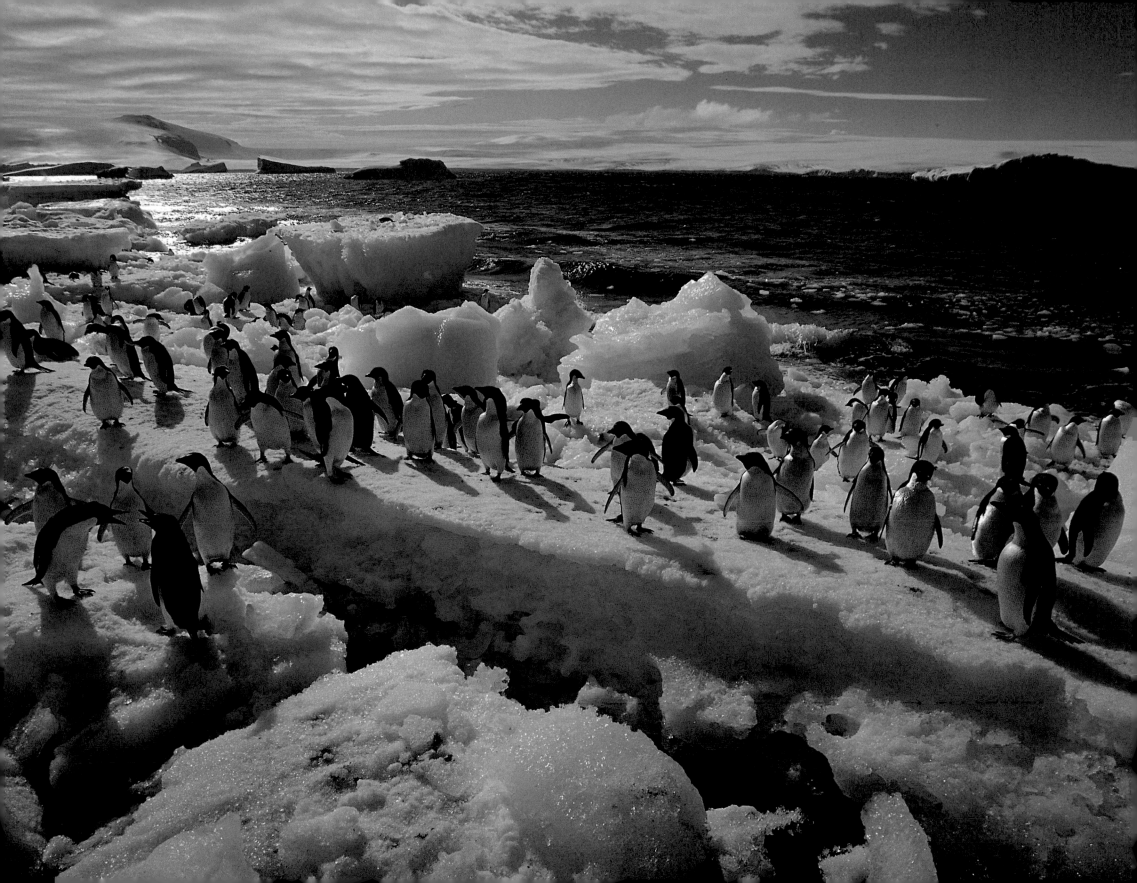

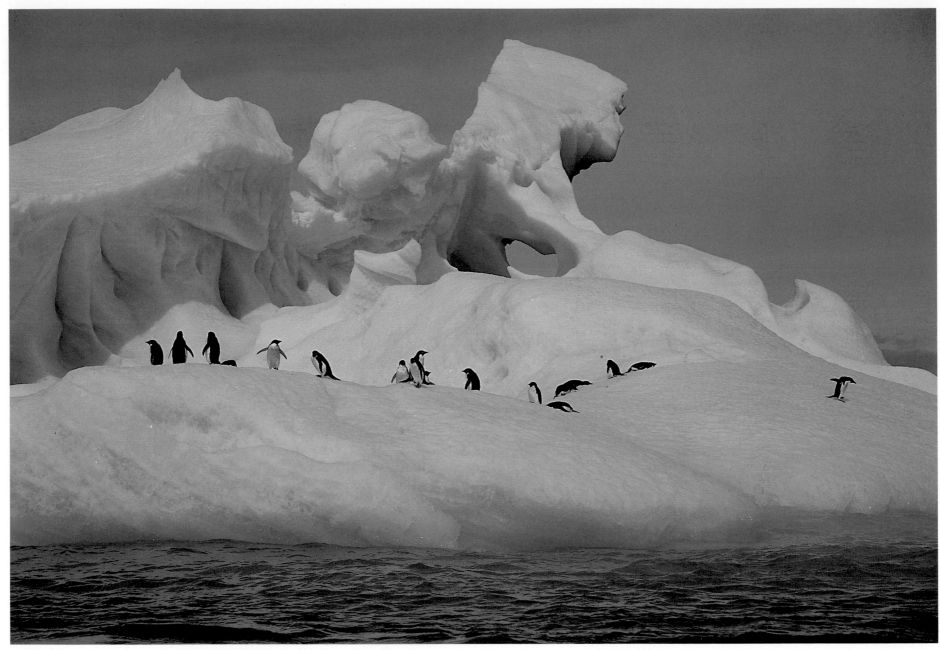

Adelie penguins can be commonly seen hitching a ride on overturned icebergs as they take a rest from searching for krill in the Southern Ocean. This small but highly sculpted iceberg is drifting in the Weddell Sea.

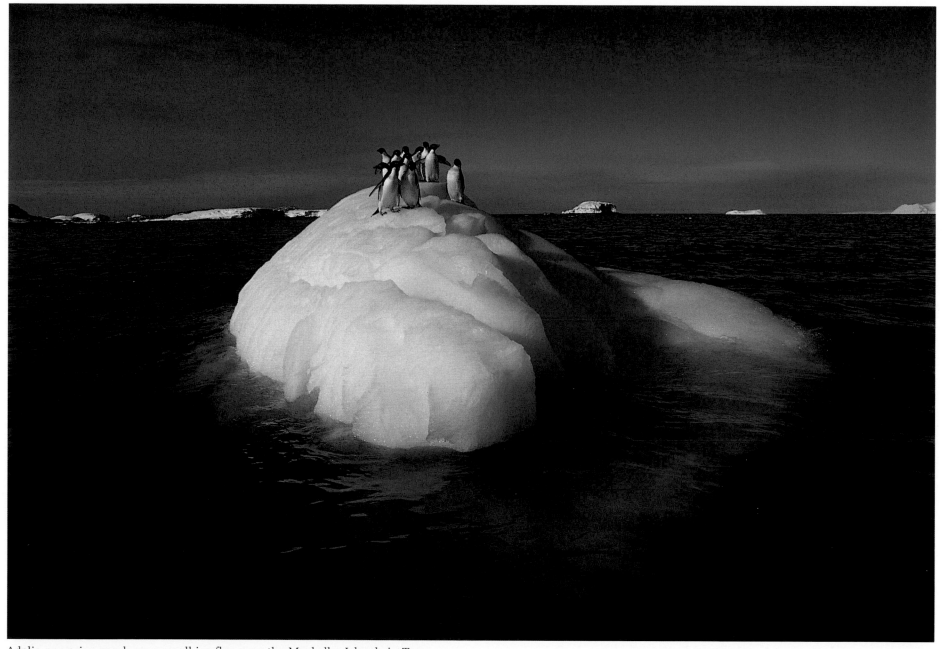

Adelie penguins perch on a small ice floe near the Mackellar Islands in Terre Adelie Land. Penguins are truly ocean-going birds that only need to return to land to breed during the brief Antarctic summer.

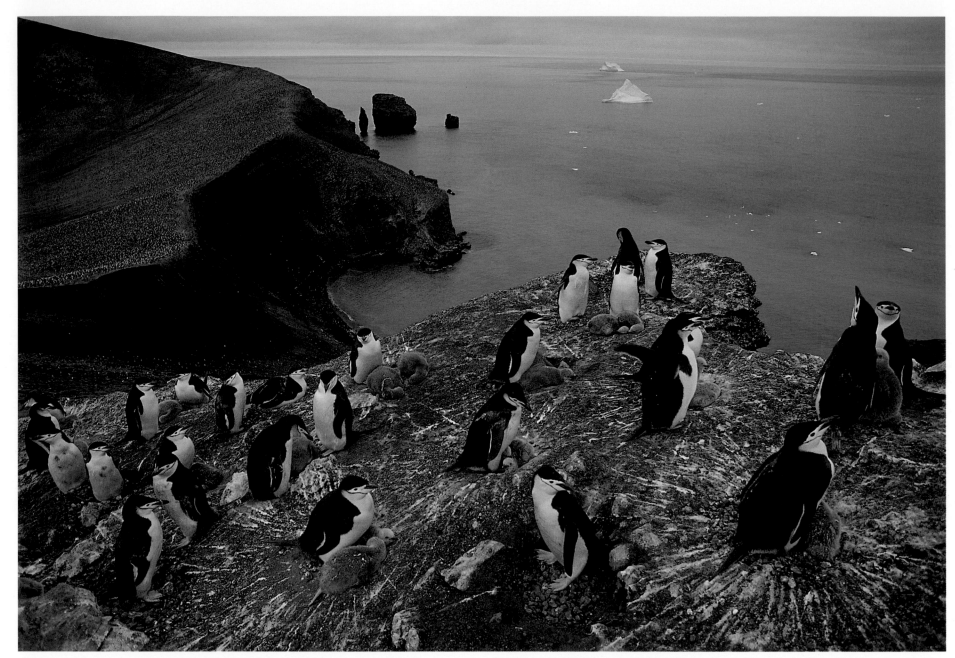

Above: Bailey Head on Deception Island is covered with several hundred thousand breeding chinstrap penguins (*Pygoscelis antarctica*). Adult birds must commute from this cliff top to the ocean to bring back food for hungry chicks.

Opposite: A chinstrap penguin "porpoises" for breath while others rest on an iceberg in the South Sandwich Islands.

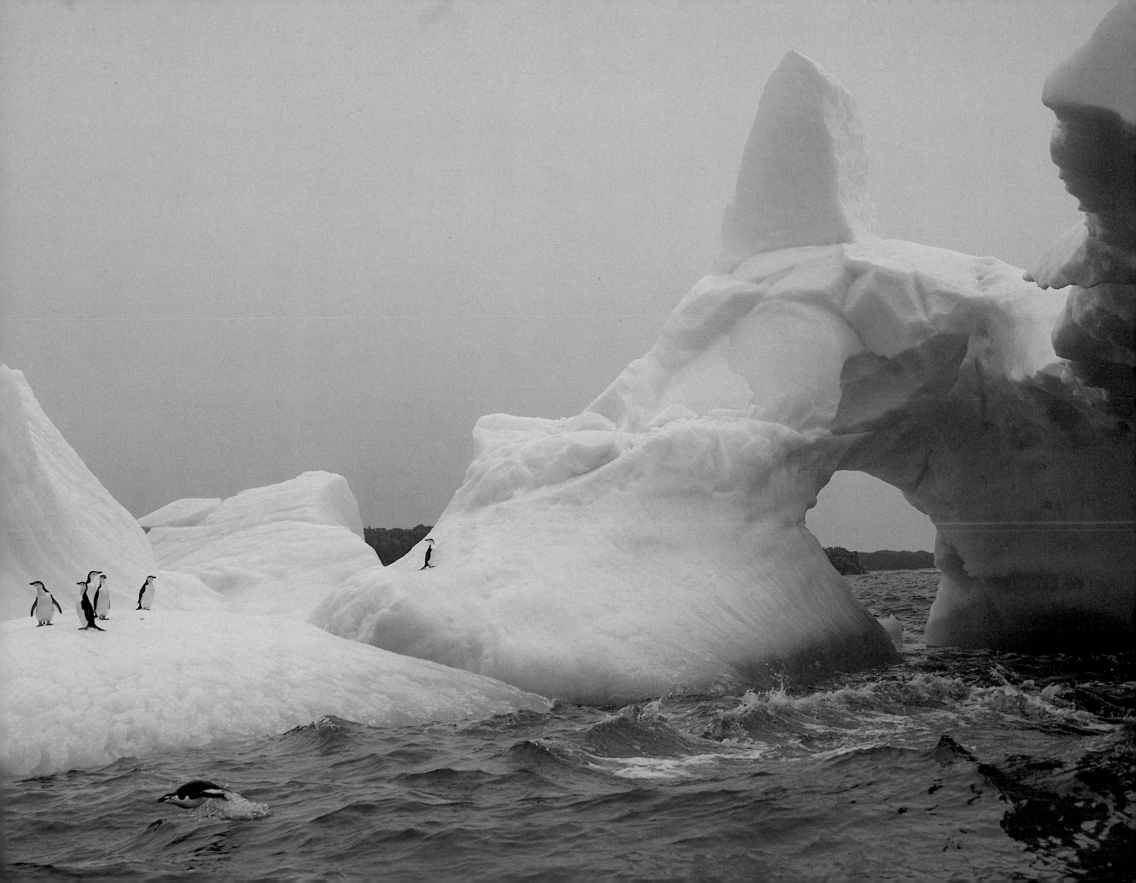

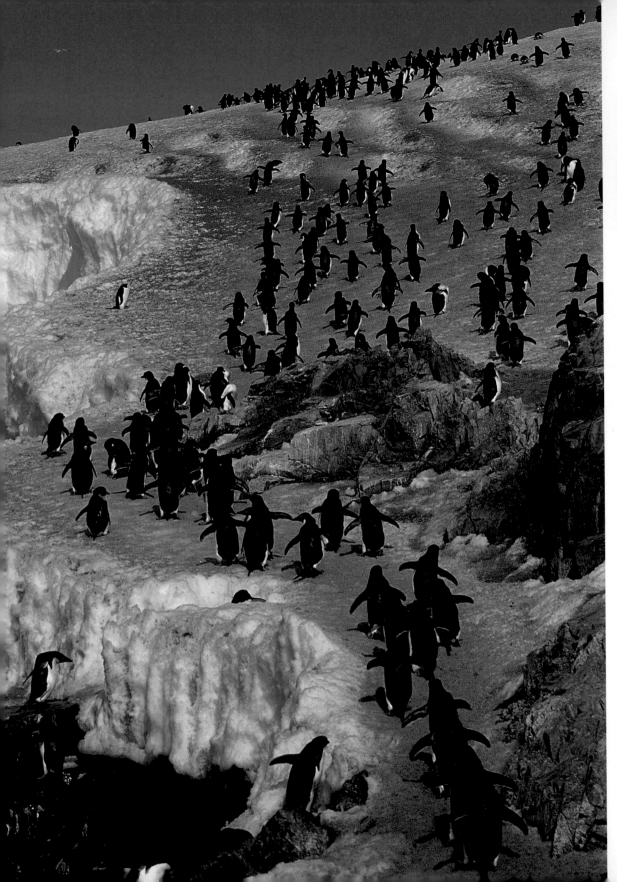

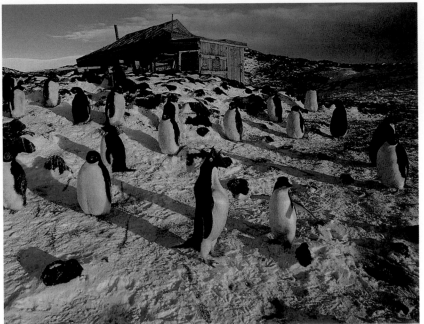

Above: Molting Adelie penguins with a topknot of downy feathers argue with adult birds in front of Shackleton's hut at Cape Royds on Ross Island. Penguins must complete their molt to adult plumage before they go to sea for the winter. Cape Royds at 77°30'S is the southernmost Adelie colony.

Left: Like commuters in a Tokyo subway, Adelie penguins stream up a snow bank in Hope Bay on the northern tip of the Antarctic Peninsula. They are returning to nesting sites to feed voraciously hungry chicks with a pink slurry of krill.

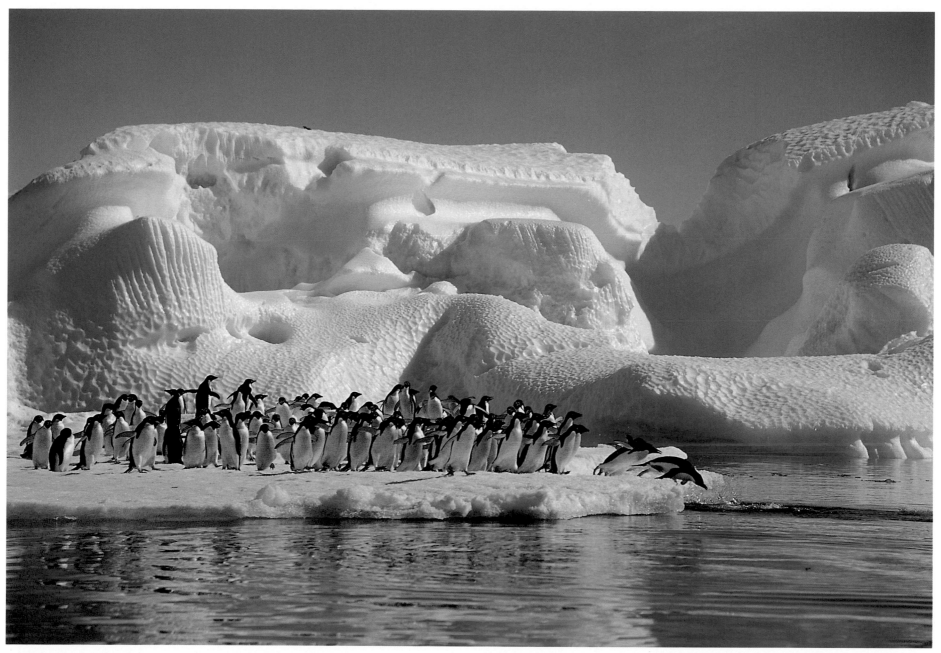

131

Adelie penguins dive from an ice floe in Hope Bay on the Antarctic Peninsula. Penguins gather together on the edge of a floe or iceberg trying to summon the courage to dive in. Often their main predator, the vicious leopard seal, lurks below to grab the first hapless bird that dives, or is pushed, into the water.

In the realm of an emperor

Below: The Riiser-Larsen emperor penguin colony on the southern edge of the Weddell Sea is protected by remoteness and hundreds of miles of grinding pack ice. Making use of stranded icebergs as windbreaks, the emperors lay their eggs in midwinter. By December, the grey chicks are quite large, requiring a lot of food from their parents.

Left: Healthy grey fluff-ball emperor chicks dwarf a runt that has hatched late. Even if properly fed, this chick will not develop fast enough to reach maturity in time to go to sea before the onset of the next winter.

Right above: These chicks huddle at the Atka Bay colony in the Weddell Sea as a powerful blizzard drives powder snow into their thinly spaced down feathers.

Right below: With beak tucked under his flipper, this emperor penguin chick enjoys a snooze on a rare windless day in the Weddell Sea.

Far right: Mirror-image emperor penguin adults take a break from parenting their ever-hungry chicks in the Riiser-Larsen colony.

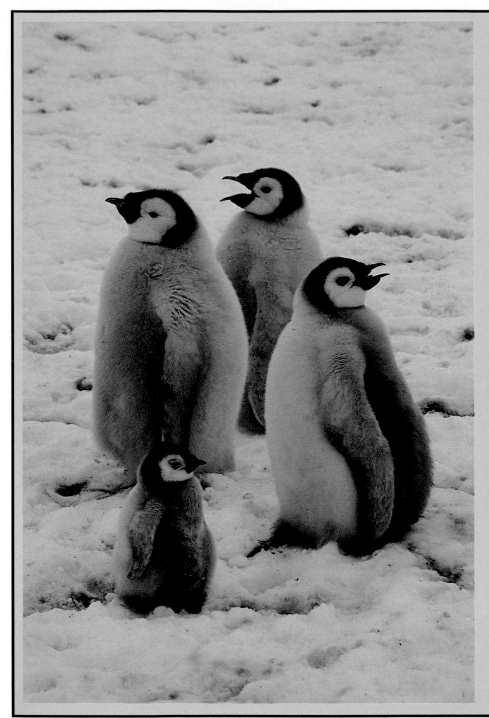

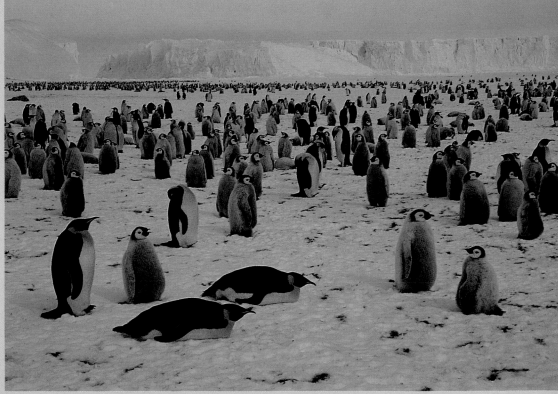

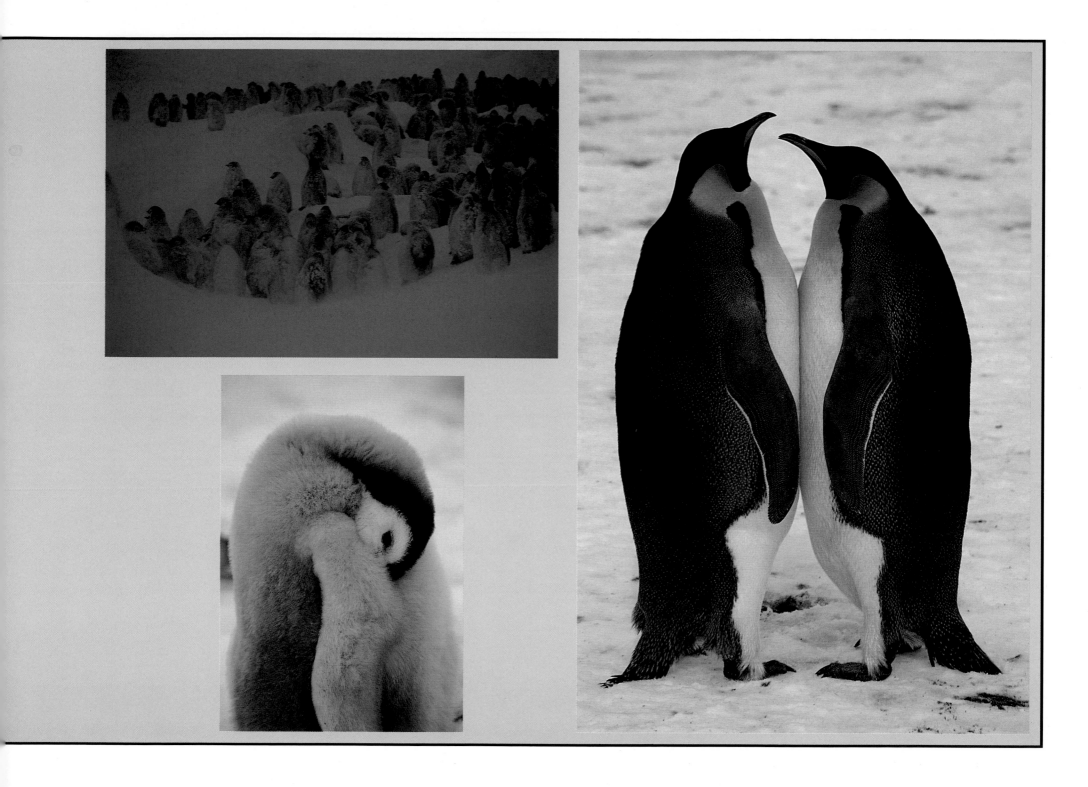

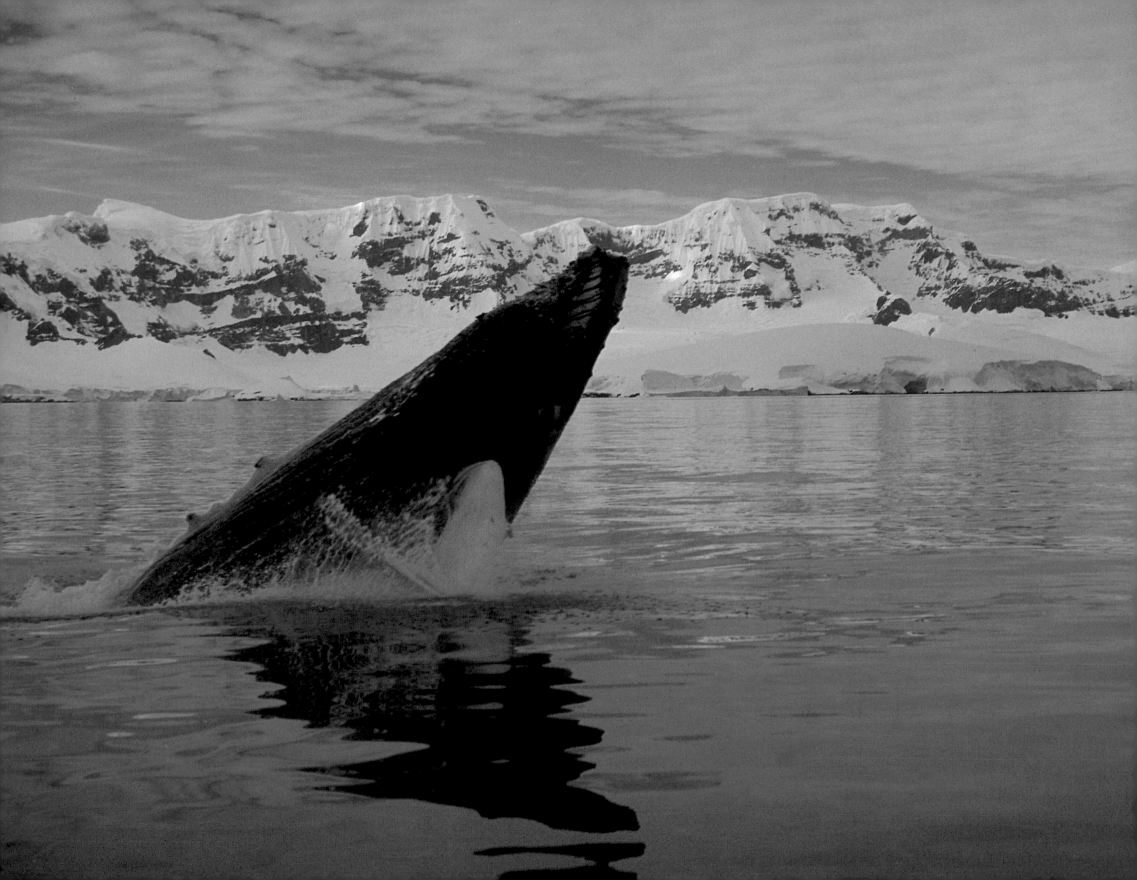

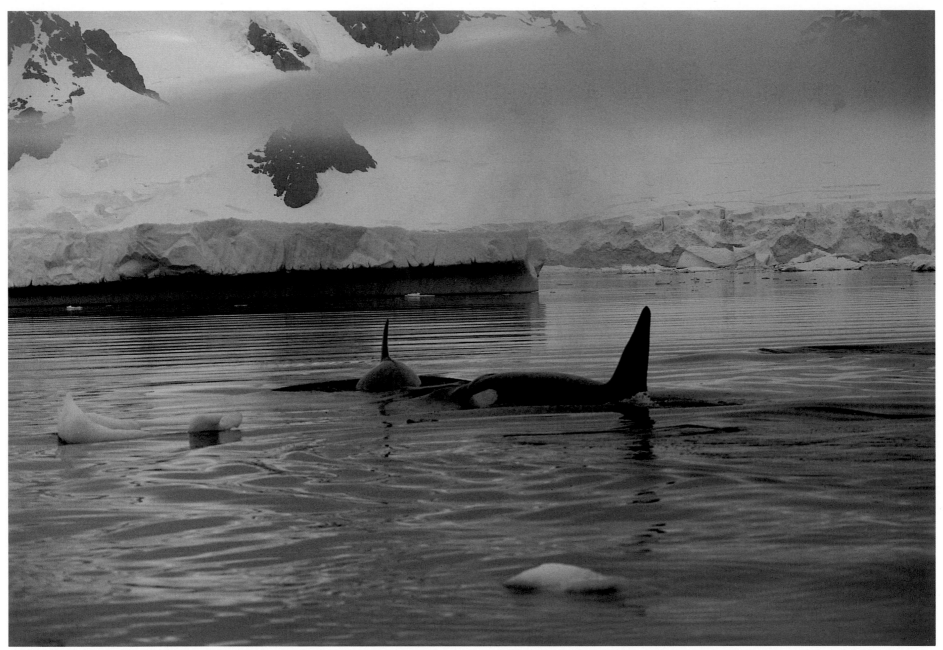

135

Above: Orcas (*Orincus orca*), the largest of the dolphins, are usually called killer whales. They are commonly found in Antarctica patrolling for seals or penguins in groups of up to forty animals. This small pod is hunting in Paradise Bay.

Opposite: Humpback whales (*Megaptera novaeangliae*) are found in increasing numbers around Antarctica. This humpback in a playful mood is breaching near the Melchior Islands.

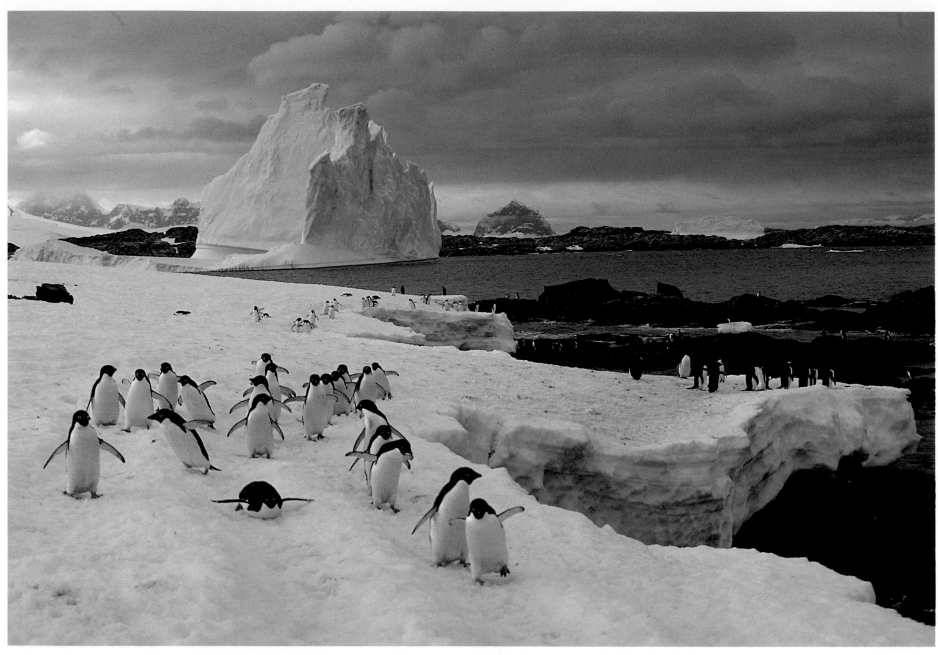

Adelie penguins on parade on Torgersen Island close to the American Palmer Station on Anvers Island. Animals living near Torgersen were affected by a major fuel spill after the Argentine resupply vessel *Bahia Paraiso* sank in 1989 when it hit rocks.

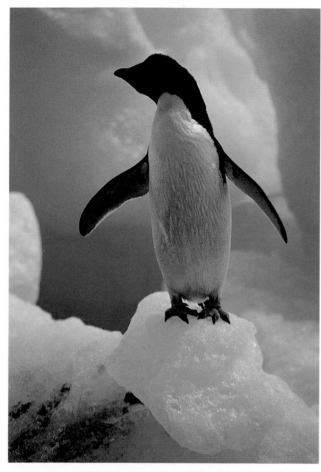

Above: An Adelie penguin perches on an ice pedestal on the beach at Paulet Island in the Weddell Sea. Along with chinstraps and gentoos, Adelies are members of the *Pygoscelis* or "bristle-tail" genus of penguins. They use their stubby tail feathers for balance on land and as rudders in the water.

Right: Adelie penguins leap from an icy ledge on the remote coast near Port Martin on Terre Adelie Land. Port Martin is the site of the abandoned French base that burned down in 1951.

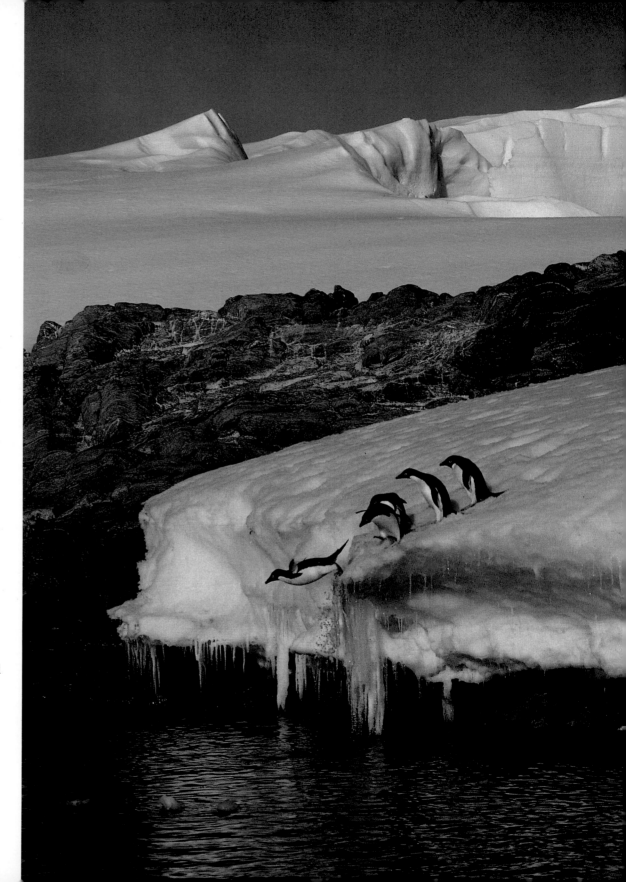

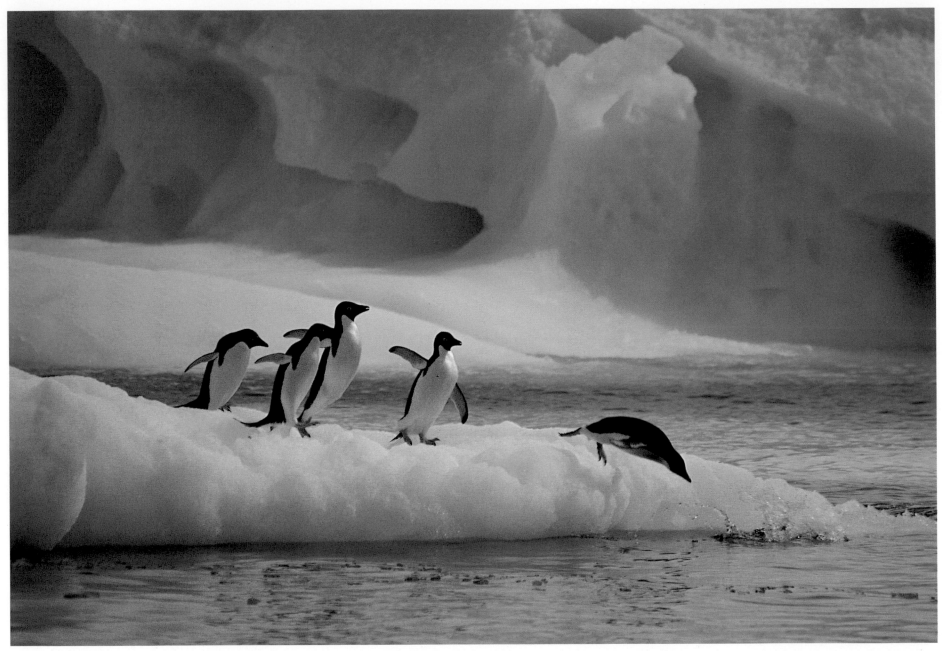

Above: Adelie penguins dive from an iceberg and head out into the Weddell Sea in search of krill.

Opposite: Adelie penguins nest alongside blue-eyed shags on Petermann Island on the Antarctic Peninsula. Penguins, like all other Antarctic animals, do not fear humans as predators. We must ensure our conduct does not destroy this trust.

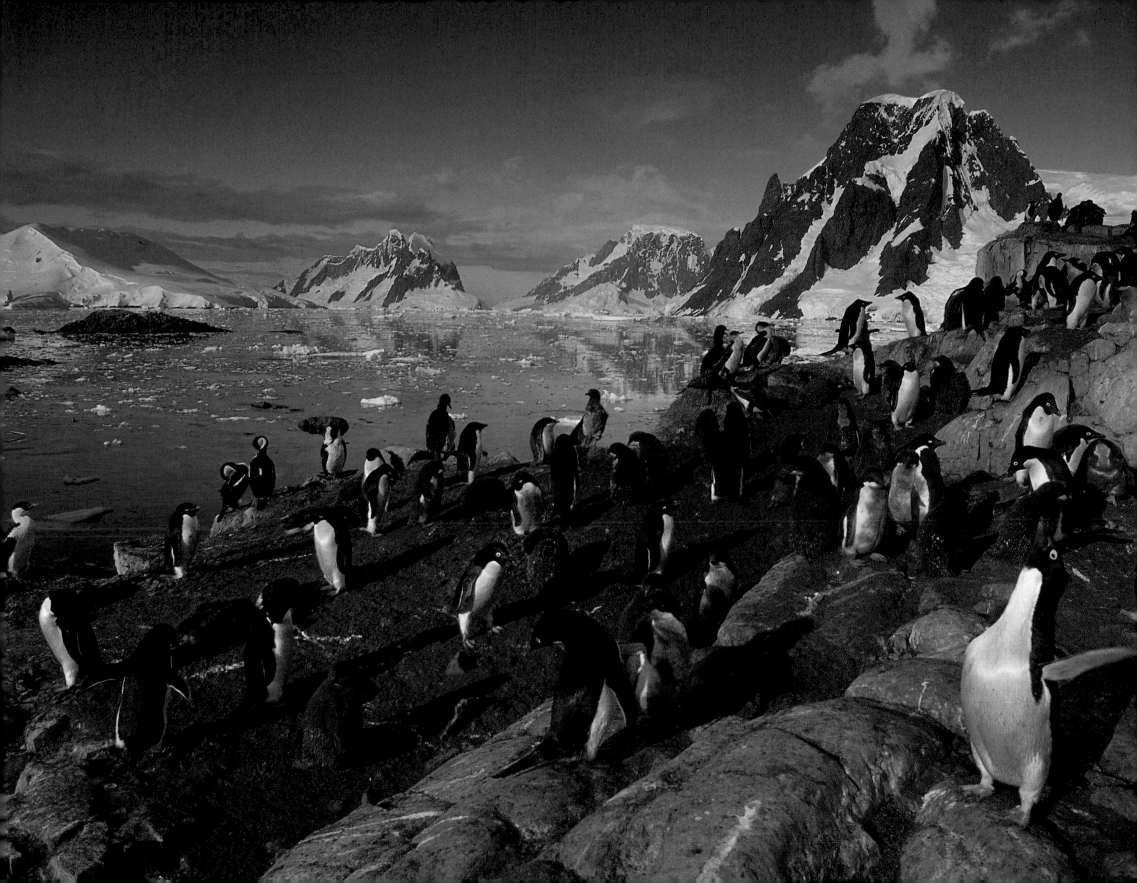

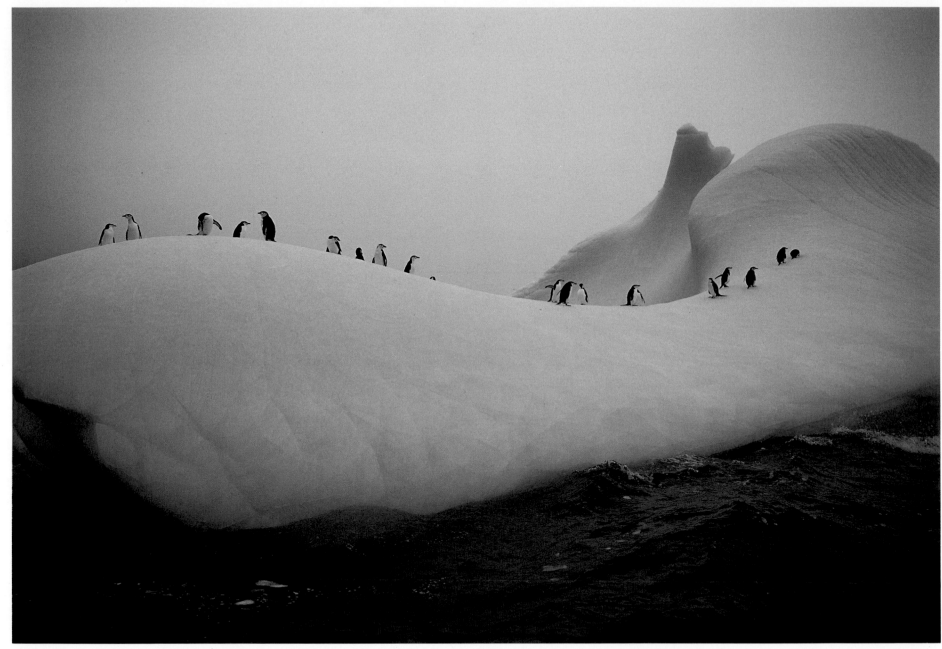

As if they are riding on the deck of a submarine, chinstrap penguins cruise the Scotia Sea on a water-worn iceberg near the South Sandwich Islands. Zavodoski, one of the nearby volcanic islands in the South Sandwich group, is home for several million breeding chinstraps.

Right: Perched on a rare blue-striped iceberg drifting near the South Sandwich Islands, chinstrap penguins look down on a storm-tossed Scotia Sea.

Below: Snarling polar bears on the Arctic Ocean pack ice north of Franz Josef Land have just finished devouring a seal.

Polar bears are great swimmers and can often be found many miles from the nearest land or ice floe. This bear, shaking itself free of water, is emerging onto a floe near Wrangel Island.

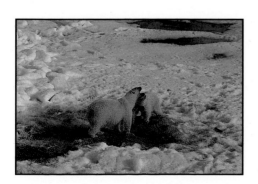

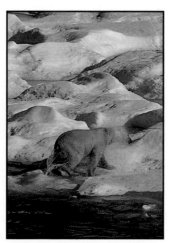

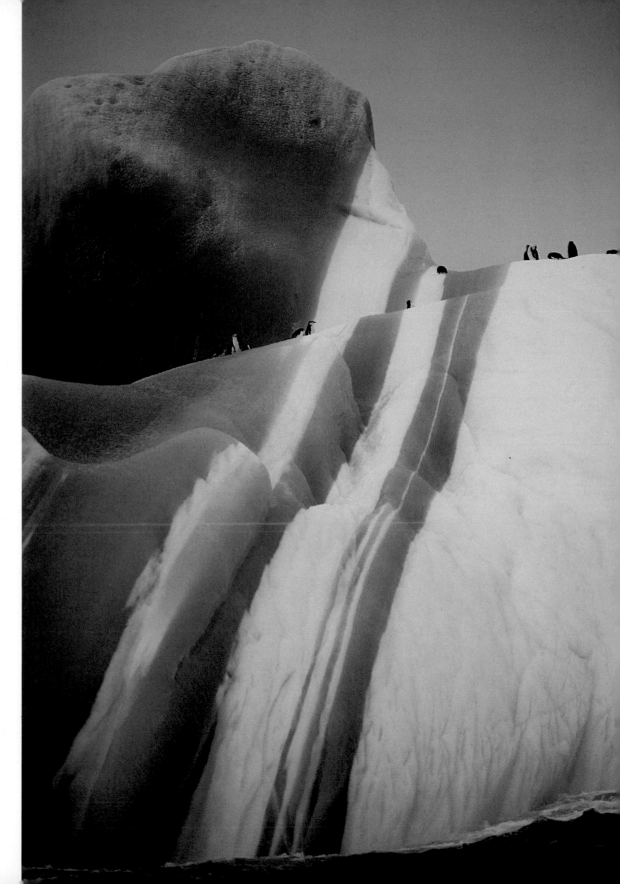

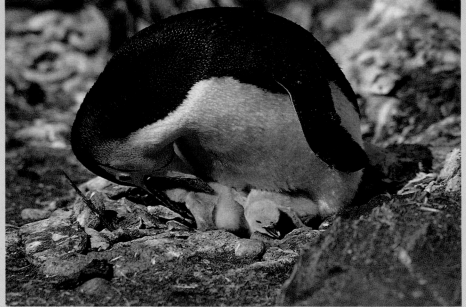

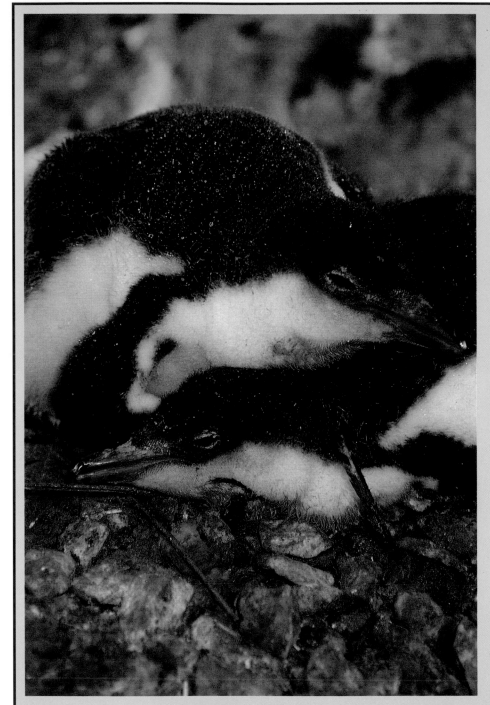

Born for a life at sea

Above: This chinstrap penguin at Point Lookout on Elephant Island is taking great care to feed its newly hatched pair of chicks. Although a chinstrap's nest is little more than a pile of pebbles, the adults, faithful to each other, will return to the same nesting site each spring.

Left: Gentoo chicks, snoozing in the sun on Cuverville Island, are really cute when they are only two weeks old.

Right above: This chinstrap chick on Deception Island seems to be gasping for cool air after sleeping beneath its mother's feathered breast.

Right below: Nibbling the beak of its parent to encourage the adult bird to regurgitate krill is the only way the chick will get fed on this busy beach on Paulet Island. The other proud parent, behind, is in an "ecstatic" display pointing its flippers and head skyward.

Far right: A month-old Adelie penguin chick on the South Orkney Islands forces its entire head inside the parent bird, eager to extract the maximum amount of regurgitated krill from its throat. The chick's twin nestles its head into the adult's breast feathers.

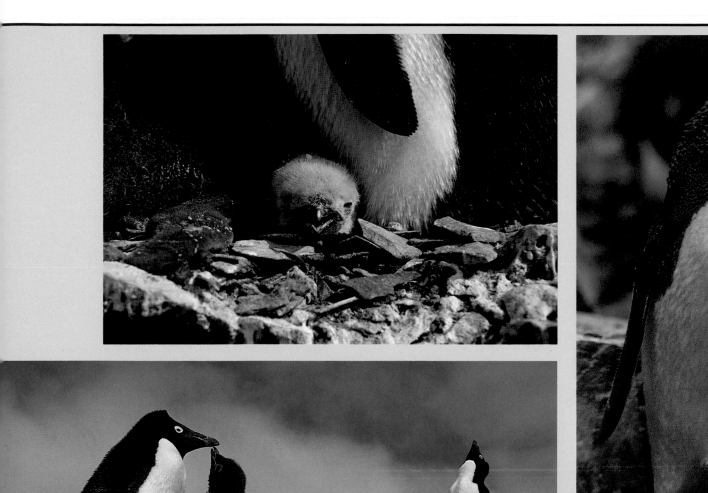

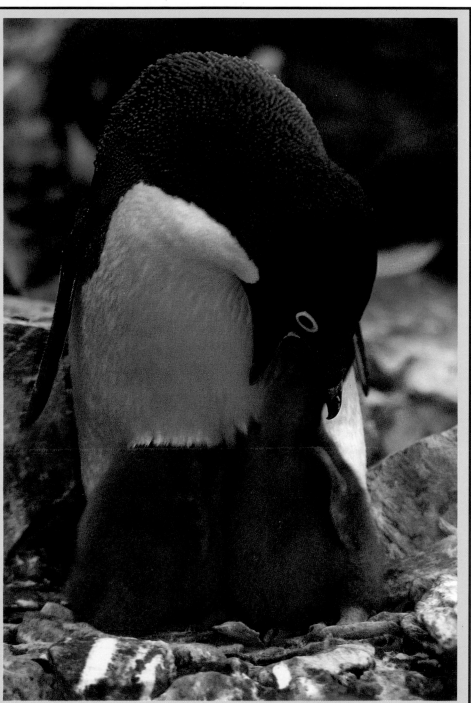

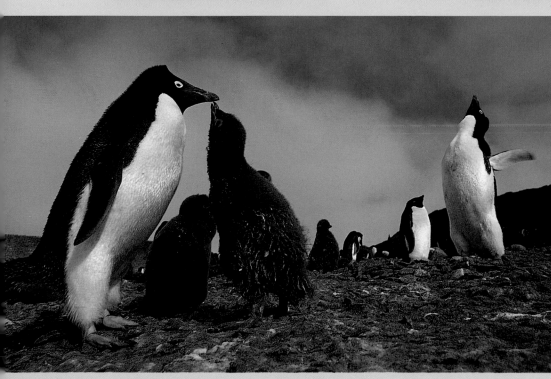

143

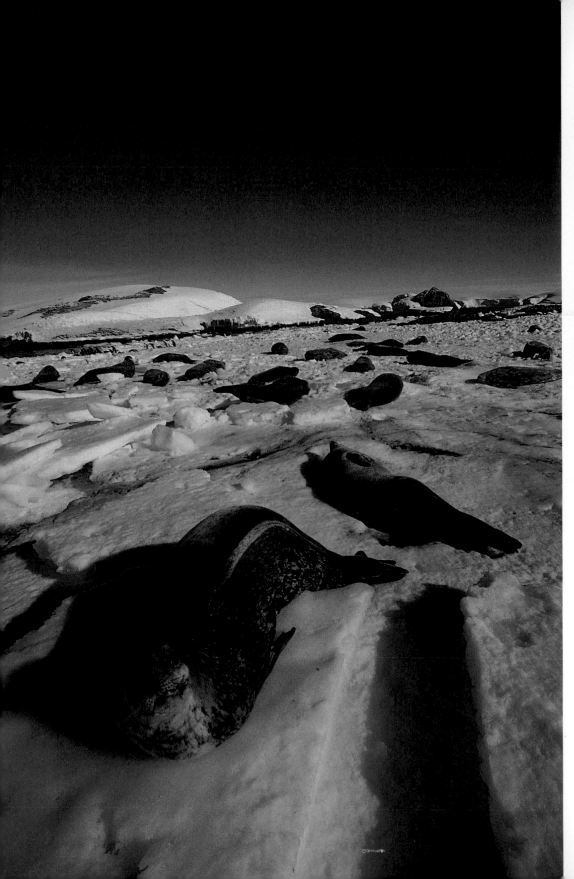

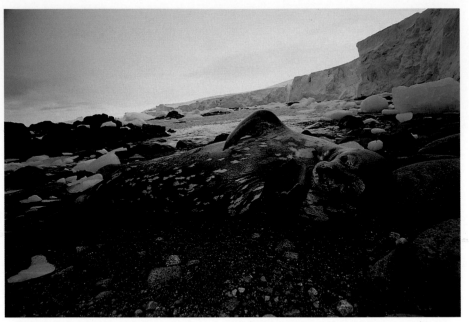

Above: The Weddell seal (*Leptonychotes weddelli*), with its distinctive silver-grey blotches and whiskered, friendly face, is a remarkable hunter of deep-dwelling Antarctic fish. This seal has hauled out on a remote beach under a glacier front on Adelaide Island.

Left: These Weddell seals on the sea ice near the Mackellar Islands have already finished rearing their pups in the early part of summer. Weddell seals live around the continent throughout the year so they must use their teeth to keep breathing holes open during winter.

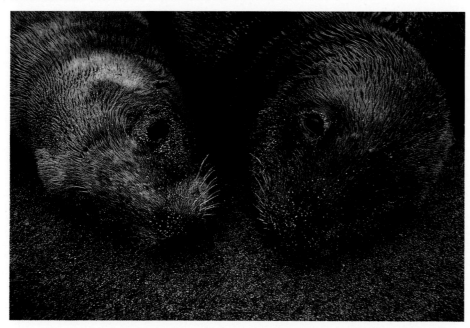

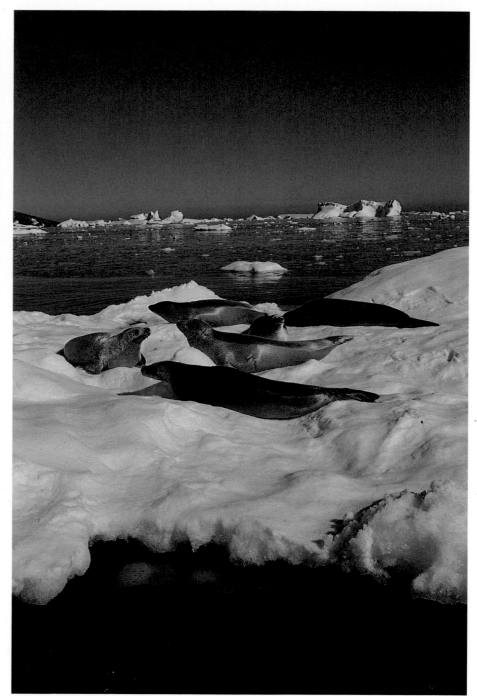

Above: Hooker's sea lion pups on Enderby Island are playful and inquisitive. The Hooker's sea lion (*Phocarctos hookeri*) remains under threat as it is often caught in fishing nets.

Right: With a population estimated to range from eight to twenty million, crabeater seals (*Lobodon carcinophagus*), seen here near Pleneau Island, are by far the most numerous Antarctic seal. Their principal diet is krill.

Below: Pacific walruses use their long curved tusks for fighting and to pull their great weight up onto a floe. Tusks are also used for rooting in the shallows for molluscs. These walruses were found on the sea ice near Wrangel Island off the Siberian coast.

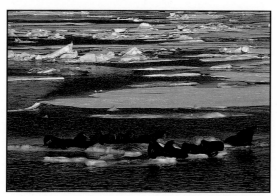

145

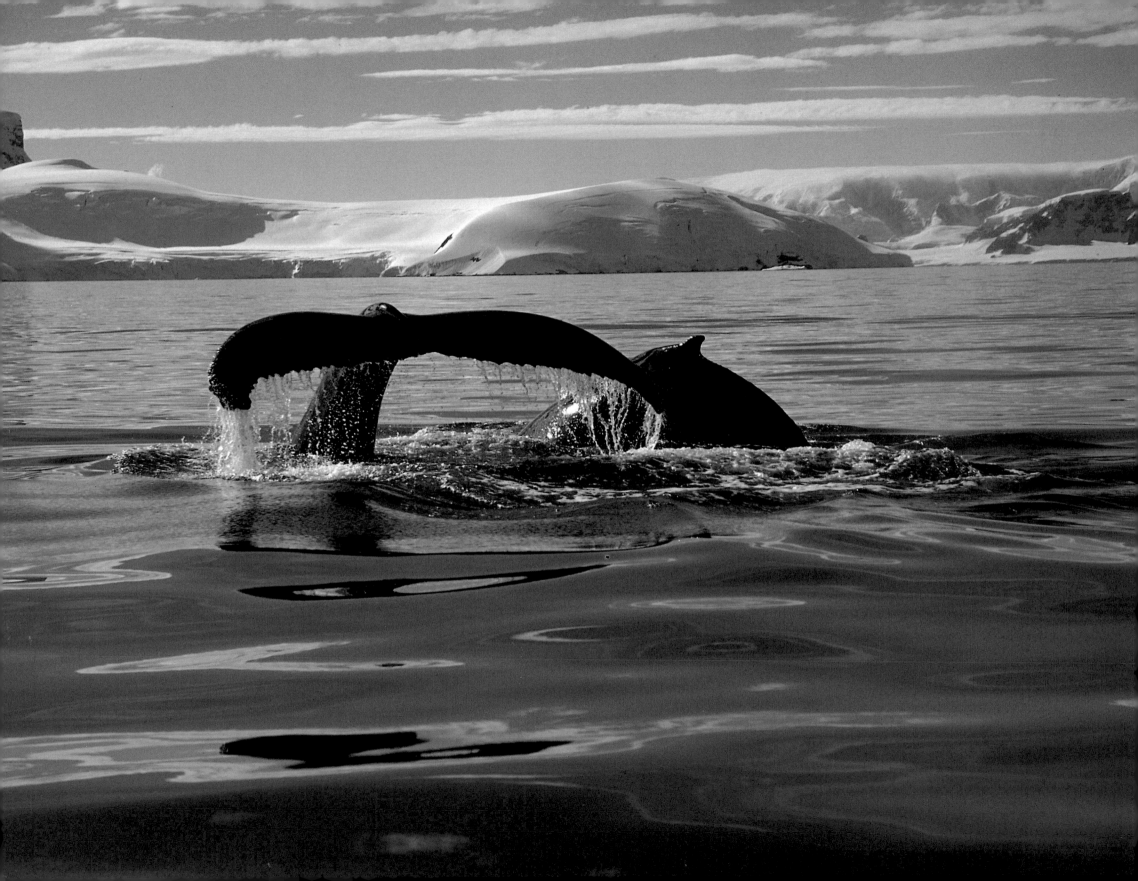

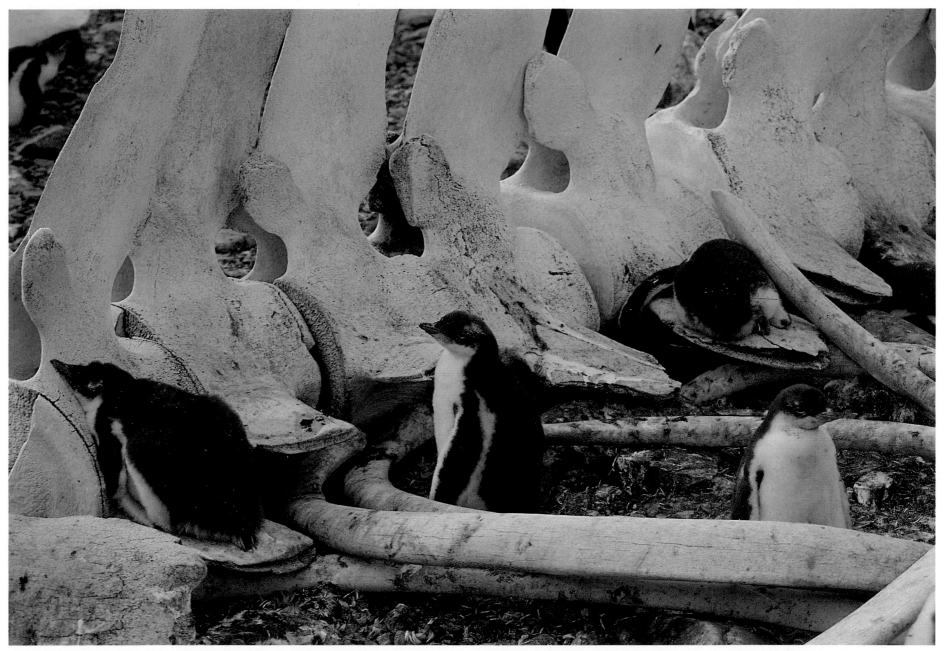

147

Above: Rather plump gentoo penguin chicks use weathered whale bones as pillows at Port Lockroy on Wiencke Island. Beaches remain cluttered with bones in sad testimony to the whaling era.

Opposite: Humpback whales migrate south to rich feeding grounds on the Antarctic Peninsula each summer. They travel up and down the Gerlache Strait in search of krill swarms.

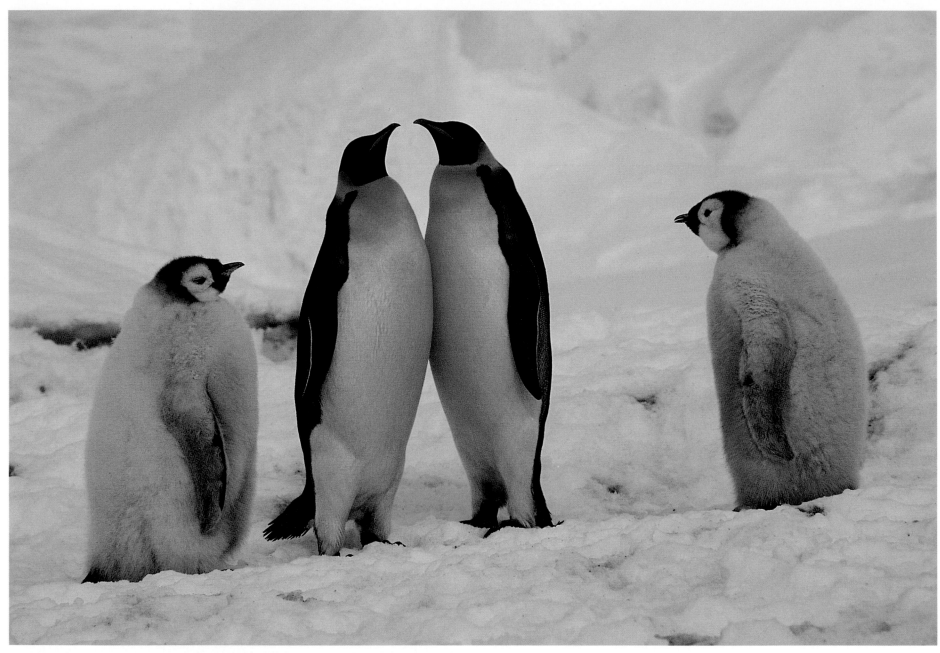

A majestic pair of emperor penguins from the Riiser-Larsen colony in the Weddell Sea is flanked by two well-grown chicks. The only bird that does not nest on land, the emperor lays its single egg on the sea ice. With a breeding cycle that begins in the chilly depths of an Antarctic winter, the emperor is a truly remarkable creature.

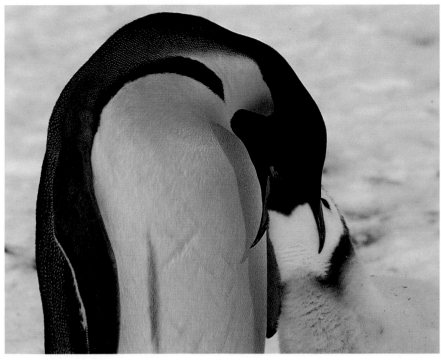

Above: Like all penguins, the emperor regurgitates food after being pestered by its chick, which often chases it through the colony in pursuit of dinner. Slightly taller and heavier than their subantarctic relative the king, emperors have exquisite head feathers and an unforgettable haunting call.

Right: Like a row of toy soldiers, emperor chicks parade along under the wall of an iceberg that is frozen in place by sea ice at the Riiser-Larsen colony.

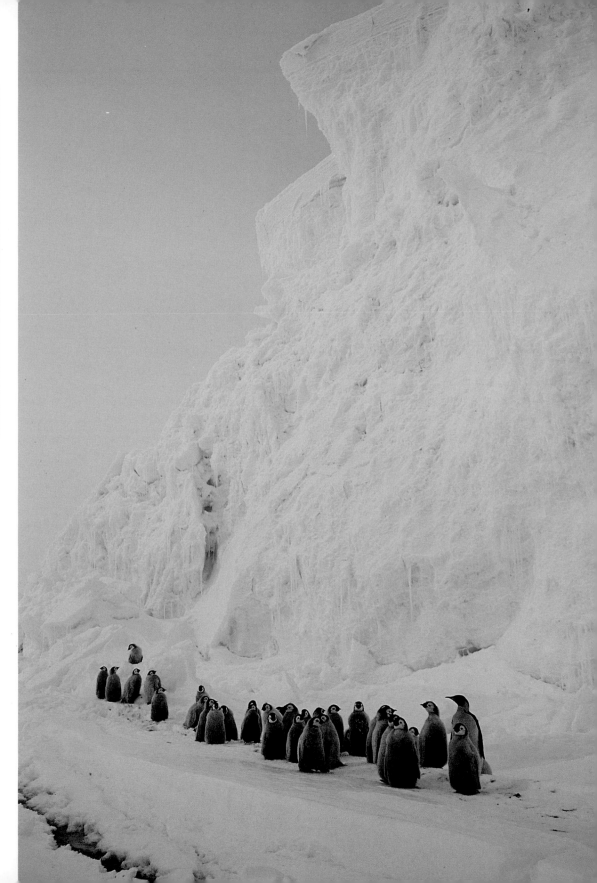

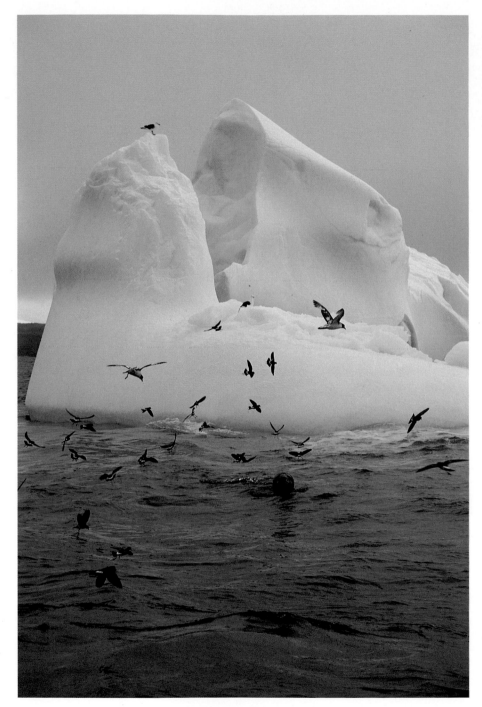

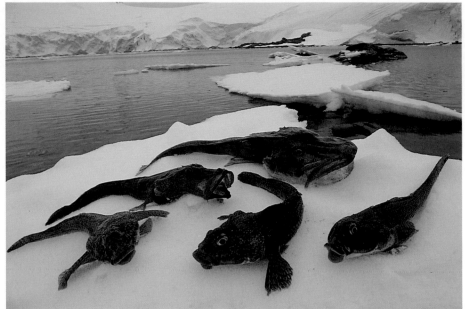

Above: Antarctic fish are strange monster-like creatures with big heads and thinly tapered bodies. Their blood has no red hemoglobin and contains a clear glycoprotein that acts as an antifreeze to enable the fish to live in very cold water. There are only about 120 species of fish in the Southern Ocean.

Left: Wilson's storm petrels (*Oceanites oceanicus*) and cape (pintado) petrels (*Daption capense*) dance over the water at Penguin Island picking up tiny droplets of oil and leftover flesh after a leopard seal has had its fill of a penguin.

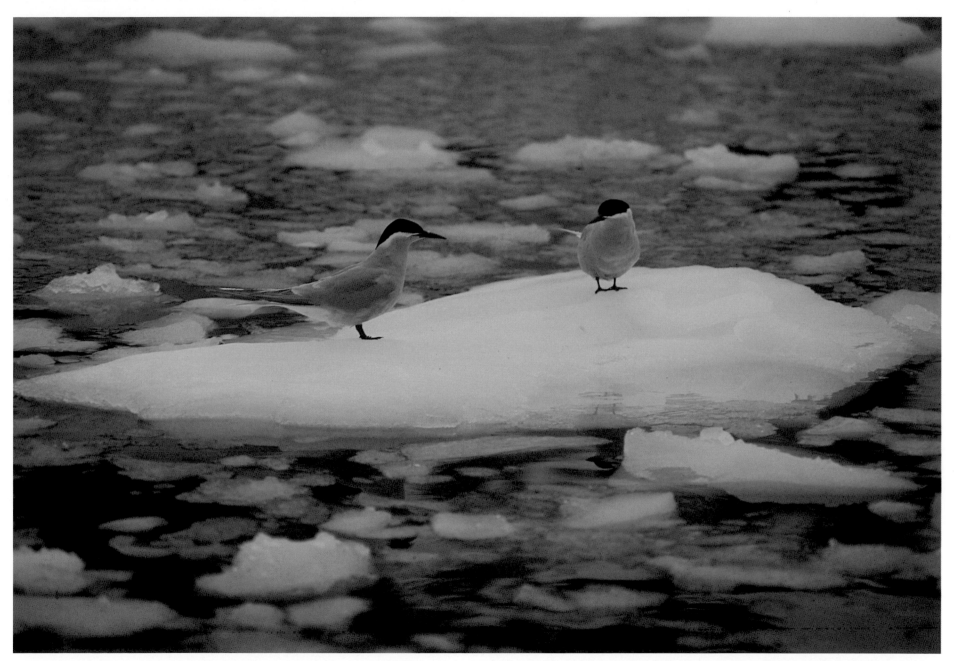

Antarctic terns (*Sterna vittata*), with their distinctive black caps, red bills and sharp-pointed wings, are aggressive and highly acrobatic hunters of small fish around Antarctic coastlines. Remarkably, the Arctic tern (*Sterna paradisaea*), a similar looking bird, migrates from its Arctic breeding grounds to feed in Antarctica during the southern summer.

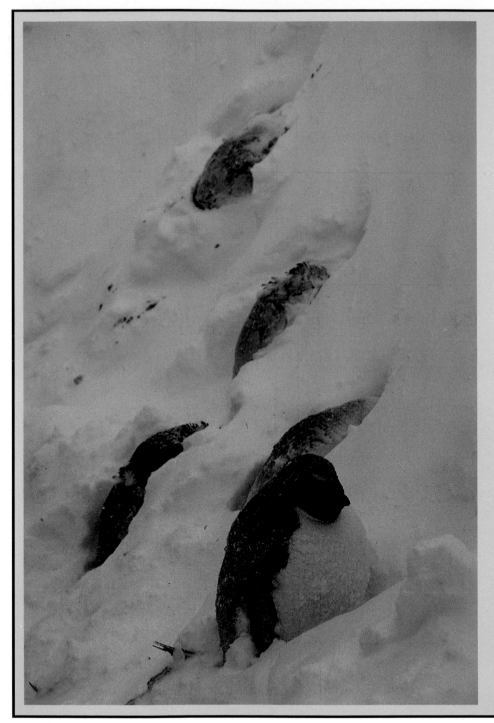

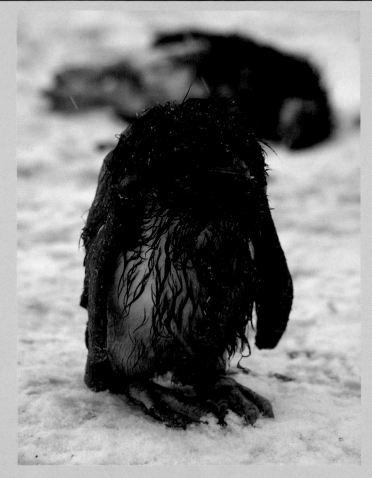

152

Shelter from the storm

Above: A little down in the mouth, this bedraggled Adelie penguin chick on Paulet Island is fighting against hypothermia as driving sleet chills its body. Many chicks, like the one behind, will not survive summer storms.

Left: Adelie penguins at Cape Royds remain on their nests during a storm.

Right above: Setting like concrete, wet driving snow from a vicious southerly blizzard at Cape Royds freezes this Adelie and its chick onto the nest.

Right below: Gasping for breath in a storm at Cape Royds, this Adelie is about to be buried by powder snow.

Far right: A juvenile Adelie penguin struggles over volcanic scoria boulders at Cape Royds to shelter near Shackleton's hut.

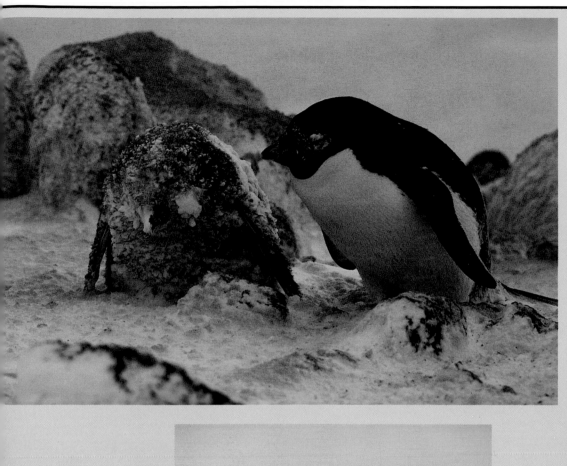

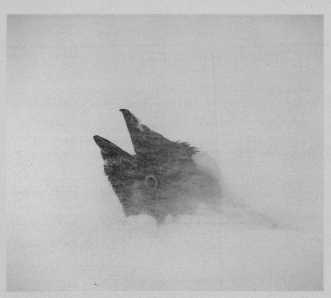

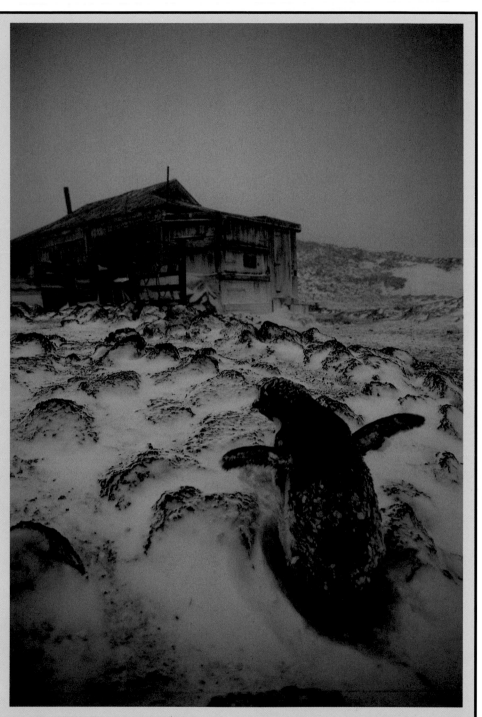

153

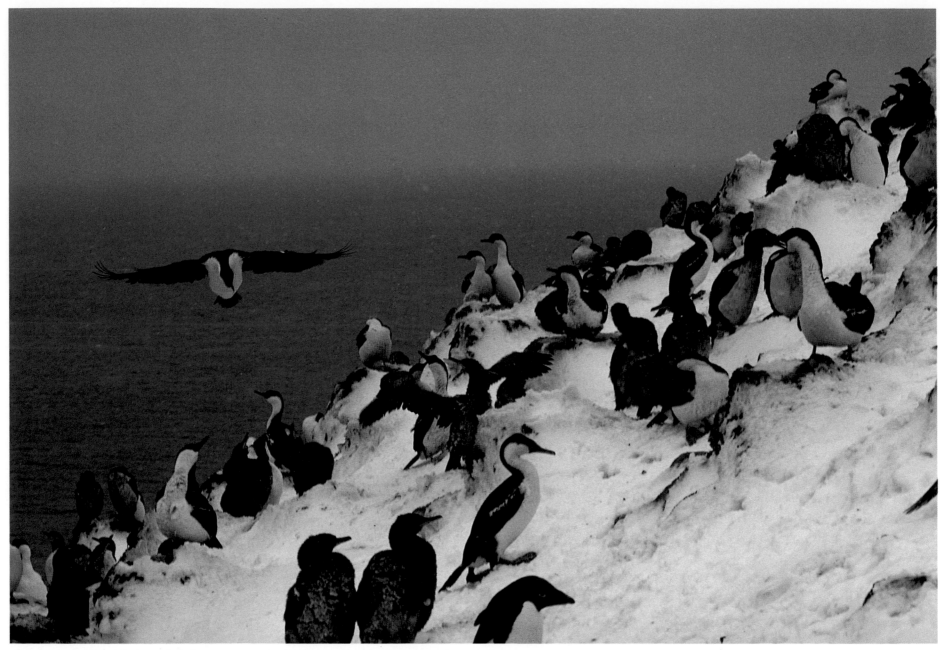

Blue-eyed or imperial shags (*Phalacrocorax atriceps*) nest on an exposed spur of the old volcano on Paulet Island. The shags exist happily alongside a massive Adelie penguin colony. Unlike albatrosses, shags do not have great wings so they concentrate their diving and fishing in waters relatively close to shore.

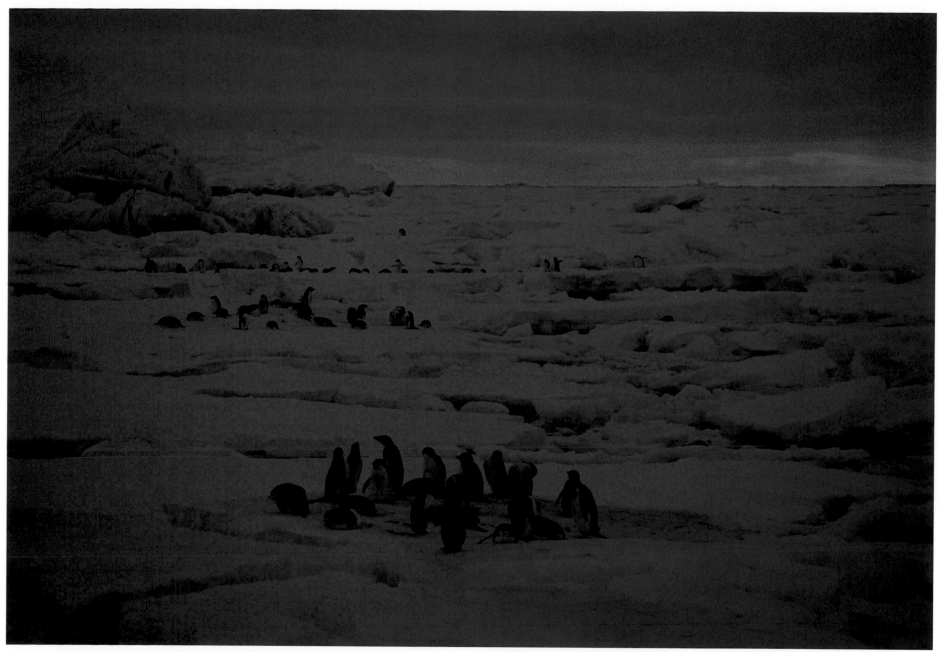

155

Thule Island in the South Sandwich Island group of the Scotia Arc is only 59°S, but it is as remote and wild as anywhere in Antarctica. Even in midsummer, heavy pack ice can be jammed around the island, making it difficult for the Adelie penguins to clamber back to their nesting sites.

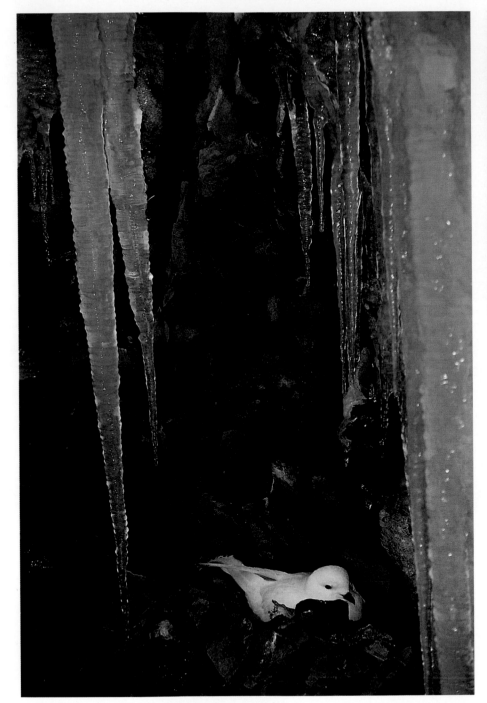

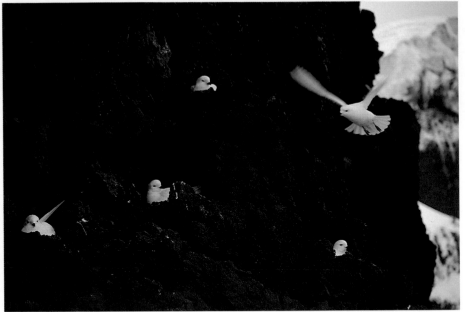

Above: Snow petrels (*Pagodroma nivea*), with their pure white plumage and black beady eyes, symbolize the spirit of the Antarctic. Here, on Thule Island in the South Sandwich Islands, snow petrels are nesting on red volcanic cliffs above the water.

Left: Sheltering in a cave overhung by icicles, this snow petrel has found a secure nesting site. Some snow petrels fly up to 125 miles inland in Antarctica to scrape out a nest on remote ledges. Snow petrels can often be seen rising from icebergs like a flurry of snowflakes.

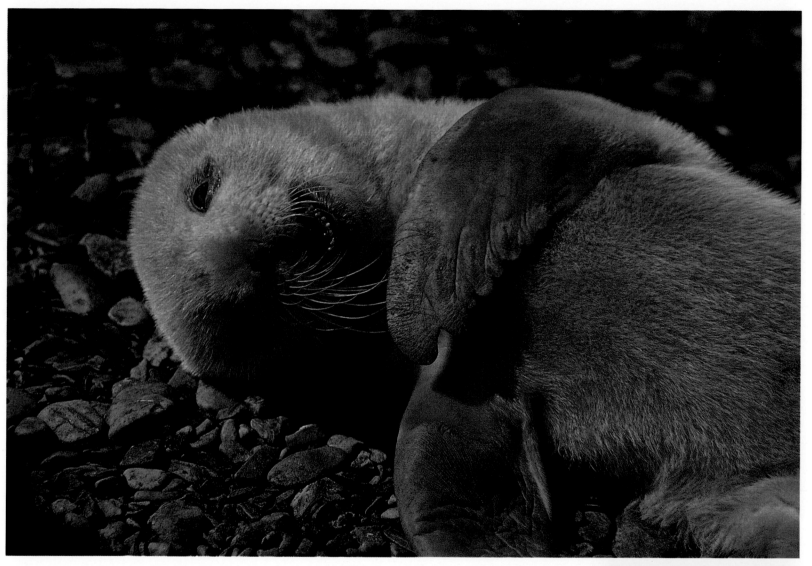

Above: A blond Antarctic fur seal pup rolls over onto its back to play after snoozing on a South Georgia beach.

Right: Sleeping walruses on Bennett Island in the Siberian Arctic show how contented and well adapted pinnipeds (seals and walruses) are to the harshness of their environment.

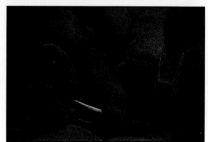

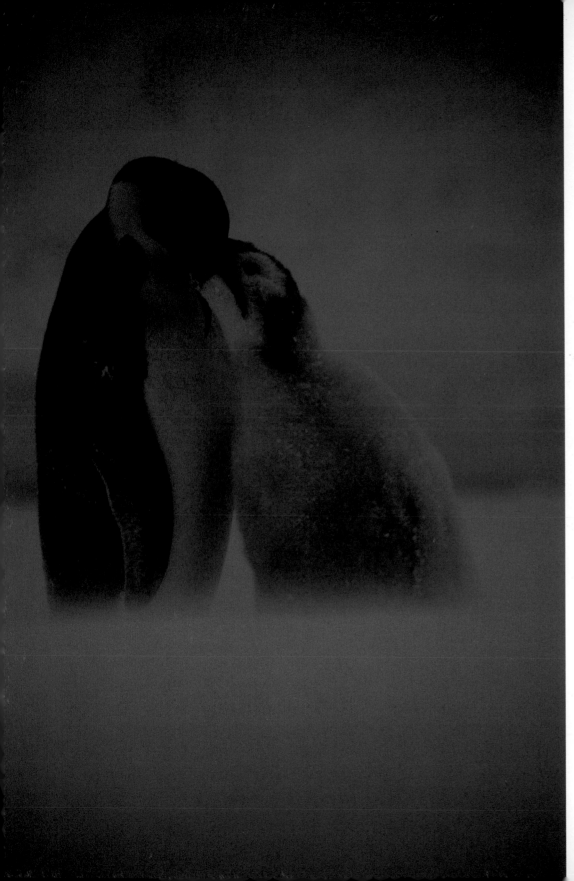

FURTHER READING

Bond, Creina, Roy Siegfried and Peter Johnson, *Antarctica: No Single Country No Single Sea*. Hamlyn, London, 1979.

De Roy, Tui, Mark Jones, Colin Monteath and Ron Naveen, *Wild Ice: Antarctic Journeys*. Smithsonian Institution Press, Washington, 1990.

Fothergill, Alastair, *Life in the Freezer: A Natural History of the Antarctic*. BBC Books, London, 1993.

Frazer, Conon, *Beyond the Roaring Forties: New Zealand's Subantarctic Islands*. Government Printing Office, Wellington, 1986.

Hatherton, Trevor (ed.), *Antarctica: The Ross Sea Region*. DSIR Publishing, Wellington, 1990.

Headland, Robert, *The Island of South Georgia*. Cambridge University Press, Cambridge, 1984.

Kooyman, Gerald, *Weddell Seal: Consummate Diver*. Cambridge University Press, Cambridge, 1981.

Knox, George, *The Southern Ocean*. Cambridge University Press, Cambridge, 1995.

Moss, Sanford, *Natural History of the Antarctic Peninsula*. Columbia University Press, New York, 1988.

Owen, Weldon, *Polar Regions: The Illustrated Library of the Earth*. Sydney, 1995.

Porter, Eliot, *Antarctica*. Hutchinson, London, 1978.

Pyne, Stephen, *The Ice: A Journey to Antarctica*. Arlington Books, London, 1986.

Reader's Digest, *Antarctica: The Extraordinary History of Man's Conquest of the Frozen Continent*. Sydney, 1985.

Rowell, Galen, *Poles Apart: Parallel Visions of the Arctic and Antarctic*. University of California Press, Berkeley, 1995.

Selkirk, P. & D., R. Seppelt, *Subantarctic Macquarie Island: Environment and Biology*. Cambridge University Press, Cambridge, 1990.

Snyder, Jim, Keith Shackleton, *Ship in the Wilderness: Voyages of the MS* Lindblad Explorer *through the Last Wild Places on Earth*. Dent and Sons, London, 1986.

Stonehouse, Bernard, *North Pole South Pole: A Guide to the Ecology and Resources of the Arctic and Antarctic*. Prion, London, 1990.

Walton, David (ed.), *Antarctic Science*. Cambridge University Press, Cambridge, 1987.

Emperor penguin feeding chick in blizzard, Atka Bay, Weddell Sea.

INDEX

159

160

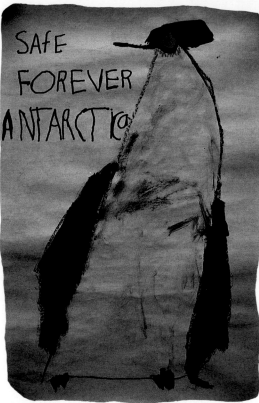

"Safe forever Antarctica,"
artwork by Andrew Woolley (aged 5).

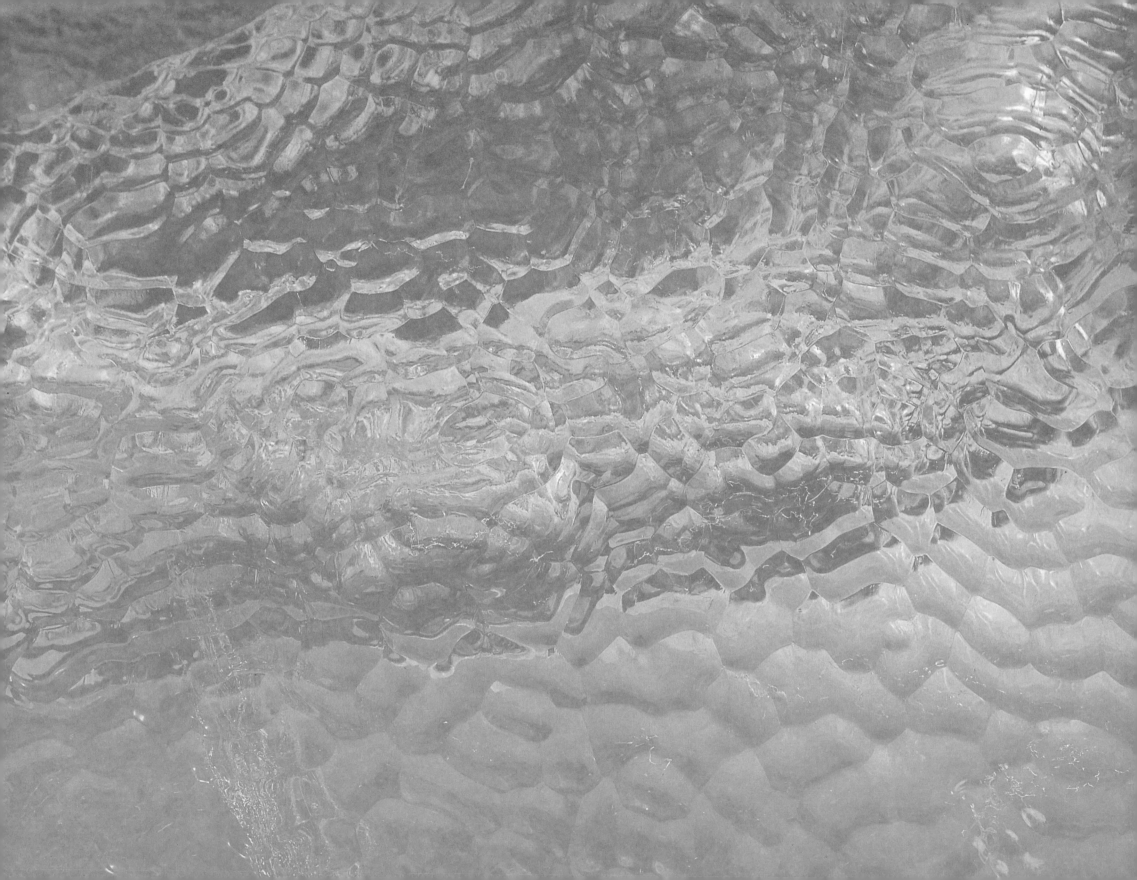